In the Name of Allah, God of all

Most Gracious, Most Merciful

From Allah we seek Help

In Allah we trust

THE COMPENDIUM OF JEWELS

ON YOUR WAY TO THE DIVINE

AL-SHARIF SAYID AL-HUSAINI

NAQSHABANDI MUJADDIDI

سلسلة تصفية التصوف (١)

Purifying Tasawwuf Series (1)

Published in February 2017 by

Author: Dr Sharif Sayid Alhusaini

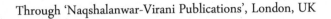

Through 'Naqshalanwar-Virani Publications', London, UK

Book Title: The Compendium of Jewels - on your Way to the Divine

ISBN: 978-0-9956656-0-6

All designs by: Alsharif Naqshalanwar Designers ©

Printed in UK

"You need to be constantly available in a state of inner awareness that you have arrived to earth from the presence of infinity and that to this presence of infinity you are returning. In between is just a glitter, which is definitely not gold."

Al-Sharif Sayid Al-Husaini

Table of Blessed Contents

Book of Truth 107

Book of Prayers.. 165

Book of Salawat 193

Book of Safety 231

Book of Sacred Images 261

ABBREVIATIONS AND ARABIC TERMS

AH	After Hijra (Prophet's Migration)
(AS) 'alaihis-salam (or 'alaihas-salam)	peace be upon him (or upon her)
awliya	Friends of Allah, Saints
azhan	call for compulsory prayer
BH	Before Hijra (Prophet's Migration)
bint	daughter of
ibn/Ibn	son of
iqamah	call for starting the compulsory prayer
fitnah (pl. fitan)	tribulation(s); dark plot(s)
khulafa	spiritual vicegerents of Allah / and of His Holy Messenger (pbuh)
latifah (pl. lataif)	spiritual subtlety in the human body
Masjid Nabawi	The Messenger's Mosque in Madinah
mizaj	one's inner state of mind, moods and inclinations
muraqabah	meditation with focus on the heart or any other inner subtlety
murid	seeker

(RA)	raDiya Allahu 'anhu (or 'anha or 'anhum) Allah is pleased with him (or her or them)
raka'at	a unit of Islamic prayer containing one bow and two prostrations
(pbuh)	peace be upon him (as translation for Salla Allahu 'alaihi wasallam)
Sahabah	Companions of the Holy Messenger
Salla Allahu 'alaihi wasallam	peace and blessings be upon him
Sayyiduna	our Master
Sayyidah	our Honourable Lady (female of Master)
Tariqa	the path of inner purification leading to knowing Allah Almighty
Qaddasa Allahu sirrahu	one with Sacred Heart (Allah has sanctified his inner reality)
zhikr / zhikrullah	remembrance of Allah

ENGLISH EQUIVALENTS OF SOME ARABIC LETTERS

Arabic Letter	English Equivalent
أ	' (glottal stop)
ث	th
ج	j
ح	H
خ	kh
ذ	zh
ز	z
ص	S
ض	D
ط	T
ظ	Z
غَ غِ غُ	'a, 'e, 'i, 'u
غ	gh
ق	q

PREFACE OF ENLIGHTENMENT

In the Name of Allah, Most Gracious, Most Merciful.

With all my humbleness and servitude to The Divine, I praise God, Allah Almighty, with what is majestically due to His Glory of Perfect Praise. I humbly implore Allah Almighty to send His further Blessings and Salutations upon His Beloved, Sayyiduna Muhammad, the Makki, the Madani - Master of all messengers and prophets of God, and upon his Noble Family (Ahlul-Bayt), the ever-shining Stars, and upon his blessed Companions (Sahabah), the bright Lights in the dark sky.

This book is a great compendium of enlightened inspirations for the serious seeker who is travelling to God Almighty with awareness, through this wonderful journey to the Divine Secret – union with Perfect, Eternal Happiness. This book has all the necessary means for your success, all in this world, in the transitory grave world, and in the everlasting hereafter life. The Book will help protect you from the common confusion prevalent in the world today and provides you with spiritual and emotional energy to experience The Truth for yourself.

I acknowledge that our Master Muhammad is the last of God's messengers and prophets sent by God Almighty to humanity. The mission of the Holy Messenger (pbuh) was to revive the dead hearts and to purify the ailing souls. He has beautifully enlightened many men and women and made them masters in spiritual medicine that they themselves can also cure others. He authorised them to manifest his shining lights unto the souls that are destined for blissful eternity. He continues to enlighten more and more people and give them spiritual support wherever they may be throughout time, and until the Last Hour.

This poor slave also comes to humanity as one of the deputies, and on behalf of my Master, Sayyiduna Muhammad (Salla Allahu 'alaihi wasallam), with that same blessed Muhammadi manifestation of Divine Love and Universal Compassion. I invite my fellow human beings to take this Path to purify their hearts, minds, self/egos and all their inner faculties, and to revive their spiritual subtleties so that they are in constant Presence of God Almighty. This is what all human beings need, and this is what the Holy Messenger (Salla Allahu 'alaihi wasallam) came to provide for humankind. This is the perfect meaning of the Holy Quranic verse, "We have only sent you (Muhammad) as Mercy to the worlds."

His beautiful mission is my mission. My Path springs from, and is connected to, the same Source that flows unto the hearts of the Friends of God: Sayyiduna Muhammad (pbuh). When you come to me, you will be coming to perfect purity and lasting happiness. May The Divine Accept you.

LOVE OF MY SEEKER

O seeker of The Divine!

My love for you

is but pure sheer honey

Transcended from heart to heart.

Now, reflect: where is your heart

From this Divine Presence,

where you are the lover and the beloved?

I have wounded my soul with your love

but you did not realise my pain and hurt!

Reflect, and look deep into this heart of mine

It is but your destined abode.

You will soon realise

your soul has long dwelt here!

Reflect, and you will soon find –

You are the seeker and the sought!

Book of Tariqah

Book of Tariqah

The Master of Tariqah

"The authorised Shaykh of Tariqah is a Vicegerent of the Holy Messenger, Sayyiduna Muhammad (pbuh), in that the Shaykh reflects the Messenger's heart, spiritual lights and his Sunnah way of life in everything the Shaykh feels, thinks, does and experiences."

Al-Sharif Sayid Al-Husaini

Book of Tariqah

Introduction to the Jewel of Life: Tariqah

Everybody needs a path to lead them to Divine Pleasure and Divine Presence. The Muhammadan connected Tariqah is that special Path. Every servant of Allah needs this Path to take him/her towards knowing Allah Almighty and for the attainment of His Pleasure, which means everlasting happiness. Tariqah is the efficient and safe way to realising the deep and sacred meanings of the Divine Covenant: "There is no god but God; Muhammad is the Messenger of God" (la ilaha illa-Allah, Muhammad-un rasool-ullah).

Beloved brothers and sisters! Without Tariqah linked through a connected chain from this present time all the way to the Source of Enlightenment, the Holy Messenger of Allah (pbuh), it is impossible for one's non-physical faculties to be purified from the evils and the veils of the nafs (ego and desires) and from one's worldly affairs and attachments. When you are internally purified, only then you will be qualified to attain everlasting blissful life in the Hereafter, without going through trouble in the transition, such as torture in the grave, standing under the heat of the sun for 50,000 years and entering Hell for a period of time.

Tariqah is also the way of happiness in this worldly life. It allows you to rise above troubles of the world and above your base desires.

When you become needless of everything and everyone, you will then experience the greatest joy of freedom — freedom from the prisons of your clay nature, your material attachments, and from Satanic influence.

You can only be free when you submit yourself to the Mentor who is empowered to uplift your soul with the Power of Love — Divine Love. God Almighty has veiled Himself from creation by Veils of Glory and Light. Moreover, one is obstructed behind the veils of mental incapacity and physical feebleness which veil those who are not devout to Him. Allah Almighty says:

{وخلق الإنسان ضعيفا}

"Man has been created feeble" (Surat Al-Nisa: 28)

Allah Almighty, on the other hand, has commanded man to strive on this earth by travelling on a journey to know Him and to reach His Divine Pleasure. Only Allah can remove these veils, and only He has the Power to allow any creation to know Him. It is His Divine Wisdom that He connected His Path with His beloved, devout ones, whom He had chosen to be His messengers and Friends and gave them the keys to His Divine Presence. Allah Almighty concluded the Guiding Sources on His Path with His last messenger, Sayyiduna Muhammad (pbuh), who in turn transmits his lights and wisdom to those who come on his Path (Tariqah).

Our Madani Naqshabandi Tariqah is so pure and original in its approaches and is spiritually connected to a great extent that we see the pure glorious light all the way from our end to the End where the Holy Messenger, Muhammad (pbuh) stands. As we meditate through zhikrullah, focusing on our inner subtleties, while being connected to the blessed heart of Sayyiduna Muhammad (pbuh), we become spiritually cleansed and enlightened.

Tazkiyah (inner purification) through a true Tariqah does not replace nor abrogate any good work that a Muslim may engage in, whether individually or collectively with other people. Instead, Tariqah supports good works and gives soul to their ways and results. Tariqah strongly supports da'wah (preaching), for zhikrullah is the aim of da'wah. Tariqah strongly supports seeking knowledge, for Allah cannot be worshiped in ignorance. Tariqah strongly supports charity works, for universal compassion is an outcome of inner purification. In fact, Tariqah is the basis of all good works. Without Tariqah, seekers would be working in vacuum.

May Allah, the All Merciful, accept us as faithful servants on the Way of His Beloved Vicegerent, Sayyiduna Muhammad, Salla Allahu 'alaihi wasallam, the Seal of Divine Revelation.

Book of Tariqah

الورد النقشبندي الشريف

برابطة الشيخ
الشريف ابن هاشم عبد الله الحسيني المدني

THE BLESSED NAQSHABANDI WIRD

And Al-Sharif's English Translation

With the Rabitah (Spiritual Connection) of Shaykh
Al-Sharif ibn-Hashim Abdullah Al-Husaini

Our Crown Masters: Muhammad the Messenger of Allah (pbuh), Abu-Bakr AS-Siddiq, Omar ibn Al-khattab,
Othman ibn Affan (RA), {Ali ibn Abi-Talib, Fatima Az-zahra, Al-Hasan and Al-Husain (AS)}

Authorization by Alsharif Alhusaini

I would like to give permission to my English-speaking murids who have difficulty in reading Arabic to read my English translation of the Blessed Naqshabandi Wird. I would like to encourage them, however, to make every effort to learn to read the Arabic text of the blessed Wird so to receive its full spiritual benefits.

May Allah Almighty give you this Wird's numerous blessings, its glorious spiritual flow of Divine Light and its protective power from internal and external harms. Amen.

1 بِسْمِ اللهِ الرَّحْمَنِ الرَّحِيمِ ❁ اَللّٰهُمَّ أَنْتَ الْمَلِكُ الْحَيُّ الْقَيُّومُ ❁

2 الْحَقُّ الْمُبِينُ الَّذِي لَا إِلَهَ إِلَّا هُوَ ❁ أَنْتَ رَبِّي خَلَقْتَنِي وَأَنَا عَبْدُكَ

3 وَأَنَا عَلَى عَهْدِكَ وَوَعْدِكَ مَا اسْتَطَعْتُ ❁ أَعُوذُ بِكَ مِنْ شَرِّ مَا

4 صَنَعْتُ ❁ أَبُوءُ لَكَ بِنِعْمَتِكَ عَلَيَّ ❁ وَأَبُوءُ بِذَنْبِي فَاغْفِرْ لِي

5 ذُنُوبِي ❁ فَإِنَّهُ لَا يَغْفِرُ الذُّنُوبَ إِلَّا أَنْتَ ❁

6 سُبْحَانَ اللهِ وَالْحَمْدُ لِلّٰهِ وَلَا إِلَهَ إِلَّا اللهُ وَاللهُ أَكْبَرُ ❁ وَلَا حَوْلَ

7 وَلَا قُوَّةَ إِلَّا بِاللهِ الْعَلِيِّ الْعَظِيمِ ❁ هُوَ الْأَوَّلُ وَالْآخِرُ وَالظَّاهِرُ

8 وَالْبَاطِنُ وَهُوَ بِكُلِّ شَيْءٍ عَلِيمٌ ❁ يُحْيِي وَيُمِيتُ وَهُوَ عَلَى كُلِّ

9 شَيْءٍ قَدِيرٌ ❁ سُبْحَانَكَ يَا عَظِيمُ ❁ سُبْحَانَكَ يَا مُعَظِّمُ ❁

10 سُبْحَانَكَ يَا مُقْتَدِرُ ❁ سُبْحَانَكَ يَا عَالِمَ السِّرِّ وَالْخَفِيَّاتِ ❁

11 سُبْحَانَكَ يَا بَاعِثَ مَنْ فِي الْجَدَالَةِ وَالْمَسْوُكَاتِ ❁ سُبْحَانَكَ يَا

12 مُسْتَعْبَدَ جَمِيعَ الْخَلَائِقِ ❁ سُبْحَانَكَ يَا مُقَدِّرَ الْوُجْدِ

13 وَالصَّوَافِتِ ❁ سُبْحَانَكَ يَا مَنْ لَا تَطْرَأُ عَلَيْهِ الْآفَاتُ ❁ سُبْحَانَكَ

14 يَا مُكَوِّنَ الْأَزْمِنَةِ وَالْأَوْقَاتِ ❁ عَلَا قَدْرُكَ ❁ وَتَعَالَيْتَ عَمَّا يَقُولُ

15 الظَّالِمُونَ عُلُوًّا كَبِيرًا ❁

16   سُبْحَانَكَ يَا مُعْتِقَ الرِّقَابِ ۞ سُبْحَانَكَ يَا مُسَبِّبَ الْأَسْبَابِ ۞

17   سُبْحَانَكَ يَا حَيُّ يَا قَيُّومُ لَا يَمُوتُ ۞ سُبْحَانَكَ يَا إِلَهِي وَإِلَهَ

18   النَّاسُوتِ ۞ خَلَقْتَنَا رَبَّنَا بِيَدِكَ وَفَضَّلْتَنَا عَلَى كَثِيرٍ مِنْ خَلْقِكَ

19   تَفْضِيلًا ۞ فَلَكَ الْحَمْدُ وَالنَّعْمَاءُ وَلَكَ الطَّوْلُ وَالْآلَاءُ ۞ رَبَّنَا

20   تَبَارَكْتَ وَتَعَالَيْتَ ۞ نَسْتَغْفِرُكَ وَنَتُوبُ إِلَيْكَ ۞

21   أَنْتَ الْأَوَّلُ فَلَا شَيْءَ قَبْلَكَ ۞ وَأَنْتَ الْآخِرُ فَلَا شَيْءَ بَعْدَكَ ۞

22   وَأَنْتَ الظَّاهِرُ فَلَا شَيْءَ يُشْبِهُكَ ۞ وَأَنْتَ الْبَاطِنُ فَلَا شَيْءَ

23   يَرَاكَ ۞ وَأَنْتَ الْوَاحِدُ بِلَا كَثِيرٍ ۞ وَأَنْتَ الْقَادِرُ بِلَا وَزِيرٍ ۞ وَأَنْتَ

24   الْمُدَبِّرُ بِلَا مُشِيرٍ ۞ قُلِ اللَّهُمَّ مَالِكَ الْمُلْكِ تُؤْتِي الْمُلْكَ مَنْ

25   تَشَاءُ وَتَنْزِعُ الْمُلْكَ مِمَّنْ تَشَاءُ وَتُعِزُّ مَنْ تَشَاءُ وَتُذِلُّ مَنْ

26   تَشَاءُ بِيَدِكَ الْخَيْرُ إِنَّكَ عَلَى كُلِّ شَيْءٍ قَدِيرٌ ۞ تُولِجُ اللَّيْلَ فِي

27   النَّهَارِ وَتُولِجُ النَّهَارَ فِي اللَّيْلِ وَتُخْرِجُ الْحَيَّ مِنَ الْمَيِّتِ وَتُخْرِجُ

28   الْمَيِّتَ مِنَ الْحَيِّ وَتَرْزُقُ مَنْ تَشَاءُ بِغَيْرِ حِسَابٍ ۞

29 يَا رَحْمَنُ فِي الدُّنْيَا وَرَحِيمُ فِي الْآخِرَةِ ۞ اِرْحَمْنِي رَحْمَةً مِنْ عِنْدِكَ

30 تُغْنِينِي بِهَا عَمَّنْ سِوَاكَ ۞

31 سُبْحَانَكَ يَا مَنِ احْتَجَبَ فِي الْأُوْلَى عَنْ جَمِيعِ الْوَرَى ۞ سُبْحَانَكَ

32 يَا مَنْ تَرَدَّى بِالْوَقَارِ وَالْكِبْرِيَاءِ ۞ سُبْحَانَكَ يَا مَالِكَ جَمِيعِ

33 الْأَشْيَاءِ ۞ سُبْحَانَكَ يَا مَنْ تَعَزَّزَ بِالْقُدْرَةِ وَالْعَلَاءِ ۞ يَا مَنْ

34 يَعْلَمُ مَا فِي الضَّوَاحِي وَالْحِسَا ۞ يَا مَنْ يَعْلَمُ مَا يَتَلَجْلَجُ فِي

35 الصُّدُورِ وَالْحَشَا ۞ يَا مَنْ شَرَّفَ الْعَرُوضَ عَلَى الْمُدُنِ وَالْقُرَى ۞

36 يَا مَنْ يَعْلَمُ مَا تَحْتَ الْحِبَبِ وَالثَّرَى ۞ سُبْحَانَكَ يَا مَنْ تَعَالَى

37 وَلَطُفَ عَنْ أَنْ يُرَى ۞ تَبَارَكْتَ رَبَّنَا وَتَعَالَيْتَ ۞ لَا رَبَّ وَلَا قَاهِرَ

38 سِوَاكَ ۞

39 اَللَّهُمَّ أَنْتَ الْمُنْعِمُ الْمُتَفَضِّلُ الشَّكُورُ ۞ وَأَشْهَدُ أَنَّكَ أَنْتَ اللهُ

40 الَّذِي لَا إِلَهَ إِلَّا أَنْتَ ۞ أَنْتَ رَبِّي وَرَبُّ كُلِّ شَيْءٍ ۞ فَاطِرَ السَّمَاوَاتِ

41 وَالْأَرْضِ عَالِمَ الْغَيْبِ وَالشَّهَادَةِ الْعَلِيُّ الْكَبِيرُ الْمُتَعَالِ ۞

42   طسٓمٓ ۞ طسٓ ۞ مَرَجَ ٱلْبَحْرَيْنِ يَلْتَقِيَانِ ۞ بَيْنَهُمَا بَرْزَخٌ لَّا

43   يَبْغِيَانِ ۞

44   ٱللَّهُ لَا إِلَٰهَ إِلَّا هُوَ ٱلْحَيُّ ٱلْقَيُّومُ لَا تَأْخُذُهُ سِنَةٌ وَلَا نَوْمٌ لَّهُ مَا فِي

45   ٱلسَّمَٰوَٰتِ وَمَا فِي ٱلْأَرْضِ مَن ذَا ٱلَّذِي يَشْفَعُ عِندَهُ إِلَّا بِإِذْنِهِ

46   يَعْلَمُ مَا بَيْنَ أَيْدِيهِمْ وَمَا خَلْفَهُمْ وَلَا يُحِيطُونَ بِشَيْءٍ مِّنْ

47   عِلْمِهِ إِلَّا بِمَا شَآءَ وَسِعَ كُرْسِيُّهُ ٱلسَّمَٰوَٰتِ وَٱلْأَرْضَ وَلَا يَئُودُهُ

48   حِفْظُهُمَا وَهُوَ ٱلْعَلِيُّ ٱلْعَظِيمُ ۞

49   حمٓ حمٓ حمٓ حمٓ حمٓ حمٓ حمٓ ۞ حمٓ ٱلْأَمْرُ وَجَاءَ ٱلنَّصْرُ

50   فَعَلَيْنَا لَا يُنْصَرُونَ ۞ حمٓ ۞ تَنْزِيلُ ٱلْكِتَابِ مِنَ ٱللَّهِ ٱلْعَزِيزِ

51   ٱلْعَلِيمِ ۞ غَافِرِ ٱلذَّنْبِ وَقَابِلِ ٱلتَّوْبِ شَدِيدِ ٱلْعِقَابِ ذِي ٱلطَّوْلِ

52   لَا إِلَٰهَ إِلَّا هُوَ إِلَيْهِ ٱلْمَصِيرُ ۞ يَفْعَلُ مَا يَشَاءُ بِقُدْرَتِهِ

53   وَيَحْكُمُ مَا يُرِيدُ بِعِزَّتِهِ ۞ وَلَا مُنَازِعَ لَهُ فِي جَبَرُوتِهِ ۞ وَلَا

54   شَرِيكَ لَهُ فِي مُلْكِهِ ۞ سُبْحَانَ اللهِ وَبِحَمْدِهِ ۞ لَا قُوَّةَ إِلَّا بِاللهِ ۞

55　مَا شَاءَ اللّٰهُ كَانَ ۞ وَمَا لَمْ يَشَأْ لَمْ يَكُنْ ۞ أَعْلَمُ أَنَّ اللّٰهَ عَلَى كُلِّ

56　شَيْءٍ قَدِيرٌ ۞ وَأَنَّ اللّٰهَ قَدْ أَحَاطَ بِكُلِّ شَيْءٍ عِلْماً ۞ اَللّٰهُمَّ لَا

57　تَقْتُلْنَا بِغَضَبِكَ ۞ وَلَا تُهْلِكْنَا بِإِمْلَائِكَ وَعَذَابِكَ ۞ وَعَافِنَا قَبْلَ

58　ذَلِكَ ۞ سُبْحَانَ الْمَلِكِ الْقُدُّوسِ ۞ سُبْحَانَ ذِي الْعِزَّةِ وَالْعَظَمَةِ

59　وَالْقُدْرَةِ وَالْقُوَّةِ وَالْكِبْرِيَاءِ وَالْجَبَرُوتِ ۞ سُبْحَانَ الْمَلِكِ الْحَقِّ

60　الْحَيِّ الَّذِي لَا يَنَامُ وَلَا يَمُوتُ ۞ سُبُّوحٌ قُدُّوسٌ ۞ رَبُّنَا وَرَبُّ

61　الْمَلَائِكَةِ وَالرُّوحِ ۞

62　اَللّٰهُمَّ عَلِّمْنَا مِنْ عِلْمِكَ ۞ وَفَهِّمْنَا عَنْكَ ۞ وَقَلِّدْنَا بِصَمْصَامِ

63　نَصْرِكَ ۞ اَللّٰهُمَّ اجْعَلْنِي شَاكِرًا لَكَ ۞ ذَاكِرًا لَكَ ۞ رَاهِبًا لَكَ ۞

64　مِطْوَاعًا لَكَ ۞ وَاجْعَلْنِي هَيِّنًا مُخْبِتًا إِلَيْكَ أَوَّاهًا مُنِيبًا ۞ اَللّٰهُمَّ

65　تَقَبَّلْ تَوْبَتَنَا ۞ وَاغْسِلْ حَوْبَتَنَا ۞ وَسَدِّدْ مَقَاوِلَنَا ۞ وَاسْلُلْ

66　سَخِيمَةَ صُدُورِنَا ۞ وَأَذْهِبِ الدَّخَلَ وَالرَّانَ وَالْأَجِنَّةَ مِنْ

67　قُلُوبِنَا ۞

---

68   اَللَّهُمَّ إِنَّا نَعُوذُ بِكَ مِنْ جُدَاعِ الْفَجْأَةِ ۞ وَمِنْ حِرَاقِ الْمَأْرُوْشَةِ

69   وَمِنَ الْإِلْحَادِ وَالْغِرَّةِ ۞ وَمِنَ الْجَمِّ وَالْعَنَتِ وَمِنَ الْأُمُوْرِ

70   الْمُطْغِرَاتِ ۞

71   اَللَّهُمَّ اقْسِمْ لَنَا مِنْ خَشْيَتِكَ مَا يَحُوْلُ بَيْنَنَا وَبَيْنَ

72   مَعَاصِيكَ ۞ وَمِنْ طَاعَتِكَ مَا تُبَلِّغُنَا بِهِ جَنَّتَكَ ۞ وَمِنَ الْيَقِينِ

73   مَا يُهَوِّنُ عَلَيْنَا مَصَائِبَ الدُّنْيَا ۞ وَمَتِّعْنَا بِأَسْمَاعِنَا وَأَبْصَارِنَا

74   وَقُوَّتِنَا مَا أَحْيَيْتَنَا ۞ وَاجْعَلْهُ الْوَارِثَ مِنَّا ۞ وَاجْعَلْ ثَأْرَنَا عَلَى

75   مَنْ ظَلَمَنَا ۞ وَانْصُرْنَا عَلَى مَنْ عَادَانَا وَلَا تَجْعَلْ مُصِيبَتَنَا فِي

76   دِينِنَا ۞ وَلَا تَجْعَلِ الدُّنْيَا أَكْبَرَ هَمِّنَا ۞ وَلَا مَبْلَغَ عِلْمِنَا ۞ وَلَا

77   تُسَلِّطْ عَلَيْنَا مَنْ لَا يَرْحَمُنَا يَا أَرْحَمَ الرَّاحِمِينَ ۞

78   اَللَّهُمَّ إِنَّا نَسْأَلُكَ رَحْمَةً مِنْ عِنْدِكَ تَهْدِي بِهَا رُوْعَنَا ۞ وَتَلُمُّ

79   بِهَا شَعَثْنَا ۞ وَتَجْمَعُ بِهَا شَمْلَنَا ۞ وَتَشْفِي بِهَا مَرْضَانَا ۞ وَتُزَكِّي

80   بِهَا أَعْمَالَنَا وَأَقْوَالَنَا ۞ وَتُلْهِمُنَا بِهَا رُشْدَنَا ۞ اَللَّهُمَّ إِنَّا نَسْأَلُكَ

81   ۞ بِصَمَدَانِيَّتِكَ وَبِوَحْدَانِيَّتِكَ وَبِفَرْدَانِيَّتِكَ ۞ وَبِعِزَّتِكَ الْبَاهِرَةِ ۞

82   وَبِرَحْمَتِكَ الْوَاسِعَةِ ❖ أَنْ تَجْعَلَ لَنَا نُورًا فِي مَسَامِعِنَا ❖ وَنُورًا فِي

83   أَعْيُنِنَا ❖ وَنُورًا فِي أَحْدَاقِنَا ❖ وَنُورًا فِي قُلُوبِنَا ❖ وَنُورًا فِي

84   حَوَاسِّنَا ❖ وَنُورًا فِي نَسَمِنَا ❖ وَنُورًا مِنْ بَيْنِ أَيْدِينَا ❖

85   اَللّٰهُمَّ زِدْنَا عِلْمًا وَنُورًا وَحِلْمًا ❖ وَآتِنَا نِعْمَةً ظَاهِرَةً وَنِعْمَةً

86   بَاطِنَةً ❖ حَسْبُنَا اللهُ لِدِينِنَا ❖ حَسْبُنَا اللهُ لِدُنْيَانَا ❖ حَسْبُنَا اللهُ

87   لِمَا أَهَمَّنَا ❖ حَسْبُنَا اللهُ الْحَلِيمُ الْقَوِيُّ لِمَنْ بَغَى عَلَيْنَا ❖ حَسْبُنَا

88   اللهُ الرَّحِيمُ عِنْدَ السَّامِ ❖ حَسْبُنَا اللهُ الرَّءُوْفُ عِنْدَ الْمَسْأَلَةِ

89   فِي الْجَدَثِ ❖

90   حَسْبِيَ اللّٰهُ لَا إِلَهَ إِلَّا هُوَ عَلَيْهِ تَوَكَّلْتُ وَهُوَ رَبُّ الْعَرْشِ الْعَظِيمِ ❖

91   حَسْبِيَ اللّٰهُ لَا إِلَهَ إِلَّا هُوَ عَلَيْهِ تَوَكَّلْتُ وَهُوَ رَبُّ الْعَرْشِ الْعَظِيمِ ❖

92   حَسْبِيَ اللّٰهُ لَا إِلَهَ إِلَّا هُوَ عَلَيْهِ تَوَكَّلْتُ وَهُوَ رَبُّ الْعَرْشِ الْعَظِيمِ ❖

93   حَسْبِيَ اللّٰهُ لَا إِلَهَ إِلَّا هُوَ عَلَيْهِ تَوَكَّلْتُ وَهُوَ رَبُّ الْعَرْشِ الْعَظِيمِ ❖

94   حَسْبِيَ اللّٰهُ لَا إِلَهَ إِلَّا هُوَ عَلَيْهِ تَوَكَّلْتُ وَهُوَ رَبُّ الْعَرْشِ الْعَظِيمِ ❖

95   حَسْبِيَ اللّٰهُ لَا إِلَهَ إِلَّا هُوَ عَلَيْهِ تَوَكَّلْتُ وَهُوَ رَبُّ الْعَرْشِ الْعَظِيمِ ❖

96 حَسْبِيَ ٱللَّهُ لَا إِلَهَ إِلَّا هُوَ عَلَيْهِ تَوَكَّلْتُ وَهُوَ رَبُّ ٱلْعَرْشِ ٱلْعَظِيمِ ❁

97 مَرْحَبًا مَرْحَبًا بِالصَّبَاحِ وَالْيَوْمِ ¹ الْجَدِيدَيْنِ ❁ وَبِالْإِبَانِ

98 وَالْفِئَةِ السَّعِيدَيْنِ ❁ وَبِالسَّافِرِ الشَّهِيدِ ❁ اُكْتُبْ لَنَا مَا

99 نَقُولُ ❁ بِسْمِ اللَّهِ الْحَمِيدِ الرَّفِيعِ الْوَدُودِ الْمُحِيطِ الْفَعَّالِ فِي

100 خَلْقِهِ لِمَا يُرِيدُ ❁ وَهُوَ أَقْرَبُ إِلَيْهِمْ مِنْ حَبْلِ الْوَرِيدِ ❁

101 أَصْبَحْتُ ² بِاللَّهِ مُؤْمِنًا ❁ وَبِلِقَائِهِ مُصَدِّقًا ❁ وَبِحُجَّتِهِ مُعْتَرِفًا ❁

102 وَبِسِوَى اللَّهِ فِي الْأُلُوهِيَّةِ جَاحِدًا ❁ وَعَلَى اللَّهِ مُتَوَكِّلًا ❁ نُشْهِدُ

103 اللَّهَ وَنُشْهِدُ مَلَائِكَتَهُ وَأَنْبِيَاءَهُ وَرُسُلَهُ وَحَمَلَةَ عَرْشِهِ وَجَمِيعَ

104 خَلْقِهِ ❁ بِأَنَّهُ هُوَ اللَّهُ لَا إِلَهَ إِلَّا هُوَ وَحْدَهُ ❁ وَبِأَنَّ سَيِّدَنَا مُحَمَّدًا

105 عَبْدُهُ وَرَسُولُهُ ❁ وَأَنَّ الْجَنَّةَ حَقٌّ ❁ وَأَنَّ النَّارَ حَقٌّ ❁ وَأَنَّ الْحَوْضَ

106 حَقٌّ ❁ وَأَنَّ الشَّفَاعَةَ حَقٌّ ❁ وَأَنَّ السُّؤَالَ حَقٌّ ❁ وَأَنَّ مُنْكَرًا

107 وَنَكِيرًا حَقٌّ ❁ وَأَنَّ وَعْدَكَ حَقٌّ ❁

---

¹ In the evening: بِالْمَسَاءِ وَاللَّيْلِ

² أَمْسَيْتُ

108 وَأَنَّ ٱلسَّاعَةَ آتِيَةٌ لَا رَيْبَ فِيهَا وَأَنَّ ٱللَّهَ يَبْعَثُ مَنْ فِي ٱلْقُبُورِ ❁

109 عَلَى ذَلِكَ نَحْيَا وَعَلَيْهِ نَمُوتُ ❁ وَعَلَيْهِ نُبْعَثُ غَدًا لَا نَرَى عَذَابًا

110 إِنْ شَاءَ اللَّهُ تَعَالَى ❁

111 اَللَّهُمَّ إِنَّا ظَلَمْنَا أَنْفُسَنَا ❁ فَاغْفِرْ لَنَا أَوْزَارَنَا الْكَبَائِرَ وَاللَّمَمَ ❁

112 فَإِنَّهُ لَا يَغْفِرُهَا إِلَّا أَنْتَ ❁ وَاهْدِنَا لِأَحْسَنِ الْأَخْلَاقِ ❁ فَإِنَّهُ لَا

113 يَهْدِي لِأَحْسَنِهَا إِلَّا أَنْتَ ❁ لَبَّيْكَ وَسَعْدَيْكَ ❁ وَالْخَيْرُ كُلُّهُ

114 بِيَدَيْكَ ❁ نَسْتَغْفِرُكَ وَنَتُوبُ إِلَيْكَ ❁ آمَنَّا وَصَدَّقْنَا اللَّهُمَّ بِمَا

115 أَرْسَلْتَ مِنْ رَسُولٍ ❁ وَآمَنَّا وَصَدَّقْنَا بِمَا أَنْزَلْتَ مِنْ كِتَابٍ ❁

116 اَللَّهُمَّ امْلَأْ وُجُوهَنَا مِنْكَ حَيَاءً ❁ وَقُلُوبَنَا مِنْكَ حُبُوراً ❁ اَللَّهُمَّ

117 اجْعَلْنِي لُهُمُوماً ظَلَفاً ❁ وَلَا تَجْعَلْنِي ضَنِينًا وَعِبِّينًا ❁ وَنَبِيئًا

118 وَنَفَّاجاً وَدَاحِساً ❁ اَللَّهُمَّ إِنَّا نَعُوذُ بِكَ مِنَ الْهَبْرَمَةِ ❁ وَمِنَ

119 الْجَأْوَةِ وَمِنَ الْعُتُوِّ وَمِنَ الْخَطْرَبَةِ وَالْخَيْلُولَةِ وَالْفَيْهَجِ وَالرَّثْعِ

120 وَالْعَتْلِ وَالرَّمَاءِ وَالْفِتْنَةِ الدَّهْمَاءِ وَالْمَعِيشَةِ الضَّنْكَى ❁

121 اَللّٰهُمَّ اجْعَلْ أَوَّلَ يَوْمِنَا ³ هٰذَا صَلَاحًا ❈ وَأَوْسَطَهُ فَلَاحًا ❈ وَآخِرَهُ

122 نَجَاحًا ❈ اَللّٰهُمَّ اجْعَلْ أَوَّلَهُ رَحْمَةً ❈ وَأَوْسَطَهُ زَهَادَةً ❈ وَآخِرَهُ

123 تَكْرِمَةً ❈ اَللّٰهُمَّ ارْزُقْنَا مِنَ الْعَيْشِ أَرْغَدَهُ ❈ وَمِنَ الْعُمْرِ

124 أَسْعَدَهُ ❈ وَمِنَ الرِّزْقِ أَوْسَعَهُ وَأَنْفَعَهُ ❈

125 اَللّٰهُمَّ اعْفُ عَنَّا بِعَفْوِكَ ❈ وَاحْلُمْ عَلَيْنَا بِفَضْلِكَ ❈ سُبْحَانَكَ

126 اللّٰهُمَّ وَبِحَمْدِكَ ❈ لَا أُحْصِي ثَنَاءً عَلَيْكَ ❈ أَنْتَ كَمَا أَثْنَيْتَ عَلَى

127 نَفْسِكَ ❈ عَزَّ جَارُكَ ❈ وَجَلَّ ثَنَاؤُكَ ❈ وَلَا يُهْزَمُ جُنْدُكَ ❈ وَلَا

128 يُخْلَفُ وَعْدُكَ ❈ وَلَا إِلٰهَ غَيْرُكَ ❈

129 سُبْحَانَكَ مَا عَبَدْنَاكَ حَقَّ عِبَادَتِكَ يَا مَعْبُودُ ❈ سُبْحَانَكَ مَا

130 عَرَفْنَاكَ حَقَّ مَعْرِفَتِكَ يَا مَعْرُوفُ ❈ سُبْحَانَكَ مَا ذَكَرْنَاكَ حَقَّ

131 ذِكْرِكَ يَا مَذْكُورُ ❈ سُبْحَانَكَ مَا شَكَرْنَاكَ حَقَّ شُكْرِكَ يَا

132 مَشْكُورُ ❈ اَللّٰهُمَّ أَوْزِعْنَا شُكْرَ مَا أَنْعَمْتَ بِهِ عَلَيْنَا ❈ فَإِنَّكَ أَنْتَ

133 اللّٰهُ الَّذِي ارْتَفَعْتَ عَنْ صِفَةِ الْجِبِلِّ صِفَاتُ قُدْرَتِكَ ❈

---

³ لَيْلِنَا

134 وَلَا ضِدَّ شَهِدَكَ حِينَ فَطَرْتَ الْمَأْرُوْشَاتِ وَلَا نِدَّ حَجَزَكَ حِينَ

135 بَرَأْتَ الْحَوْبَاوَاتِ ۞

136 اَللَّهُمَّ إِنَّا نَعُوْذُ بِكَ مِنْ جَحْمَةٍ لَا تَدْمَعُ ۞ وَمِنْ جَنَانٍ لَا

137 يَخْشَعُ ۞ وَمِنْ عِلْمٍ لَا يَنْفَعُ ۞ وَمِنْ نَفْسٍ لَا تَشْبَعُ ۞ وَمِنْ

138 دُعَاءٍ لَا يُسْمَعُ ۞ وَمِنْ عِوَازِ الْمَاعُوْنِ ۞

139 اَللَّهُمَّ فَهِّمْنَا أَسْرَارَكَ ۞ وَأَلْبِسْنَا مَلَابِسَ أَنْوَارِكَ ۞ وَاغْمِسْنَا فِي

140 رَامُوْزِ اللَّطَائِفِ ۞ وَأَفِضْ عَلَيْنَا مِنْ عَوَارِفِ الْمَعَارِفِ ۞ يَا نُوْرَ

141 الْأَنْوَارِ ۞ يَا لَطِيْفُ يَا سَتَّارُ ۞ نَسْأَلُكَ أَنْ تُصَلِّيَ عَلَى سَيِّدِنَا

142 مُحَمَّدٍ نِبْرَاسِ الْأَنْبِيَاءِ ۞ وَنَيِّرِ الْأَوْلِيَاءِ ۞ وَزِبِرْقَانِ الْأَصْفِيَاءِ

143 وَيُوْحِ الثَّقَلَيْنِ ۞ وَضِيَاءِ الْخَافِقَيْنِ ۞ وَأَنْ تَرْفَعَ وُجُوْدَنَا إِلَى

144 فَلَكِ الْعِرْفَانِ ۞ وَتُثْبِتَ شُهُوْدَنَا فِي مَقَامِ الْإِحْسَانِ ۞

145 يَا اَللهُ يَا نُوْرُ يَا وَاسِعُ يَا غَفُوْرُ ۞ يَا مَنِ السَّمَاءُ بِأَمْرِهِ مَبْنِيَّةٌ ۞

146 وَالْغَبْرَاءُ بِقُدْرَتِهِ مَدْحِيَّةٌ ۞ وَالشَّوَاهِقُ بِحِكْمَتِهِ مَرْسِيَّةٌ ۞

147 وَأَنْوَارُ الْقَمَرَيْنِ بِفَضْلِهِ مُضِيْئَةٌ ۞

148 ❖ نَسْأَلُكَ بِاسْمِكَ الَّذِي تَرَقْرَقَتْ بِهِ الخُنَّسُ وَالْأَزْهَرَانُ ❖

149 وَتَبَلَّجَتْ مِنْهُ الْعَنَانُ ❖ حِرْزًا مَانِعًا وَنُورًا سَاطِعًا خَاشِعًا ❖ يَكَادُ

150 سَنَا بَرْقِهِ يَذْهَبُ بِالْأَبْصَارِ ❖ يُقَلِّبُ اللَّهُ اللَّيْلَ وَالنَّهَارَ إِنَّ فِي

151 ذَلِكَ لَعِبْرَةً لِّأُولِي الْأَبْصَارِ ❖

152 طس ❖ طسم ❖ وَنَعُوذُ بِاللَّهِ الْعَظِيمِ ❖ مِنَ الْمَعَازِفِ وَالْعَضَهِ

153 وَالْمَحْظُورِ وَالْمُمَاحَلَةِ وَالْغِمَارِ وَمِنْ كَيْدِ الْفُجَّارِ وَحَوَادِثِ

154 الْعَصْرَيْنِ وَمِنْ شَرِّ الْأَجْرَيْنِ ❖ يَا حَفِيظُ احْفَظْنَا ❖ يَا وَالِي يَا

155 عَلِيُّ يَا عَالِي ❖ يَا مَنْ لَا إِلَهَ إِلَّا هُوَ ❖ وَلَا يَعْلَمُ أَحَدٌ كَيْفَ هُوَ إِلَّا

156 هُوَ ❖ يَا اللَّهُ يَا حَيُّ يَا قَيُّومُ ❖ يَا حَقُّ يَا وَكِيلُ يَا وَاحِدُ يَا أَحَدُ

157 يَا فَرْدُ يَا صَمَدُ ❖ يَا وَهَّابُ يَا فَتَّاحُ يَا مُحْيِي يَا مُمِيتُ ❖ سَلَامٌ

158 قَوْلًا مِّن رَّبٍّ رَّحِيمٍ ❖ فَسَيَكْفِيكَهُمُ اللَّهُ وَهُوَ السَّمِيعُ الْعَلِيمُ ❖

159 هُوَ اللَّهُ الَّذِي لَا إِلَهَ إِلَّا هُوَ الرَّحْمَنُ الرَّحِيمُ الْمَلِكُ الْقُدُّوسُ

160 السَّلَامُ الْمُؤْمِنُ الْمُهَيْمِنُ الْعَزِيزُ الْجَبَّارُ الْمُتَكَبِّرُ الْخَالِقُ

161 الْبَارِئُ الْمُصَوِّرُ الْغَفَّارُ الْقَهَّارُ الْوَهَّابُ الرَّزَاقُ الْفَتَّاحُ الْعَلِيمُ

162   السَّمِيعُ   الْمُعِزُّ الْمُذِلُّ   الْخَافِضُ الرَّافِعُ   الْقَابِضُ الْبَاسِطُ

163   الْحَلِيمُ الْعَظِيمُ   اللَّطِيفُ الْخَبِيرُ   الْحَكَمُ الْعَدْلُ   الْبَصِيرُ

164   الْحَسِيبُ   الْحَفِيظُ الْمُقِيتُ   الْعَلِيُّ الْكَبِيرُ   الْغَفُورُ الشَّكُورُ

165   الْوَدُودُ   الْوَاسِعُ الْحَكِيمُ   الرَّقِيبُ الْمُجِيبُ   الْجَلِيلُ الْكَرِيمُ

166   الْوَلِيُّ   الْحَقُّ الْوَكِيلُ الْقَوِيُّ الْمَتِينُ   الْمَجِيدُ الْبَاعِثُ الشَّهِيدُ

167   الْحَيُّ   الْمُحْيِي الْمُمِيتُ   الْمُحْصِي الْمُبْدِئُ الْمُعِيدُ   الْحَمِيدُ

168   الْقَادِرُ   الْفَرْدُ الصَّمَدُ   الْوَاحِدُ الْأَحَدُ   الْوَاجِدُ الْمَاجِدُ   الْقَيُّومُ

169   الْوَالِي   الظَّاهِرُ الْبَاطِنُ   الْأَوَّلُ الْآخِرُ   الْمُقَدِّمُ الْمُؤَخِّرُ   الْمُقْتَدِرُ

170   مَالِكُ الْمُلْكِ   الرَّءُوفُ   الْعَفُوُّ   الْمُنْتَقِمُ   التَّوَّابُ   الْبَرُّ   الْمُتَعَالِ

171   الْمُعْطِي   الْغَنِيُّ الْمُغْنِي   الْجَامِعُ الْمُقْسِطُ   ذُو الْجَلَالِ وَالْإِكْرَامِ

172   الْوَارِثُ   الْبَدِيعُ الْبَاقِي   النُّورُ الْهَادِي   الضَّارُّ النَّافِعُ   الْمَانِعُ

173   الرَّشِيدُ الصَّبُورُ ❁ اَلَّذِي لَيْسَ كَمِثْلِهِ شَيْءٌ وَهُوَ السَّمِيعُ الْبَصِيرُ ❁

174   حَسْبُنَا اللَّهُ وَنِعْمَ الْوَكِيلُ ❁ نِعْمَ الْمَوْلَى وَنِعْمَ النَّصِيرُ ❁

175   غُفْرَانَكَ رَبَّنَا وَإِلَيْكَ الْمَصِيرُ ❁

176 يَا دَائِمًا بِلَا فَنَاءٍ ❁ وَيَا بَاقِيًا بِلَا زَوَالٍ ❁ وَيَا مُدَبِّرًا بِلَا وَزِيرٍ ❁

177 سَهِّلْ عَلَيْنَا وَعَلَى أَبَوَيْنَا كُلَّ عَسِيرٍ ❁

178 اَللَّهُمَّ لَا مَانِعَ لِمَا أَعْطَيْتَ ❁ وَلَا مُعْطِيَ لِمَا مَنَعْتَ ❁ وَلَا رَادَّ لِمَا

179 قَضَيْتَ ❁ وَلَا مُبَدِّلَ لِمَا حَكَمْتَ ❁ وَلَا هَادِيَ لِمَا أَضْلَلْتَ ❁ وَلَا

180 مُضِلَّ لِمَا هَدَيْتَ ❁ وَلَا مُيَسِّرَ لِمَا عَسَّرْتَ ❁ وَلَا مُعَسِّرَ لِمَا

181 يَسَّرْتَ ❁ وَلَا يَنْفَعُ ذَا الْجَدِّ مِنْكَ الْجَدُّ ❁

182 سُبْحَانَ رَبِّيَ الْعَلِيِّ الْعَظِيمِ ❁ الْحَسِيبِ الْحَكَمِ الْعَدْلِ الرَّقِيبِ ❁

183 اَلْبَاذِخِ الشَّامِخِ ❁ الْمُجِيبِ الْغَنِيِّ الرَّشِيدِ الصَّبُورِ ❁ الْجَلِيلِ

184 الْمُقْسِطِ الْمُعْطِي الْمَانِعِ ❁

185 لَا إِلٰهَ إِلَّا اللهُ الْوَكِيلُ الشَّهِيدُ ❁ لَا إِلٰهَ إِلَّا اللهُ الْمَتِينُ الْمَجِيدُ ❁

186 لَا إِلٰهَ إِلَّا اللهُ الْوَاجِدُ الْوَالِي ❁ لَا إِلٰهَ إِلَّا اللهُ الْمَاجِدُ الْمُتَعَالِ ❁

187 أَعَدَدْنَا لِكُلِّ هَوْلٍ لَا إِلٰهَ إِلَّا اللهُ ❁ وَلِكُلِّ رَغْسٍ الْحَمْدُ لِلّٰهِ ❁

188 وَلِكُلِّ أُعْجُوبَةٍ سُبْحَانَ اللهِ ❁ وَلِكُلِّ لَزْنٍ حَسْبِيَ اللهُ ❁ وَلِكُلِّ

189 شَجْوٍ مَا شَاءَ اللهُ ❁ وَلِكُلِّ قَضَاءٍ وَقَدَرٍ تَوَكَّلْتُ عَلَى اللهِ ❁

190 وَلِكُلِّ مُصِيبَةٍ إِنَّا لِلّٰهِ ❁ وَلِكُلِّ طَاعَةٍ وَمَعْصِيَةٍ لَا حَوْلَ وَلَا قُوَّةَ

191 إِلَّا بِاللّٰهِ ❁ وَلِكُلِّ شَجِبٍ اسْتَعَنْتُ بِاللّٰهِ ❁

192 اَللّٰهُمَّ إِنَّا أَصْبَحْنَا⁴ نُشْهِدُكَ وَنُشْهِدُ مَلَائِكَتَكَ وَأَنْبِيَاءَكَ

193 وَرُسُلَكَ وَجَمِيعَ خَلْقِكَ ❁ بِأَنَّنَا نَشْهَدُ أَنَّكَ أَنْتَ اللّٰهُ وَحْدَكَ لَا

194 شَرِيكَ لَكَ ❁ وَأَنَّ سَيِّدَنَا مُحَمَّداً عَبْدُكَ وَرَسُولُكَ ❁

195 اَللّٰهُمَّ إِنَّا أَصْبَحْنَا⁴ نُشْهِدُكَ وَنُشْهِدُ مَلَائِكَتَكَ وَأَنْبِيَاءَكَ

196 وَرُسُلَكَ وَجَمِيعَ خَلْقِكَ ❁ بِأَنَّنَا نَشْهَدُ أَنَّكَ أَنْتَ اللّٰهُ وَحْدَكَ لَا

197 شَرِيكَ لَكَ ❁ وَأَنَّ سَيِّدَنَا مُحَمَّداً عَبْدُكَ وَرَسُولُكَ ❁

198 اَللّٰهُمَّ إِنَّا أَصْبَحْنَا⁴ نُشْهِدُكَ وَنُشْهِدُ مَلَائِكَتَكَ وَأَنْبِيَاءَكَ

199 وَرُسُلَكَ وَجَمِيعَ خَلْقِكَ ❁ بِأَنَّنَا نَشْهَدُ أَنَّكَ أَنْتَ اللّٰهُ وَحْدَكَ لَا

200 شَرِيكَ لَكَ ❁ وَأَنَّ سَيِّدَنَا مُحَمَّداً عَبْدُكَ وَرَسُولُكَ ❁

---

⁴ أَمْسَيْنَا

201 اَللّٰهُمَّ إِنَّا أَصْبَحْنَا ⁴ نُشْهِدُكَ وَنُشْهِدُ مَلَائِكَتَكَ وَأَنْبِيَاءَكَ

202 وَرُسُلَكَ وَجَمِيعَ خَلْقِكَ ❊ بِأَنَّنَا نَشْهَدُ أَنَّكَ أَنْتَ اللّٰهُ وَحْدَكَ لَا

203 شَرِيكَ لَكَ ❊ وَأَنَّ سَيِّدَنَا مُحَمَّداً عَبْدُكَ وَرَسُولُكَ ❊

204 وَلَا حَوْلَ وَلَا قُوَّةَ إِلَّا بِاللّٰهِ الْعَلِيِّ الْعَظِيمِ ❊ يَا رَحْمَنَ الدُّنْيَا

205 وَرَحِيمَ الْآخِرَةِ ❊ فَاعْفُ عَنَّا وَاغْفِرْ لَنَا وَارْحَمْنَا ❊ وَأَنْتَ أَرْحَمُ

206 الرَّاحِمِينَ ❊

207 بِسْمِ اللّٰهِ الشَّافِي هُوَ اللّٰهُ ❊ بِسْمِ اللّٰهِ الْكَافِي هُوَ اللّٰهُ ❊ بِسْمِ اللّٰهِ

208 الْمُعَافِي هُوَ اللّٰهُ ❊ بِسْمِ اللّٰهِ الَّذِي لَا يَضُرُّ مَعَ اسْمِهِ شَيْءٌ فِي

209 الْأَرْضِ وَلَا فِي السَّمَاءِ وَهُوَ السَّمِيعُ الْعَلِيمُ ❊ بِسْمِ اللّٰهِ الَّذِي لَا

210 يَضُرُّ مَعَ اسْمِهِ شَيْءٌ فِي الْأَرْضِ وَلَا فِي السَّمَاءِ وَهُوَ السَّمِيعُ

211 الْعَلِيمُ ❊ بِسْمِ اللّٰهِ الَّذِي لَا يَضُرُّ مَعَ اسْمِهِ شَيْءٌ فِي الْأَرْضِ وَلَا

212 فِي السَّمَاءِ وَهُوَ السَّمِيعُ الْعَلِيمُ ❊

213 فَاللّٰهُ خَيْرٌ حَافِظاً وَهُوَ أَرْحَمُ الرَّاحِمِينَ ❊

214 يَا مُحْيِيُ أَحْيِنَا حَيَاةً طَيِّبَةً بِالصِّحَّةِ وَالعَافِيَةِ فِي الدُّنْيَا

215 وَالآخِرَةِ ۞ إِنَّكَ عَلَى كُلِّ شَيْءٍ قَدِيرٌ ۞

216 وَٱللَّهُ مِن وَرَائِهِم مُّحِيطٌ ۞ بَلْ هُوَ قُرْآنٌ مَّجِيدٌ ۞ فِي لَوْحٍ

217 مَّحْفُوظٍ ۞ حَافِظُواْ عَلَى الصَّلَوَاتِ وَالصَّلَوٰةِ الْوُسْطَىٰ وَقُومُواْ لِلَّهِ

218 قَانِتِينَ ۞ إِن كُلُّ نَفْسٍ لَّمَّا عَلَيْهَا حَافِظٌ ۞ نِعْمَ ٱلْحَافِظُ اللَّهُ ۞ يَا

219 حَفِيظُ احْفَظْنَا ۞ يَا حَفِيظُ احْفَظْنَا ۞ يَا حَفِيظُ احْفَظْنَا

220 ثُمَّ أَنزَلَ عَلَيْكُم مِّنۢ بَعْدِ ٱلْغَمِّ أَمَنَةً نُّعَاسًا يَغْشَىٰ طَآئِفَةً

221 مِّنكُمْ وَطَآئِفَةٌ قَدْ أَهَمَّتْهُمْ أَنفُسُهُمْ يَظُنُّونَ بِٱللَّهِ غَيْرَ ٱلْحَقِّ

222 ظَنَّ ٱلْجَاهِلِيَّةِ يَقُولُونَ هَل لَّنَا مِنَ ٱلْأَمْرِ مِن شَيْءٍ قُلْ إِنَّ ٱلْأَمْرَ

223 كُلَّهُ لِلَّهِ يُخْفُونَ فِي أَنفُسِهِم مَّا لَا يُبْدُونَ لَكَ يَقُولُونَ لَوْ كَانَ

224 لَنَا مِنَ ٱلْأَمْرِ شَيْءٌ مَّا قُتِلْنَا هَاهُنَا قُل لَّوْ كُنتُمْ فِي بُيُوتِكُمْ لَبَرَزَ

225 ٱلَّذِينَ كُتِبَ عَلَيْهِمُ ٱلْقَتْلُ إِلَىٰ مَضَاجِعِهِمْ وَلِيَبْتَلِيَ ٱللَّهُ مَا فِي

226 صُدُورِكُمْ وَلِيُمَحِّصَ مَا فِي قُلُوبِكُمْ وَٱللَّهُ عَلِيمٌ بِذَاتِ ٱلصُّدُورِ ۞

227 ٱلَّذِينَ يَقُولُونَ رَبَّنَا إِنَّنَا آمَنَّا فَٱغْفِرْ لَنَا ذُنُوبَنَا وَقِنَا عَذَابَ

228 ٱلنَّارِ ۞

229   ٱلصَّابِرِينَ وَٱلصَّادِقِينَ وَٱلْقَانِتِينَ وَٱلْمُنفِقِينَ وَٱلْمُسْتَغْفِرِينَ

230   بِٱلْأَسْحَارِ ۞ شَهِدَ ٱللَّهُ أَنَّهُ لَا إِلَٰهَ إِلَّا هُوَ وَٱلْمَلَائِكَةُ وَأُولُو ٱلْعِلْمِ

231   قَائِمًا بِٱلْقِسْطِ لَا إِلَٰهَ إِلَّا هُوَ ٱلْعَزِيزُ ٱلْحَكِيمُ ۞ إِنَّ ٱلدِّينَ عِندَ

232   ٱللَّهِ ٱلْإِسْلَامُ ۞ فَسُبْحَانَ ٱللَّهِ حِينَ تُمْسُونَ وَحِينَ تُصْبِحُونَ ۞

233   وَلَهُ ٱلْحَمْدُ فِي ٱلسَّمَاوَاتِ وَٱلْأَرْضِ وَعَشِيًّا وَحِينَ تُظْهِرُونَ ۞

234   يُخْرِجُ ٱلْحَيَّ مِنَ ٱلْمَيِّتِ وَيُخْرِجُ ٱلْمَيِّتَ مِنَ ٱلْحَيِّ وَيُحْيِي

235   ٱلْأَرْضَ بَعْدَ مَوْتِهَا وَكَذَٰلِكَ تُخْرَجُونَ ۞

236   إِنِّي تَوَكَّلْتُ عَلَى ٱللَّهِ رَبِّي وَرَبِّكُم مَّا مِن دَآبَّةٍ إِلَّا هُوَ آخِذٌ

237   بِنَاصِيَتِهَا إِنَّ رَبِّي عَلَى صِرَاطٍ مُّسْتَقِيمٍ ۞ وَمَا لَنَا أَلَّا نَتَوَكَّلَ عَلَى

238   ٱللَّهِ وَقَدْ هَدَانَا سُبُلَنَا وَلَنَصْبِرَنَّ عَلَى مَا آذَيْتُمُونَا وَعَلَى ٱللَّهِ

239   فَلْيَتَوَكَّلِ ٱلْمُتَوَكِّلُونَ ۞ قُل لَّن يُصِيبَنَا إِلَّا مَا كَتَبَ ٱللَّهُ لَنَا هُوَ

240   مَوْلَانَا وَعَلَى ٱللَّهِ فَلْيَتَوَكَّلِ ٱلْمُؤْمِنُونَ ۞ وَمَا مِن دَآبَّةٍ فِي ٱلْأَرْضِ

241   إِلَّا عَلَى ٱللَّهِ رِزْقُهَا وَيَعْلَمُ مُسْتَقَرَّهَا وَمُسْتَوْدَعَهَا كُلٌّ فِي كِتَابٍ

242   مُّبِينٍ ۞ وَكَأَيِّن مِّن دَآبَّةٍ لَّا تَحْمِلُ رِزْقَهَا ٱللَّهُ يَرْزُقُهَا وَإِيَّاكُمْ

243   وَهُوَ ٱلسَّمِيعُ ٱلْعَلِيمُ ۞

244 مَّا يَفْتَحِ اللهُ لِلنَّاسِ مِن رَّحْمَةٍ فَلَا مُمْسِكَ لَهَا وَمَا يُمْسِكْ فَلَا

245 مُرْسِلَ لَهُ مِن بَعْدِهِ وَهُوَ الْعَزِيزُ الْحَكِيمُ ❖ وَلَئِن سَأَلْتَهُم مَّنْ

246 خَلَقَ السَّمَاوَاتِ وَالْأَرْضَ لَيَقُولُنَّ اللهُ قُلْ أَفَرَأَيْتُم مَّا تَدْعُونَ

247 مِن دُونِ اللهِ إِنْ أَرَادَنِيَ اللهُ بِضُرٍّ هَلْ هُنَّ كَاشِفَاتُ ضُرِّهِ ❖ أَوْ

248 أَرَادَنِي بِرَحْمَةٍ هَلْ هُنَّ مُمْسِكَاتُ رَحْمَتِهِ   قُلْ حَسْبِيَ اللهُ عَلَيْهِ

249 يَتَوَكَّلُ الْمُتَوَكِّلُونَ ❖ وَمَا جَعَلَهُ اللهُ إِلَّا بُشْرَىٰ لَكُمْ وَلِتَطْمَئِنَّ

250 قُلُوبُكُم بِهِ وَمَا النَّصْرُ إِلَّا مِنْ عِندِ اللهِ الْعَزِيزِ الْحَكِيمِ ❖

251 كهيعص ❖ حم ❖ عسق ❖ اِكْفِنَا وَارْحَمْنَا ❖ هُوَ اللهُ الْقَادِرُ

252 الْقَاهِرُ الظَّاهِرُ الْبَاطِنُ ❖ الْفَاطِرُ اللَّطِيفُ الْخَبِيرُ ❖

253 قَوْلُهُ الْحَقُّ وَلَهُ الْمُلْكُ يَوْمَ يُنفَخُ فِي الصُّورِ عَالِمُ الْغَيْبِ

254 وَالشَّهَادَةِ وَهُوَ الْحَكِيمُ الْخَبِيرُ ❖

255 تَحَصَّنْتُ بِالْقَوِيِّ الْمَتِينِ اللَّطِيفِ الْكَافِي الْحَفِيظِ الْحَيِّ الْقَيُّومِ

256 الَّذِي لَا تَأْخُذُهُ سِنَةٌ وَلَا نَوْمٌ ❖ الْحَنَّانِ الْمَنَّانِ ❖ يَا بَدِيعَ

257 السَّمَاوَاتِ وَالْأَرْضِ ❖ يَا حَيُّ يَا قَيُّومُ ❖ يَا ذَا الْجَلَالِ وَالْإِكْرَامِ ❖

258   نَسْأَلُكَ بِعَظِيمِ اللَّاهُوتِيَّةِ ❖ أَنْ تَنْقُلَ طِبَاعَنَا مِنْ طِبَاعِ

259   الْبَشَرِيَّةِ ❖ وَأَنْ تَرْفَعَ مُهَجَنَا مَعَ مَلَائِكَتِكَ الْعُلْوِيَّةِ ❖

260   يَا مُحَوِّلَ الْحَوْلِ وَالْأَحْوَالِ حَوِّلْ حَالَنَا إِلَى أَحْسَنِ حَالٍ ❖

261   يَا مُحَوِّلَ الْحَوْلِ وَالْأَحْوَالِ حَوِّلْ حَالَنَا إِلَى أَحْسَنِ حَالٍ ❖

262   يَا مُحَوِّلَ الْحَوْلِ وَالْأَحْوَالِ حَوِّلْ حَالَنَا إِلَى أَحْسَنِ حَالٍ ❖

263   سُبْحَانَكَ اللَّهُمَّ وَبِحَمْدِكَ أَشْهَدُ أَنْ لَا إِلَهَ إِلَّا أَنْتَ أَسْتَغْفِرُكَ

264   وَأَتُوبُ إِلَيْكَ ❖

265   اَللَّهُمَّ صَلِّ عَلَى سَيِّدِنَا مُحَمَّدٍ صَلَاةً تُنْجِينَا بِهَا مِنْ جَمِيعِ

266   الْأَهْوَالِ وَالْآفَاتِ ❖ وَتَقْضِي لَنَا بِهَا جَمِيعَ الْحَاجَاتِ ❖ وَتُطَهِّرُنَا

267   بِهَا مِنْ جَمِيعِ السَّيِّئَاتِ ❖ وَتَرْفَعُنَا بِهَا عِنْدَكَ أَعْلَى الدَّرَجَاتِ

268   وَتُبَلِّغُنَا بِهَا أَقْصَى الْغَايَاتِ ❖ مِنْ جَمِيعِ الْخَيْرَاتِ فِي الْحَيَاةِ

269   وَبَعْدَ الْمَمَاتِ ❖ وَعَلَى آلِهِ وَصَحْبِهِ وَسَلِّمْ تَسْلِيمًا كَثِيرًا ❖

270   اَللَّهُمَّ صَلِّ عَلَى سَيِّدِنَا مُحَمَّدٍ ۞ اَلسَّابِقِ إِلَى الْأَنَامِ نُورُهُ ۞

271   اَلرَّحْمَةِ لِلْعَالَمِينَ ظُهُورُهُ ۞ عَدَدَ مَنْ مَضَى مِنَ الْبَرِيَّةِ وَمَنْ

272   بَقِيَ ۞ وَمَنْ سَعِدَ مِنْهُمْ وَمَنْ شَقِيَ ۞ صَلَاةً تَسْتَغْرِقُ الْعَدَّ

273   وَتُحِيطُ بِالْحَدِّ ۞ لَا غَايَةَ لَهَا وَلَا انْتِهَاءَ وَلَا أَمَدَ ۞ صَلَاتَكَ الَّتِي

274   صَلَّيْتَ عَلَيْهِ صَلَاةً دَائِمَةً ۞ وَعَلَى آلِهِ وَأُسْرَتِهِ وَسَلِّمْ تَسْلِيمًا

275   مِثْلَ ذَلِكَ ۞ وَالْحَمْدُ لِلَّهِ رَبِّ الْعَالَمِينَ ۞

End of the Blessed Naqshabandi Wird

تم الورد الشريف

TRANSLATION OF THE BLESSED NAQSHABANDI WIRD

(The Naqshabandi Daily Supplications)

1   In the Name of Allah, Most Gracious, Most Merciful.

2   O Allah, You are The Divine King, The Ever-Living, The Self-
3   Subsisting, The Truth, The Manifest. There is no God but You. You
4   are my Lord. You Created me and I am Your slave; I will abide by
5   Your Covenant and Command to the best of my capacity. I seek
6   refuge in You from the evil I have committed. I acknowledge Your
7   Favours upon me and I confess to You all my sins. I beg Your
8   Forgiveness, for certainly none can forgive sins but You.

9   Glory be to Allah. Praise be to Allah. There is no God but Allah.
10   Allah is The Greatest. There is no power and no might except with
11   Allah, The Most High, The Great One. He is The First and He is
12   The Last. He is The Apparent and The Hidden. He is All Knowing
13   and All-Aware of all things. He is The Giver of life and death, and
14   He is All-Competent at all things.

15   Praise be to You, Glorious One. Praise be to You, Most High. Praise
16   be to You, Most Powerful. Praise be to You, Knower of all that is
17   secret and all that is most concealed. Praise be to You, The One
18   Who Resurrects beings on earth and in the heavens. Praise be to

19 You, Controller of all creation. Praise be to You; You Have
20 Predestined all wealth and earnings.

21 Praise be to You, Free from fault. Praise be to You, Maker of time.
22 You are Most Sublime. You are High above what they describe You
23 to be. Praise be to You; You Grant freedom from Hellfire. Praise be
24 to you, The Creator of all means and causes. Praise be to you, Ever-
25 Living, Eternal. Praise be to You, my Lord and The Lord of all
26 mankind. Our Lord! You created us with Your Power, and You
27 Have Favoured us over many of Your creation. All Praise and Grace
28 are due to You. All favours we have are due to You. You are Most
29 Gracious, Most High. We seek Your Pardon and to You we repent.

30 You are The First, there was none before You. You are The Last,
31 there is none after You. You are The Apparent, there is none like
32 unto You. You are The Concealed, none can behold You. You are
33 The One God; You have no need for partners. You are All-Powerful;
34 You have no need for ministers. You are The Supreme Commander;
35 You have no need for advisors. Say, O Allah! Lord of All Power
36 and All Kingdom, You Empower whomever You Wish, and You
37 Forbid power from whomever You Wish. You Honour whomever
38 You Wish, and You Disgrace whomever You Wish: In Your Hands
39 lie all good. Verily, You have all Power over all things.

40 You Make the night gain on the day, and You Make the day gain
41 on the night; You Bring forth the living out of the dead, You Bring

42   forth the dead out of the living; You give sustenance to whomever
43   You Wish without count or measure.

44   O Most Compassionate in this life, Most Merciful in the hereafter!
45   Glory be to You, The One, Veiled from the creation in this life.
46   Glory be to You, The One, Distinguished with Grandeur and Pride.
47   Glory be to You, The Owner of all things. Glory be to You, The
48   Honourable One with Power and Highness. O You, Knower of all
49   that is in the heavens and in the earth! O You, Knower of all that
50   which flutters in our hearts and of that within our chests! O You,
51   Who Have Honoured the Two Holy Lands (Makkah and Madinah)
52   over other towns and places! O You, Knower of all that is beneath
53   the sand and the soil.

54   Glory be to You, Most High, You Are so Subtle that You Are not
55   realised by our cognitive senses. Our Lord. You are Most Blessed,
56   Supreme; there is no Lord other than You, there is no Overpowering
57   Deity except You. O Allah, You are The Kind Giver, The Source
58   of Grace, The Grateful. I bear witness that You are God, Allah, there
59   is no god but You. You are my Lord and the Lord of all things, the
60   Creator of the heavens and the earth, Knower of the seen and the
61   unseen, Most High, Most Glorious, The Supreme One. Taa-seen-
62   meem. Taa-seen. Allah has joined the two seas but with an invisible
63   barrier in between, and they cannot transgress against one another.

64 "Allah. There is no god but He, The Living, The Self-Subsisting,
65 The Eternal. No slumber nor sleep can seize Him. His are all things
66 in the heavens and the earth. Who is there that can intercede in His
67 Presence except with His Divine Permission! He Knows what is
68 before them and what is behind them. Nor shall they compass aught
69 of His knowledge except as He Wills. His Throne encompasses all
70 the heavens and the earths. He never suffers any fatigue in guarding
71 and preserving them, He is Most High, Supreme in Glory".

72 Haam-meem, Haam-meem, Haam-meem, Haam-meem, Haam-
73 meem, Haam-meem, Haam-meem. The matter has been fulfilled
74 and victory has come - the enemies shall not be helped. Haam-
75 meem. The revelation of the Holy Book is from Allah, The Mighty,
76 The All-Wise. He is The Forgiver of sins; He Accepts repentance,
77 yet His Punishment is severe. He is The Kind Giver. There is no
78 god but He: to Him is the final destination. He is Able to do
79 anything with His Own Power. He Governs as He Wills with His
80 Might. No one can share His Power and He has no partner in His
81 Kingdom.

82 Glory and Praise be to Allah. There is no Might except with Allah.

83 Whatever Allah Wills happens and that which He Does not Will
84 cannot happen. I confirm that Allah Owns Power over all things
85 and that Allah Has Full Knowledge of all things.

86 O Allah, do not kill us by Your Wrath, nor destroy us by leaving us
87 engrossed in the passions of this world! Protect us so that Your
88 punishment may never befall us! Glory be to You, The King, Most
89 Holy. Glory be to You, Lord of Honour, Glory, Greatness, Power,
90 Pride and Might! Glory be to The Majesty, The Truth, The Ever-
91 Living, Who is never taken by sleep nor by death. The Pure One,
92 The Holy One. You Are our Lord and The Lord of all angels and
93 You are The Lord of the Spirit (Archangel Gabriel).

94 O Allah, grant us knowledge from Your Knowledge, make us have
95 better understanding of what You Mean. Bless us with the Power of
96 Your Help and Victory. O Allah, make me thank You, remember
97 You, worship You, obey You and be totally devoted to You. Make
98 me good-natured, soft hearted, supplicant to You and oft-repentant
99 unto You. O Allah, accept our repentance, wash away our
100 wrongdoing and keep our tongues free from error. Take away all
101 hatred that is within us and cleanse our hearts from all deceitfulness,
102 corruption and cowardice.

103 O Allah, we seek refuge in You from sudden death, from moral
104 corruption, from abandoning truth and from negligence.

105 Protect us from amassing wealth, from all means of corruption and
106 from all causes of our doom.

107 O Allah, grant us enough reverence for You that can save us from
108 falling into error against You. Grant us enough obedience to You
109 that allows us to enter Your Garden. Grant us enough certainty of
110 Faith that reduces the misery of calamities in this world. O Allah,
111 bless us to enjoy our hearing, our sight and our strength as long as
112 we are destined to live, and make these blessings last for us to the
113 end. O Allah, grant us power against those who oppress us, and
114 support us against those who show enmity to us. O Allah, allow not
115 calamity to come to our Faith, nor let this worldly life be our major
116 concern, nor our share of knowledge. O Most Merciful One! Let us
117 not be oppressed by those who show no mercy to us.

118 O Allah, we ask of Your Grace that by which You Guide our hearts,
119 You Mend our torn pieces, You Unite our broken relations, You
120 Cure our ill ones, You Purify our deeds and speech and You Inspire
121 us with righteousness. O Allah, we ask You through Your Divine
122 Power, through Your Oneness, through Your Dominant Glory and
123 Your Extensive Mercy, to grant us light in our hearing, light in our
124 eyesight, light in our eyes and light in our hearts. Grant us light in
125 our senses, light in our souls and light in front of us.

126 O Allah, grant us more true knowledge, light and wisdom, and grant
127 us plenty of the outer and inner bounties. Allah is Sufficient for us
128 for our Faith and for our worldly life. Allah is Sufficient for us for
129 all of our worries and concerns.

130   Allah, Most Wise, Most Powerful, is Sufficient for us against those
131   who wronged us. Allah, Most Merciful, is Sufficient for us at the
132   time of death. Allah, Most Kind, is Sufficient for us when questioned
133   in the grave.

134   "Allah is Sufficient for me: there is no god but He. On Him do I
135   rely, Lord of The Throne". (Repeat 7 times)

136   O new morning and new day! (If in the evening: O new evening
137   and new night!) Welcome, welcome to you. Welcome to the angel
138   of witness: register what we say. In the name of Allah, Most
139   Gracious, Most High, Most Loving, All Encompassing, Free to do
140   with His creation as He Wills. He is closer to them than their
141   jugular veins.

142   I know I have woken up this morning a believer in Allah: believing
143   in my ultimate meeting with Him, confirming His rights over me,
144   denying divinity to any other than Allah, and putting my complete
145   trust in Allah alone.

146   We bear witness before Allah, and before His angels, His Prophets
147   and Messengers, the Bearers of His Throne and before all of His
148   creation, that there is no other god beside Allah and that our Master,
149   Muhammad, is His Servant and Messenger. We bear witness that
150   Heaven is true, the Fire is true, the Sacred Spring (HawD) is true,
151   the Messenger's Intercession is true, Questioning in the grave is

152 true, the two Angels of the grave, Munkar and Nakeer, are true, that
153 Your Promise is true, that the Last Hour is undoubtedly coming,
154 and that Allah resurrects those in the graves. On this belief, we shall
155 live and die, and with this belief, we shall be resurrected, and God
156 willing, we shall not suffer any torture.

157 O Allah! We have wronged ourselves, forgive us all our sins, the
158 major and the minor sins, for surely, none can forgive them except
159 You. Guide us to the best of manners, for none can guide us to the
160 best of manners except You. My Lord! Here I am forever Yours; all
161 good is with You. From You do we ask for pardon and to You do
162 we repent. We have believed in Your Messenger and in Your Holy
163 Book.

164 O Allah, decorate our faces with modesty in Your Presence, and fill
165 our hearts with happiness with You. O Allah, make me generous
166 and noble, and do not make me stingy, a frequent sinner, a reporter
167 of gossip, arrogant or corruptive. O Allah, we seek refuge in You
168 from excessive eating and excessive talking, from extreme worry and
169 sadness, from pride, from living in hardship, from mistrust, from
170 intoxicants, from greed, from laziness, from falsehood, from evil
171 temptations and from living in misery.

172 O Allah, make the beginning of this day (or, "the beginning of this
173 night") righteous, and the middle of it prosperous and the end of it

174 success. O Allah, make the beginning of it full of mercy, the middle
175 of it free from need of worldly things, and the end of it filled with
176 honour. O Allah, make our life a blissful life, give us happiness in
177 our time here, and give us plentiful provision that is beneficial for
178 us.

179 O Allah, pardon us with Your Pardon, and be kind to us with Your
180 Kindness. Glory and praise be to You. I am incapable of praising
181 You the way You deserve to be praised. You are praiseworthy in the
182 manner that You have Praised Yourself. Those are honoured who
183 seek Your Protection. Your Tribute is most great. Your soldiers are
184 never defeated. Your Promise is never broken; there is no god but
185 You.

186 Glory be to You, The Worshiped One: we have not worshiped You
187 as You deserve to be worshiped. Glory be to You, The Known One:
188 we have not known You in the right manner You ought to be
189 known. Glory be to You, Most Remembered One: we have not
190 remembered You as You deserve to be remembered. Glory be to
191 You, The Most Thanked One: we have not been thankful to You as
192 You deserve to be thanked. O Allah! Grant us the proper manner
193 to thank You for the favours that you have bestowed upon us.

194 You are God, Whose Powerful Attributes are High above human
195 attributes. No partner has witnessed You when You created the

196 creation, and there was no equal being to You who could prevent
197 You from creating the souls You created.

198 O Allah! We seek refuge in You from tearless eyes, from hearts that
199 do not tremble with Your reverence, from knowledge that is not
200 beneficial to us, from egos that are never satisfied, from unanswered
201 prayers and from dire poverty.

202 O Allah! Allow us to realise and understand Your Concealed
203 Knowledge. Clothe us with the garments of Your Light. Submerse
204 us in the ocean of spiritual subtleties, and shower us with the
205 blessings of knowing You. O Light of Lights! O Most Kind,
206 Concealer of sins! We ask You to send Your Blessings upon our
207 Master, Sayyiduna Muhammad, the guiding light of all prophets
208 and friends of Allah, the bright full moon to all the pure ones, the
209 shining sun to both mankind and spirits, the radiance for both the
210 East and the West. We beg You to raise our existence to be in the
211 sphere of Divine Knowledge, and to secure our presence in the
212 Station of Perfection.

213 O Allah, O Light! O You through Whose Command the sky was
214 built, through Whose Power the earth was laid down, through
215 Whose Wisdom the mountains were fixed firm, and through Whose
216 Favour the sun and the moon were granted light.

217 We ask You by Your Name through Which the sun and the bright
218 planets have been illuminated, and the heavens have been
219 brightened, to give us a protective shield against all harm, and an
220 overwhelmingly brilliant light that blind the eyes. Allah alternates
221 the Night and the Day: verily in this reality is a great sign for those
222 who have true insight.

223 Ta-Seen, Ta-Seen-Meem. We seek refuge in Allah The Magnificent
224 from time-wasting instruments, from lying and slandering, from the
225 prohibited things, from deceit, from the oppression of people, from
226 the evil plots of the corrupt people, from the tribulations that
227 emerge during the day or during the night, and from the horrors of
228 torture in both this world and the hereafter. O Guardian, guard us
229 from all harm. O Protector, Most High, Most Eminent, The One
230 beside Whom there is no other god. No one except You knows how
231 You truly are. O Allah, Ever-Living, Self-Existing, The Truth,
232 Sufficient Protector, The One, Indivisible One, The Distinguished,
233 Self-Subsisting, Giver, Opener and Source of life and death.

234 Peaceful salutation is a Word from The Lord, Most Merciful. Allah
235 will Suffice you as against others, for He is All-Hearing, All-
236 Knowing.

237 He is God, Allah, there is no god but He: The Compassionate, The
238 Merciful, The Sovereign, The Holy, The All-Peace, The Source of
239 Security, The Perfect Guardian, The Almighty, The Compeller, The

240 Supreme, The Creator, The Originator, The Designer of forms, The

241 Oft-Forgiving, The Dominant, The All-Giving, The All-Provider,

242 The Opener, The All-Knowing, The Causer of compression, The

243 Causer of expansion, The Abaser, The Exalter, The Giver of honour,

244 The Giver of disgrace, The All-Hearing, The All-Seeing, The Judge,

245 The Just, The Subtle, The All-Aware, The All-Clement, The All-

246 Glorious, The Forgiver, The Thankful, The Sublime, The Great, The

247 Protector, The Sustainer, The Reckoner, The Omnipotent, The All-

248 Generous, The Watchful, The One Who Answers prayers, The All-

249 Comprehending, The All-Wise, The All-Loving, The Majestic, The

250 Resurrector, The All-Witness, The Truth, The Universal Trustee,

251 The All-Strong, Unyielding in Power, The True Friend, The

252 Praiseworthy, The Reckoner, The Originator, The Restorer, The

253 Giver of Life, The Life-Taker, The Ever-Living, The Eternal, The

254 Wealthy, The Most Noble, The One, The Everlasting Refuge, The

255 Powerful, The Prevailing, The Promoter, The Detainer, The First,

256 The Last, The Manifest, The Hidden, The Protector.

257 He is The All-Exalted, The Beneficent, The Acceptor of Repentance,

258 The Avenger, The Forgiving, The Gentle, The Lord of the Kingdom,

259 The Lord of Majesty and Generosity, The Lord of Justice, The

260 Gatherer, The Self-Sufficient, The Enricher, The Withholder, The

261 Afflicter, The Beneficent, The Light, The Guide, The Innovator, The

262 Everlasting, The Inheritor, The Righteous, The Forbearing. Nothing

263
264
is like unto Him, He is The All-Hearing, The All-Seeing. Allah is sufficient for us.

265
266
267
He is The Best Trustee, The Best Disposer of affairs, The Best Protective Friend and the Best Supporter. Our Lord, Your forgiveness do we seek, and to You we shall return.

268
269
270
271
272
273
274
275
276
277
O my Lord, Ever Living without demise, Most Persistent without decay, The Divine Director without assistants, turn all difficulties into ease for us and for our parents. O Allah, nothing can deprive us of what You Have Given us and nothing can give us what You Have Denied us. Nothing can reject what You have Willed, and nothing can change what You Have Decreed. No one can guide the one You Have Misled, and no one can mislead the one You Have Guided. No one can make easy what You Have Made difficult, and no one can make difficult what You Have made Easy. No one can benefit from their good deeds except if they are accepted by You.

278
279
280
281
Glory be to my Great High Lord, The Reckoner, The All-Ruler, The All Just, The All-Watchful, The All-Great, The Sublime, The One Who Answers prayers, The Wealthy, The Righteous, The Most Patient, The Almighty, The Equitable, The Giver, The Withholder.

282
283
There is no god but Allah, The Divine Trustee, The All-Witness. There is no god but Allah, The Unyielding in Power, The Majestic.

284   There is no god but Allah, The Absolute in Wealth, The True
285   Friend. There is no god but Allah, The Most Noble, The Exalted.

286   We have prepared for every horror: la ilaha illallah "There is no god
287   but Allah", and for every favour: alhamdu-lillah "Praise be to
288   Allah", and for every evil eye: subhan-allah "Glory be to Allah", and
289   for every difficulty hasbiy-allah "Allah is Sufficient Power for me",
290   and for every misery: masha-allah "Everything is the Will of Allah",
291   and for every fate and destiny: tawakkaltu 'alallah "I rely only on
292   Allah", and for every calamity: innaa-lillah "we belong to Allah",
293   and for every act of obedience and disobedience: la Hawla walaa
294   quwwata illa-billah "There is no power nor means of help except by
295   Allah", and for every need: ista'antu billah "I seek the Support of
296   Allah".

297   "O Allah, this morning (or "evening"), we bear witness before You
298   and before Your angels, Your Prophets, Your Messengers, and
299   before all of Your creation, that You are The True God Alone,
300   without any partners, and that our Master, Muhammad, is Your
301   servant and messenger". (Repeat 4 times).

302   In The Name of Allah, The Curer, He is Allah. In The Name of
303   Allah, The All-Sufficient, He is Allah. In The Name of Allah, The
304   Healer, He is Allah.

305 "In the name of Allah, with Whose Name nothing in the heavens
306 or in the earth can harm us, He is All-Seeing, All-Knowing." (Repeat
307 3 times). Surely, Allah is The Best Protector, Most Merciful.

308 O Giver of Life, grant us a good life: in health and in safety both in
309 this life and in the next. You are surely Able to do anything.

310 Allah encompasses them from all directions. Surely, this is the
311 Glorious Quran, in the Heavenly Tablet Preserved! Guard strictly
312 your prayers, and take extra care of the Middle Prayer; and stand
313 before Allah in a devout condition. There is no soul but has a
314 protector over it, and Allah is the Best of Protectors.

315 "O Protector, Protect us." (Repeat 3 times)

316 Then, after the distress that befell you, He Sent down calm on a
317 band of you overcome with slumber, while another band was stirred
318 to anxiety by their own feelings, moved by wrong suspicions of
319 Allah: suspicions due to ignorance.

320 They said, "What affair is this of ours?" Say, "Indeed, this affair is
321 wholly of Allah." They hide in their hearts what they dare not reveal
322 to you. They say, 'If we had the power to do anything with this
323 affair, we would not have been in the slaughter here.' Say, 'Even if
324 you had remained in your own homes, those for whom death was
325 decreed would certainly have come forth to the places of their

326 death;' but that Allah may test what is in your chests and purge

327 what is in your hearts. For Allah knows well the deepest secrets in

328 your hearts. Those who say, "Our Lord! We have indeed believed:

329 forgive us, then, our sins, and save us from the agony of the Fire of

330 Hell.

331 Those who show patience, firmness and self-control; who are true

332 in word and in deed; who worship devoutly; who spend in the Way

333 of Allah; and who spend the night praying for forgiveness. There is

334 no god but He: That is the witness of Allah, His angels, and of those

335 endued with knowledge, standing firm on justice. Surely, there is no

336 god but He, The Exalted in Power, The Wise. With Allah, the true

337 Religion is Islam. So glorify Allah, when you reach eventide and

338 when you rise in the morning; to Him be praise, in the heavens and

339 on earth; and in the evening and when the day begins to decline.

340 It is He Who brings out the living from the dead, and brings out

341 the dead from the living, and Who gives life to the land after it is

342 dead: and thus will you too be brought out from the dead.

343 I put my trust in Allah, my Lord and your Lord! There is not a

344 moving creature, but He has full grasp of its forelock. Verily, it is

345 my Lord Who is on the Straight Path. No reason have we why we

346 should not put our trust in Allah. Indeed, He Has guided us to our

347 good ways. We shall certainly bear with patience all the hurt that

348 you may cause us. For those who put their trust should put their

349 trust in Allah. Say, "Nothing will happen to us except what Allah

350 has decreed for us: He is our Protector", and on Allah, the Believers

351 should put their trust. There is no living creature on earth but its

352 sustenance depends on Allah. He knows the time and place of its

353 definite abode and its temporary deposit: All is recorded in a clear

354 Register. How many a creature that does not carry its own

355 sustenance but Allah provides it its sustenance and the same for

356 you, for He is The All-Hearing, All Knowing.

357 What Allah, out of His Mercy, Does Bestow upon mankind, none

358 can withhold: what He Does Withhold, none can grant, apart from

359 Him; He is The Exalted in Power, All-Wise. If indeed you ask them

360 who it is that created the heavens and the earth, they would surely

361 say, "Allah".

362 Say, "Can you not see then? The things that you invoke besides

363 Allah, can they, if Allah wills some Penalty on me, remove His

364 Penalty? Or if He Wills some grace for me, can they prevent His

365 Grace?" Say, "Sufficient is Allah for me! In Him trust those who put

366 their trust." Allah Has Sent it but a message of hope for you, and

367   an assurance to your hearts - there is no true help except from Allah.
368   The Exalted, the Wise.

369   Kaaf-ha-yaa-'ayn-SaaD. Haa-meem. 'ayn-seen-qaaf: Suffice us with
370   Your Power and have mercy upon us. He is Allah, The Able, The
371   Dominant, The Manifest, The Concealed, The Originator, The
372   Most Kind, The All-Aware. His Word is the Truth, and His will be
373   the Dominion on the Day when the Trumpet will be blown. He is
374   All-Knowing of hidden and the seen; He is All Wise, Well
375   Acquainted with all things.

376   I am in the Protection of Allah, The All-Strong, The Firm One, The
377   Most Kind, The Subsisting, The Protector, The Ever Living. The
378   One Who neither fatigue nor sleep can overtake Him. The Most
379   Compassionate, The Most Kind. O Most Magnificent, Originator
380   of the heavens and the earth, Ever Living, Eternal. O Possessor of
381   Majesty and Honour, we ask You by Your Great Lordship to change
382   our inner selves from that of the human nature and to raise our
383   souls to be with Your high Angels.

384   "O Transformer of states and conditions, turn our condition into
385   the best of conditions". (Repeat 3 times)

386   Glory and Praise be to You. I bear witness that there is no god but
387   You. I beg for Your forgiveness and to You I do repent.

388 O Allah, send Your Blessings upon our Master, Muhammad;
389 blessings that will be the means of our salvation from all the horrors
390 and trauma of the Day of Judgment. Send upon him Blessings that
391 will fulfill all of our needs and that which will purify us from all of
392 our sins. Send upon him Blessings that will raise our stations to the
393 highest of all stations. Send upon him Blessings that will raise us to
394 the highest of virtuous destinations in this world and after death.
395 Send abundant Blessings and Greetings upon him and upon his
396 Family and Companions.

397 O Allah, send Your Blessings upon our Master, Muhammad, whose
398 light preceded the existence of mankind, and whose coming to earth
399 is mercy for all mankind. Allah, send upon him as many Blessings
400 as the number of mankind who have passed away and the number
401 of those who remain to come, and as many as those who are
402 fortunate and as many as those who are wretched. O Allah, send
403 upon Sayyiduna Muhammad continuous Blessings that encompass
404 all the creation, Blessings that have no limit and that never stop and
405 never end, the Blessings that You have already been sending upon
406 him from time immemorial. Allah, send similar Blessings upon his
407 Family, Ahlul-Bayt, and upon all of his Supporters. All praise be to
408 Allah, Lord of the worlds.

End of the Blessed Wird Translation

TAZKIYAH: PURIFICATION OF THE INNER SELF

Beloved murid!

This life is a life of great joy and happiness; do not let it pass by in misery. Enjoy being the servant of Allah, The King of kings, the All Glorious, All Merciful, All Beautiful. If you are a true believer and submit to your Creator, Allah, then enjoy your submission. Enjoy your Islam - do not live it as a burden on your shoulders.

Allah has given you such a wonderful reality, a miraculous subtlety, which is your spiritual heart — but only one heart. This heart is a diamond in which Divine meanings can be inscribed. By this heart, you can receive and understand Divine communication. You must know, however, Allah is Glorious and Majestic and He does not inscribe His Divine Meanings in a diamond that has already been used by someone or something else. A single heart cannot serve as abode for two opposite things. If the heart is filled with the forms of sensory perceptions, it becomes unable to perceive Divine Meanings. When your heart is clean from all that is 'other-than-God', you will experience Divine bliss even in this very world. Then, when your heart utters 'Allah' once, you will find such bliss and out-of-this-world joy that your tongue can never describe.

The more problems there are between one's self and one's effort for good deeds, the clearer are the signs of illness in his heart.

The more unrest (hatred, jealousy, etc.) there is between believers, the greater the risk of dying without attainment of a clean, sound heart. One's life is but counted breaths: if you do not stop at a certain breath to reflect upon the condition of your heart and take action, you will only suddenly wake up with the last breath.

Sayyiduna Muhammad, the last Messenger of Allah (pbuh), said, "People are often asleep; as soon as they die they wake up!" From this kind of sleep, the future of such people is but utter ruin. The intelligent ones, on the other hand, as the holy Messenger (pbuh) also noted, are "those who wake up before death wakes them up."

The eyes of the heart open only when the heart is in the state of constant remembrance of Allah, a state that is Divinely gifted, but only to those who are devoted to Allah in every breath they take. When one reaches this state, Divine Light permeates the heart of the murid, by means of which the murid can perceive what was previously veiled or hidden from him. As a result, the murid's mind can now perceive a more comprehensive understanding of life. The manifest indication of this stage is that the heart of the seeker becomes indifferent to worldly attractions, finding no charm in them at all. The seeker's attention is wholly and constantly directed to the Absolute Truth, Allah Almighty.

Beloved murid! It is your gain when you devote your life to this blessed Tariqah, for devotion to the Path is devotion to the Destination of the Path: Allah The Magnificent.

You need to perform your silent zhikr (Divine remembrance) daily and to read your Naqshabandi Wird daily with total devotion and sincerity. The more you are steadfast on the life of this noble Path, the stronger your spiritual relationship will be with the Source of Light, the Holy Messenger of Allah, Sayyiduna Muhammad (pbuh). From his blessed heart, this Light reaches your heart through the hearts of all the great saints in this blessed Path, and you will be ultimately prepared to be ushered into Divine Presence.

Let us now focus on giving spiritual and mental attention to our saints, the pure souls who spiritually connect us to the Source of all Light, Sayyiduna Muhammad, peace be upon him and upon his noble Ahlul-Bayt. These saints are devout, pure beings, whose hearts never carry any evil nor know any vice. Their hearts are like soft, sensitive, aromatic white rose petals. They are finely Divinely cut diamonds who reflect only the Lights and Beauty of Allah The Glorious through their constant union with the purest of all saints, the last Messenger of God, Sayyiduna Muhammad, peace be upon him and his noble Ahlul-Bayt.

The spiritual and scholarly knowledge and light of these blessed saints have reached us through two chains of Muslim saints. We call the tree of saints a chain (silsilah) because each one of them is a ring that is strongly connected to, and intertwined with, the other ring so that the heat of love and faith is always transmitted from one end of the chain to the other end. One Chain, or silsilah, is called The Siddiqiya Chain, as it goes back to Sayyiduna Abu-Bakr AS-Siddiq (RA), who took the Divine Secret from the Holy Messenger (pbuh). The other Chain is The Zhahabiya (Golden) Chain, going back to Sayyiduna Ali ibn Abi-Talib (RA), who also took the Divine Secret from the Holy Messenger (pbuh), and is then transmitted to us through early Masters of Ahlul-Bayt, Allah be pleased with them. We often use the Siddiqiya Chain because its line of transmission is much shorter, which means there are less saints between me and the Holy Messenger (pbuh).

May Allah Almighty bless you with perfect light and true guidance, and may He protect you from Satan, from your own ego/self and from all other evils. Amen.

Now, bring forth all of your attention. Here is the Book that will awaken your spiritual senses, increase your subtle awareness and lead you to The Divine Presence. Enjoy your heart!

THE NOBLE SILSILAH SIDDIQIYA
(Siddiqiya Chain)

1. Master of all Masters, Sayyiduna Muhammad ibn Abdullah, last Messenger of Allah (Salla Allahu 'alaihi wasallam)

2. Master Abu-Bakr AS-Siddiq (RA)

3. Master Salman Al-farisi (RA)

4. Master Al-qasim ibn Muhammad ibn Abu-Bakr (RA)

5. Master Ja'far AS-Sadiq (RA)

6. Master Abu-Yazid Al-bistami (Tayfur ibn Eesa) (RA)

7. Master Abul-Hasan Al-kharqani (RA)

8. Master Abu-Ali Al-fadhl Al-faramdi (RA) (where both Noble Chains meet)

9. Master Abu Ya'qub Yusuf Al-hamadani (RA)

10. Master Abdul-khaliq Al-ghajdawani (RA)

11. Master Muhammad Arif Rayukari Ramitni (RA)

12. Master Mahmud Al-injir Faghnawi (RA)

13. Master Azizan An-nassaj Ramitni (RA)

14. Master Muhammad Baba As-samasi (RA)

15. Master As-saif Ameer Kulal (RA)

16. Imam of Tariqah, Sunshine of Haqiqa (The Truth), Master Muhammad Baha-uddin Shah Naqshaband Al-bukhari Al-Husaini (RA)

17. Master 'Ala-uddin Al-'attaar (RA)

18. Master Ya'qub Al-jarkhi (RA)

19. Master Nasir-uddin Ubeidullah Ahrar Samarqandi (RA)

20. Master Muhammad Az-zahid (RA)

21. Master Muhammad Darwish (RA)

22. Master Muhammad Khawajah Amkanki (RA)

23. Master Muhammad Baqi Billah Dahlawi (RA)

24. Master Ahmad Al-farouqi Sirhindi (RA)

25. Master Muhammad Ma'sum Sirhindi (RA)

26. Master Muhammad Saifuddin Farouqi (RA)

27. Master Sayyid Noor Muhammad Badawni (RA)

28. Master Shamsuddin Habibullah Mazhar Jani-Janan (RA)

29. Master Abdullah Ghulam Ali Shah Al-Ahmadi Dahlawi (RA)

30. Master Abu Sa'eed, offspring of Imam Rabbani (RA)

31. Master Ahmad ibn Sa'eed ibn Abu Sa'eed (RA)

32. Master Al-hafiz Waliyunnabi (RA)

33. Master Haji Muhammad Mujtaba Khan Rampuri (RA)

34. Master Manzur Husain Sindhi (RA)

35. Master Abul-Hasan Is-haq ibn Abdullah Al-Hasani (RA)

36. Master Abuz-zahra Uwais ibn Abdullah Al-Husaini (RA)

37. Master Al-Sharif Abdullah ibn-Hashim Al-Husaini Al-Madani
    (seeking Mercy of his Lord)

THE NOBLE SILSILAH ZHAHABIYA
(Golden Chain)

1. Master of all Masters, Sayyiduna Muhammad ibn Abdullah, last Messenger of Allah (Salla Allahu 'alaihi wasallam)

2. Master Ali ibn Abi-Talib (RA)

3. Master Al-Husain ibn Ali (RA)

4. Master Ali Zainul-'abideen ibn Al-Husain (RA)

5. Master Muhammad Al-baqir (RA)

6. Master Ja'far AS-Sadiq (RA)

7. Master Musa Al-kazim (RA)

8. Master Ali Ar-rida (RA)

9. Master Ma'ruf Al-karkhi (RA)

10. Master As-sariy As-saqati (RA)

11. Master Al-junaid Al-baghdadi (RA)

12. Master Abu-Ali Al-Ruzhabari (RA)

13. Master Abu-Uthman Al-maghribi (RA)

14. Master Abul-qasim Al-jurjani (RA)

15. Master Abu-Ali Al-fadhl Al-faramdi (RA) (where both Noble Chains meet)

16. Master Abu Ya'qub Yusuf Al-hamadani (RA)

17. Master Abdul-khaliq Al-ghajdawani (RA)

18. Master Muhammad Arif Rayukari Ramitni (RA)

19. Master Mahmud Al-injir Faghnawi (RA)

Our Crown Masters: Muhammad the Messenger of Allah (pbuh), Abu-Bakr AS-Siddiq, Omar ibn Al-khattab, Othman ibn Affan (RA), {Ali ibn Abi-Talib, Fatima Az-zahra, Al-Hasan and Al-Husain (AS)}

20. Master Azizan An-nassaj Ramitni (RA)

21. Master Muhammad Baba As-samasi (RA)

22. Master As-saif Ameer Kulal (RA)

23. Imam of Tariqah, Sunshine of Haqiqa (The Truth), Master Muhammad Baha-uddin Shah Naqshaband Al-bukhari Al-Husaini (RA)

24. Master 'Ala-uddin Al-'attaar (RA)

25. Master Ya'qub Al-jarkhi (RA)

26. Master Nasir-uddin Ubeidullah Ahrar Samarqandi (RA)

27. Master Muhammad Az-zahid (RA)

28. Master Muhammad Darwish (RA)

29. Master Muhammad Khawajah Amkanki (RA)

30. Master Muhammad Baqi Billah Dahlawi (RA)

31. Master Ahmad Al-farouqi Sirhindi (RA)

32. Master Muhammad Ma'sum Sirhindi (RA)

33. Master Muhammad Saifuddin Farouqi (RA)

34. Master Sayyid Noor Muhammad Badawni (RA)

35. Master Shamsuddin Habibullah Mazhar Jani-Janan (RA)

36. Master Abdullah Ghulam Ali Shah Al-Ahmadi Dahlawi (RA)

37. Master Abu Sa'eed, offspring of Imam Rabbani (RA)

38. Master Ahmad ibn Sa'eed ibn Abu Sa'eed (RA)

39. Master Al-hafiz Waliyunnabi (RA)

40. Master Haji Muhammad Mujtaba Khan Rampuri (RA)

41. Master Manzur Husain Sindhi (RA)

42. Master Abul-Hasan Is-haq ibn Abdullah Al-Hasani (RA)

43. Master Abuz-zahra Uwais ibn Abdullah Al-Husaini (RA)

44. Master Al-Sharif Abdullah ibn-Hashim Al-Husaini Al-Madani (seeking Mercy of his Lord)

PRAYER OF THE NOBLE NAQSHABANDI CHAIN

The blessed names of saints are connected to their blessed souls, who have authorisation from Allah Almighty to give others of their Lights and Blessings. This is why it is extremely beneficial to recite their blessed names then make a prayer for yourself so that it may bring you more virtues and grace.

There is a special prayer designated to the Blessed Chain by some of the early Naqshabandi saints. It is recommended to recite all the blessed names of the Noble silsilah Siddiqiya as above, and then recite the Prayer below in the following occasions:

- after reciting the Khatm Khawajakan

- when Shaykh gives you initiation (Talqeen)

- when beginning your individual zhikr

- after reading the Naqshabandi Wird

- This Prayer is also good for getting relief from difficulties and problems as well as for cure from illnesses.

أَسْأَلُكَ اللَّهُمَّ وَأَتُوبُ إِلَيْكَ، وَأَتَمَسَّكُ وَأَتَوَسَّلُ وَأَتَوَجَّهُ وَأَتَضَرَّعُ

وَأَتَحَفَّظُ وَأَتَحَصَّنُ وَأَسْتَشْفِي وَأَتَشَفَّعُ وَأَتَعَلَّمُ وَأَتَفَهَّمُ وَأَتَذَكَّرُ

وَأَتَفَكَّرُ وَأَتَرَيَّضُ وَأَتَرَفَّعُ وَأَتَوَصَّلُ وَأَتَقَرَّبُ بِأَسْرَارِكَ الْمُودَعَاتِ،

وَأَنْوَارِ تَجَلِّيَاتِكَ الْمَوْضُوعَاتِ وَالْمُقَرَّبَاتِ فِي هَذِهِ الطُّرُقِ الْعَلِيَّةِ،

وَبِبَرَكَاتِ الْمَشَايِخِ الْمُسْلِمِينَ، بِسَيِّدِنَا الشَّرِيفُ عَبْدُاللهِ الْحُسَيْنِي

الْمَدَنِي، وَبِسَيِّدِنَا أُوَيْسُ بْنُ عَبْدِاللهِ الْحُسَيْنِي، وَبِسَيِّدِنَا إِسْحَاقُ

بْنُ عَبْدِاللهِ الْحَسَنِي، وَبِسَيِّدِنَا مَنْظُورُ حُسَيْنُ سِنْدِي، وَبِسَيِّدِنَا

مُحَمَّدٌ مُجْتَبَى خَان، وَبِسَيِّدِنَا الْحَافِظُ وَلِيُّ النَّبِي، وَبِسَيِّدِنَا أَحْمَدُ

بْنُ سَعِيدٍ، وَبِسَيِّدِنَا أَبُوسَعِيدٍ ذُرِّيَّةُ الْإِمَامِ الرَّبَّانِي، وَبِسَيِّدِنَا

عَبْدُاللهِ شَاه غُلَامٍ، وَبِسَيِّدِنَا حَبِيبُ اللهِ جَانِيجَانَان، وَبِسَيِّدِنَا

نُورُ مُحَمَّدٌ الْبَدَاوْنِي، وَبِسَيِّدِنَا مُحَمَّدٌ سَيْفُ الدِّينِ، وَبِسَيِّدِنَا

مُحَمَّدٌ مَعْصُومٍ، وَبِسَيِّدِنَا أَحْمَدُ الْفَارُوقِي السِّرْهِنْدِي، وَبِسَيِّدِنَا

مُحَمَّدٌ الْبَاقِي بِاللهِ، وَبِسَيِّدِنَا مُحَمَّدٌ الْخَوَاجَةِ الْأَمْكَنْكِي، وَبِسَيِّدِنَا

دَرْوِيْشُ مُحَمَّدٌ، وَبِسَيِّدِنَا مُحَمَّدٌ الزَّاهِدِ، وَبِسَيِّدِنَا عُبَيْدُاللهِ

أَحْرَارٌ، وَبِسَيِّدِنَا يَعْقُوبُ ٱلْجَرْخِي، وَبِسَيِّدِنَا عَلَاءُ ٱلدِّينِ ٱلْعَطَّارِ، وَبِسَيِّدِنَا مُحَمَّدٍ شَاه نَقْشبنْدَ ٱلْبُخَارِيُّ ٱلْحُسَيْنِي، وَبِسَيِّدِنَا أَمِيرُ كُلَالٍ، وَبِسَيِّدِنَا مُحَمَّدٍ بَابَا ٱلسَّمَاسِي، وَبِسَيِّدِنَا عَلِي النَّسَّاجُ رَامِيثْنِي، وَبِسَيِّدِنَا مَحْمُودُ ٱلْإِنْجِيرِ فَغْنَوِي، وَبِسَيِّدِنَا عَارِفٌ ٱلرَّيُوكَرِي، وَبِسَيِّدِنَا عَبْدُ ٱلْخَالِقُ ٱلْغَجْدَوَانِي، وَبِسَيِّدِنَا يُوسُفُ ٱلْهَمَدَانِي، وَبِسَيِّدِنَا أَبُو عَلِي الْفَضْلُ ٱلْفَارَمِدِي، وَبِسَيِّدِنَا أَبُو ٱلْحَسَنُ ٱلْخَرْقَانِي، وَبِسَيِّدِنَا أَبُو يَزِيدُ ٱلْبِسْطَامِي، وَبِسَيِّدِنَا جَعْفَرُ ٱلصَّادِقِ، وَبِسَيِّدِنَا ٱلْقَاسِمُ بْنُ مُحَمَّدٍ بْنِ أَبِي بَكْرٍ، وَبِسَيِّدِنَا الصَّحَابِي سَلْمَانُ ٱلْفَارِسِي، وَبِسَيِّدِنَا ٱلْخَلِيفَةِ ٱلرَّاشِدُ أَبُو بَكْرٍ الصِّدِّيقُ، وَبِسَيِّدِ السَّادَاتِ، مَنْبَع ٱلْخَيْرِ وَالْبَرَكَاتِ، أَعْظَمِ ٱلْمَخْلُوقَات، سَيِّدِنَا مُحَمَّدٍ رَسُولِ اللهِ صَلَّى اللهُ عَلَيْهِ وَآلِهِ وَسَلَّمَ.

وَكَذَا، بِسَيِّدِنَا أَبُو ٱلْقَاسِمُ ٱلْجُرْجَانِي، وَبِسَيِّدِنَا أَبُو عُثْمَان ٱلْمَغْرِبِي، وَبِسَيِّدِنَا أَبُو عَلِي ٱلرُّوذَبَارِي، وَبِسَيِّدِنَا ٱلْجُنَيْدُ ٱلْبَغْدَادِي، وَبِسَيِّدِنَا السَّرِيّ ٱلسَّقَطِي، وَبِسَيِّدِنَا مَعْرُوفُ

اَلْكَرْخِي، وَبِسَيِّدِنَا عَلِيٌّ الرِّضَا، وَبِسَيِّدِنَا مُوسَى الْكَاظِمِ،
وَبِسَيِّدِنَا جَعْفَرُ الصَّادِقِ، وَبِسَيِّدِنَا مُحَمَّدٌ الْبَاقِرِ، وَبِسَيِّدِنَا عَلِيُّ
زَيْنُ الْعَابِدِينَ، وَبِسَيِّدِنَا الْحُسَيْنُ بْنُ عَلِيٍّ، وَبِسَيِّدِنَا الْخَلِيفَةِ
الرَّاشِدِ عَلِيُّ بْنُ أَبِي طَالِبٍ، وَبِسَيِّدِ السَّادَاتِ، مَنْبَعِ الْخَيْرِ وَالْبَرَكَاتِ،
أَعْظَمِ الْمَخْلُوقَاتِ سَيِّدِنَا مُحَمَّدٍ رَسُولِ اللهِ صَلَّى اللهُ عَلَيْهِ وَسَلَّمَ،
وَبِسَيِّدِنَا جِبْرِيلَ، وَبِسَيِّدِنَا مِيكَائِيلَ، وَبِسَيِّدِنَا إِسْرَافِيلَ،
عَلَيْهِمُ السَّلَامُ.

إِلَهِي أَنْتَ مَقْصُودِي، وَرِضَاكَ مَطْلُوبِي، أَعْطِنِي مَحَبَّتَكَ وَمَعْرِفَتَكَ،
فَأَسْأَلُكَ اللَّهُمَّ بِعِزَّتِكَ وَجَلَالِكَ وَجَمَالِكَ وَقُدْرَتِكَ وَكِبْرِيَائِكَ
وَعَظَمَتِكَ وَسِرِّ سِرِّ أَسْرَارِ أَسْمَائِكَ الْعِظَامِ، وَأَنْبِيَائِكَ الْكِرَامِ،
وَأَوْلِيَائِكَ الْفِخَامِ، وَمَلَائِكَتِكَ الْمُقَرَّبِينَ عَلَيْهِمُ السَّلَامِ، وَبِحَقِّ لَا
إِلَهَ إِلَّا اللهُ، مُحَمَّدٌ رَسُولُ اللهِ، وَبِحَقِّ هَذَا الِاسْمِ اللهُ اللهُ اللهُ
بِالْأَلِفِ الْقَائِمِ الَّذِي لَيْسَ قَبْلَهُ سَابِقٌ، وَلَا بَعْدَهُ لَاحِقٌ، وَبِاللَّامَيْنِ
اللَّذَيْنِ لَمَمْتَ بِهِمَا الْأَسْرَارَ وَأَخَذْتَ بِهِمَا الْعَهْدَ الْوَارِثَ، وَبِالْهَاءِ

اَلْمُحِيطَةِ الْمُحَرِّكَةِ لِلسَّوَاكِنِ وَالْجَوَامِدِ وَالنَّوَاطِقِ، أَنْ تُوَفِّقَنِي

لِلنَّظَرِ إِلَى وَجْهِكَ الْكَرِيمِ، وَتَقْضِيَ حَوَائِجِي، وَتَفْتَحَ لِي أَبْوَابَ

الْعُلُومِ وَالْكُشُوفِ، وَتُفِيضَ عَلَيَّ مِنْ بَرَكَاتِ الْعَرْشِ وَالْكُرْسِيِّ

وَاللَّوْحِ الْمَحْفُوظِ، وَتَتَجَلَّى فِي قَلْبِي بِأَنْوَاعِ التَّجَلِّيَاتِ وَالْأَنْوَارِ كَمَا

أَفَضْتَ وَتَجَلَّيْتَ عَلَى قُلُوبِ أَنْبِيَائِكَ وَأَصْفِيَائِكَ أَجْمَعِينَ، بِلُطْفِكَ

وَكَرَمِكَ يَا أَرْحَمَ الرَّاحِمِينَ. لَا إِلَهَ إِلَّا أَنْتَ سُبْحَانَكَ إِنِّي كُنْتُ مِنَ

الظَّالِمِينَ، فَاسْتَجَبْنَا لَهُ وَنَجَّيْنَاهُ مِنَ الْغَمِّ وَكَذَلِكَ نُنْجِي

الْمُؤْمِنِينَ.

اَللَّهُمَّ إِنِّي أَقَمْتُ نَفْسِي تَحْتَ الْمِيزَابِ الْمُحَمَّدِيِّ، حَقِيرًا ذَلِيلًا

مُذْنِبًا مُسْتَشْفِعًا، فَيَسِّرْ لِي أَنْوَاعَ تَجَلِّيَاتِكَ الْإِلَهِيَّةِ، وَأَسْرَارَ

مَلَائِكَتِكَ الْقُدْسِيَّةِ، وَهِمَمَ أَوْلِيَائِكَ الرَّبَّانِيَّةِ، وَفُيُوضَاتِ حَبِيبِكَ

الْمُحَمَّدِيَّةِ.

وَلَوْ أَنَّهُمْ إِذْ ظَلَمُوا أَنْفُسَهُمْ جَاؤُوكَ فَاسْتَغْفَرُوا اللَّهَ وَاسْتَغْفَرَ لَهُمُ

الرَّسُولُ لَوَجَدُوا اللَّهَ تَوَّابًا رَحِيمًا، رَبَّنَا آتِنَا فِي الدُّنْيَا حَسَنَةً وَفِي

ٱلْآخِرَةِ حَسَنَةً وَقِنَا عَذَابَ ٱلنَّارِ، رَبَّنَا لَا تُزِغْ قُلُوبَنَا بَعْدَ إِذْ هَدَيْتَنَا وَهَبْ لَنَا مِن لَّدُنْكَ رَحْمَةً إِنَّكَ أَنْتَ ٱلْوَهَّابُ، رَبَّنَا ٱغْفِرْ لِي وَلِوَالِدَيَّ وَلِلْمُؤْمِنِينَ يَوْمَ يَقُومُ ٱلْحِسَابُ، رَبَّنَا ٱغْفِرْ لَنَا وَلِإِخْوَانِنَا ٱلَّذِينَ سَبَقُونَا بِٱلْإِيمَانِ وَلَا تَجْعَلْ فِي قُلُوبِنَا غِلًّا لِّلَّذِينَ آمَنُوا رَبَّنَا إِنَّكَ رَءُوفٌ رَّحِيمٌ، سُبْحَانَ رَبِّكَ رَبِّ ٱلْعِزَّةِ عَمَّا يَصِفُونَ، وَسَلَامٌ عَلَى الْمُرْسَلِينَ، وَالْحَمْدُ لِلَّهِ رَبِّ الْعَالَمِينَ.

End of the Prayer

IMAM OF THE BLESSED TARIQAH

Sayyiduna Muhammad Baha-uddin Shah Naqshaband Albukhari Al-Hasani Al-Husaini

(Qaddasa Allahu sirrahu: the one with Sacred Heart)

Sayyiduna Muhammad Baha-uddin Shah Naqshaband (RA), the Sunshine of The Truth, the Imam of this most blessed Tariqah and the Fountain of Divine Knowledge, is from the blessed descendants of the Holy Messenger (pbuh) through his noble grandson, Imam Al-Husain ibn Ali (RA) from his father's side, and through Imam Al-Hasan ibn Ali (RA) from his mother's side.

Master Shah Naqshaband (RA) was born on 14th of Muharram, 718 AH (18 March 1318 AD), in a village called Qasr Arifan near Bukhara, (now, in Uzbekistan).

Allah Almighty blessed him from a very early age to be in the spiritual care of some of the greatest saints in the world. While still an infant, Hadrat Shah Naqshaband (RA) was accepted as a spiritual son by Sayyiduna Muhammad Baba As-samasi (RA), who raised him and educated him to the highest level of spiritual spheres that he had reached. After the departure of Hadrat As-samasi, he continued the Path of Divine Knowledge with Hadrat As-Samasi's main successor, Sayyiduna Ameer Kulal (RA), for many years.

Sayyiduna Shah Naqshaband (RA) was also spiritually instructed by Sayyiduna Abdul-khaliq Al-ghajdawani (RA), who gave him great spiritual heights in Divine Presence. Thereafter, Hadrat Shah Nashaband was Divinely inspired to resort to silent zhikr and leave vocal zhikr. This marked the crystallization of the Naqshabandi Tariqah as known today, by restricting the Path to silent zhikr, which goes back to the Righteous Caliphs, Sayyiduna Abu-Bakr (RA) and Sayyiduna Ali (RA), and since then silent zhikr became the essence of spiritual growth in this powerful and blessed Tariqah.

When Sayyiduna Shah Naqshaband (RA) fell into his final illness, he stayed in solitude in his room. As many of his murids began to visit him, he gave each one of them the last advice they needed. One day, he ordered his visitors to read Surat Yasin. When they completed the Surah, he raised his hands to heaven, then raised his right index finger and said the parting statement, 'There is no god but Allah, and Muhammad is the Messenger of Allah', and thus his blessed soul returned to Allah, The All-Merciful.

Sayyiduna Shah Naqshaband passed away on Monday, the 3rd of Rabi'ul-awwal, 791 AH (1388 CE), and his blessed body was buried in the garden of his house as he had requested, which is the place known now in Uzbekistan.

Hadrat Abdul-wahab Al-sha'rani (RA) said, 'When Sayyiduna Shah Naqshaband (RA) was buried, a great window to

Paradise was let open for him, which made his grave a wonderful Garden of Paradise. Two beautiful heavenly beings entered his presence, greeted him and said, "From the time Allah created us until now, we have been waiting for this moment to come and accompany you", but he responded to them, "I am not waiting for any other than Allah. I do not need you; I only want the Company of my Lord"'.

Someone asked Sayyiduna Shah Naqshaband (RA) about the deeper meaning of the Holy Hadith, "Removing a harmful thing from the way is part of faith"; he replied, "What the Messenger (Salla Allahu 'alaihi wasallam) meant by "harmful" is one's 'nafs' (ego/self), and what he meant by "the way" is the Way (Path) to Allah. This is similar to what Allah Almighty had said to Sayyiduna Bayazid Al-Bistami (RA), "Leave your nafs and you will be in My Presence."

Sayyiduna Shah Naqshaband (RA) was once asked, "Why are the seekers called fuqaraa (poor/helpless)?" He replied, "Because no matter how needy they are, they do not pray for help, just as when Sayyiduna Ibrahim (Salla Allahu 'alaihi wasallam) was thrown by Nemrud into fire, and Gabriel (AS) descended upon him and asked him, "Do you need any help?" Ibrahim (pbuh) replied, "No, I do not need your help. I feel no need to ask. Allah is well aware of my condition." The inner state of poverty is a sign of annihilation

of one's ego/self as well as of one's awareness of his own existence."
Sayyiduna Shah Naqshaband (RA) also said, 'The people of God do
not admire the good deeds they do; they act only out of love for
God.'

His blessed lineage to the Holy Messenger (pbuh):

He is Sayyiduna Muhammad Baha-uddin, son of Muhammad
Bukhari, son of Jalalud-din Bukhari, son of Burhanud-din, son of
Abdullah, son of Zainul-'abideen, son of Qasim, son of Sha'ban, son
of Burhanuddin, son of Mahmud, son of Bulaq, son of Taqi Sufi
Khilwati, son of Fakhruddin, son of Ali Akbar, son of Al-Hasan Al-
'askari, son of Ali Al-hadi, son of Muhammad Al-taqi, son of Ali
Ar-ridha, son of Musa Al-kazim, son of Ja'far AS-Sadiq, son of
Muhammad Al-baqir, son of Ali Zainul-'abideen, son of Al-Husain,
son of Sayyiduna Ali ibn Abu-Talib and Sayyidah Fatima Az-zhraa,
daughter of the Holy Messenger, Sayyiduna Muhammad (peace be
upon him and upon them all).

Book of Tariqah

O Allah, Most Kind! Bless our Master, the Imam of this Blessed Tariqah, Sayyiduna Muhammad Baha-uddin Shah Naqshaband, with the greatest of Your Blessings and raise his station to the highest of all heavenly stations.

O Allah, Most Gracious, grant us plenty from his shining sacred light and provide us with his beautiful flow of perfect Faith in Allah and Love for Allah, The Glorious, and of His Messenger, the Master of all Masters, Sayyiduna Muhammad, peace be upon him and upon his Noble Ahlul-Bayt. Amen.

METHOD OF SILENT ZHIKR

Beloved murid!

Silent zhikr is your life. Show extreme attentiveness and heartfelt greatness of silent zhikr, for with it you are spending time in solitude with The High Majestic Lord, Allah Almighty, The King and Creator of all. You will gain the benefits of this powerful zhikr when you observe the right etiquette and display great reverence to it in your heart and in your behaviour.

Here is the basic procedure of how to perform your daily silent zhikr session.

1. Be in a state of wudu (women should perform wudu before their zhikr even during periods of impurity)

2. Sit in solitude in a comfortable position, and:

3. Seek forgiveness (do istighfar) by repeating:

4. astaghfirullahal-'aZeem (7 times)

5. Recite Surat Fatihah once and Surat Ikhlas 3 times.

6. Gift the rewards of the recitation to the Holy Messenger (pbuh), his Noble Family, the Four Righteous Caliphs and to all our elders of the Naqshabandi Tariqah. It is preferable to read out their blessed names starting from the name of your Shaykh. During impurity, women should not read Quran; they should only do istighfar and go to the next step.

7. Engage in Connection of the Grave (rabitat qabr) for a short

while until the image of your body in your grave is clear in your heart; close your eyes, direct your head to your heart and imagine that your soul departed your body and that your body was washed, wrapped in the funeral cloth, and you were laid down in your grave. After a while, remove this image and collect your focus for the next step.

8. Engage in Connection of the Shaykh (rabitat shaykh) for a short while, until his image is very clear in your heart with intense light coming from his heart into your heart.

9. Begin your silent zhikr, with your eyes closed and your heart clear from worldly things. This zhikr is a silent repetition of the Holy Name "Allah" or "la ilaha illallah", as given by your Shaykh, for the duration or the number of times the Shaykh has assigned to you. Hold your tongue completely from saying anything throughout the zhikr session.

10. When you complete the session of silent zhikr, stop your zhikr and begin muraqabah (meditation) for around ten minutes. Muraqabah is to remain focused on your heart (or the other latifah you are doing zhikr for) watching what Divine Meanings flow into it.

11. Open your eyes and ask Allah Almighty to accept zhikr from you, and show gratefulness that He has allowed you to sit in this glorious prescence, that is, to remember Him in solitude.

After zhikr session is over, avoid eating and drinking for about 30 minutes to let the heat of zhikr take effect through the rest of your body.

O true seeker! Steadfastness is the key to success and glory in the Divine Presence. At first, silent zhikr will be like medicine that you need at regular basis and with a certain concentration. One of its fruits is gaining a state of heart that makes it always in zhikrullah even outside your silent zhikr session. Then, heart zikr will be your second nature; in fact, at some point it will be your only true nature. May Allah accept your zhikr and may He accept you amongst His true servants. Amen.

ESSENTIAL DAILY DEEDS

(For starting murids)

It is essential for your spiritual progress towards Divine Presence to be steadfast on the following daily deeds:

1. Silent zhikrullah, as prescribed to you by your Shaykh.
2. Reciting at least one chapter (1 juzu out of 30) of the Holy Quran. For non-speakers of Arabic: they may read half a chapter of Quran daily. Please note that reading English translation of the Quran is not reading Quran.
3. Reading the Tariqah's daily supplications, the Blessed Naqshabandi Wird.
4. Seeking forgiveness by repeating 500 times: astaghfirullah
5. Reading the daily praises, 100 times each:
6. subhanal-llaah. alhamdu-lillaah. la ilaha illal-llaah. Allahu-akbar
7. Recite 300 Salawat (darud sharif or prayers upon the Holy Messenger, pbuh), such as: allahumma Salli wasallim 'ala sayyidina muHammadin wa alihi.
8. Pray DuHa (pre-noon) Prayer, 2 or 4 raka'at, valid from 20 minutes after sunrise until 15 minutes before Zuhur begins.
9. Recite Ayat Al-Kursi once after each of the five obligatory prayers, before you move from your position.

The daily deeds for advanced murids are instructed to them directly by the Shaykh as they develop into higher stages when they are initiated into zhikr of each one of the seven subtleties: Heart, Soul, Secret, Hidden, Most Concealed, the Self, and Master of Zhikr. The murid is advised to keep close and respectful relationship with the Shaykh so that the murid can be blessed with more spiritual growth, and hence reach clearer manifestations of the Knowledge and Presence of Allah, by the Will of Allah.

May Allah, The Glorious, give you ability to practice these blessed deeds and steadfastness on them until the end of your worldly life. May He The Light enlighten your heart and bless you with Divine Pleasure and Divine Presence – the Bliss of Everlasting Happiness. Amen.

ETIQUETTE (ADAAB) OF THE SEEKER

Tariqah of our Master, the Messenger of Allah, peace be upon him, is all about good etiquette and noble internal and external manners. Just as the body can behave, the internal faculties also behave in a certain manner according to their condition of refinement. The person who lacks etiquette, adaab, can never approach closer to the Fountain of Muhammadi Light nor to the Ocean of Knowing Allah Almighty.

There are adaab to observe with your Lord, Allah Almighty, adaab with His Holy Messenger (pbuh), adaab with his Noble Family and Companions, adaab with your Shaykh, adaab with yourself, adaab with your fellow murids on the Path, adaab with the rest of humankind and adaab with the other created beings.

The Holy Messenger (pbuh) was exemplary in beautiful etiquette and perfect manners inwardly and outwardly. Nothing negative would ever come out of him (pbuh). He was perfect in his servitude to Allah Almighty and was perfect in dealing with others and the rest of creation. This is what his khulafa took from him by way of his inner light and guidance. O murid! If you love him, take from him his light to become like him in perfect adaab.

GENERAL ADAAB

The Divine Guidance that the Shaykh gives to his murid can be described as observing a spiritual state that makes the murid behave in a manner consistent with the Messenger's Character, which leads one to the sphere of self-realization. This can only be achieved through the murid's wilful submission to his Shaykh and his Path. This is in fact the beginning of good etiquette (adaab) with yourself and with your Guide.

The state of adaab with yourself begins from being truthful to yourself when thinking and when deciding about your travel on the Path. Never deceive yourself. Always confess to yourself your own faults and defects. The result of this truthfulness is success in taking the right Tariqah to the Almighty, Glory be to Him. The way of success in this matter is to be in the company of a living Shaykh who can accept you as his seeker.

Among other great gains, the Shaykh will help the murid to discriminate between the internal flow that comes from Allah Almighty and that which comes from your lower self. It is through the Shaykh's guidance, and through being in the community he makes, that saves you as a murid from languishing in self-involvement and transforms you into the Divine Purpose for which you have been created. Thus, you should minimise mixing with the ordinary public, and take as close friends only the God-fearing, righteous, individuals who may help you remain steadfast on the Path to Allah. One of the most dangerous obstacles in the way of the murid is spending time in the company of people engrossed in worldly affairs and people who like to argue much, as everything they do is in fact time wasting.

You must honour your fellow murids in the Tariqah. Avoid looking at their faults. Instead of being distracted by their actions, focus on your own defects. You should conceal whatever you know of their wrongs and faults. You must believe that their mistakes are better than the correct actions of others, believing that your fellow murids do things only with pure intentions.

ADAAB OF THE SEEKER WITH HIS SHAYKH

The authorised Shaykh of Tariqah is a Vicegerent of the Holy Messenger, Sayyiduna Muhammad (pbuh), in that the Shaykh reflects the Messenger's heart, spiritual lights and Sunnah way of life in everything the Shaykh feels, thinks, does and experiences.

The Shaykh is the murid's reflection of his/her inner reality, just like a mirror whose function is to reflect to you the conditions of your heart and inner self. The Shaykh is your Way to knowing the reality of the Holy Messenger of Allah (pbuh), by which you are transformed from the low qualities of the animal nature of the human being to the higher qualities of your spiritual nature. This transformation can only be fulfilled when there is love between the Shaykh and the murid. Without love, it is not possible for spiritual illumination to transcend from the Shaykh to the murid. It is Love of the Shaykh that takes the murid to the Love of the Messenger of Allah (pbuh) and ultimately to the Love of Allah Almighty.

Love of the Shaykh means a few realities together: the murid's admiration of the Shaykh, attachment, devotion and spiritual, or at least emotional, connection. The higher type of love of the Shaykh is being in a state of constant awareness of the Beauty of the Shaykh and his continuous presence in Divine Presence. This kind of love supersedes all other kinds of human love, including love between man and woman. This explains why there were men and women who loved the Holy Messenger (pbuh), and likewise their Shaykhs, more than they loved their partners, though with a higher kind of love than physical attachment. Love of the Shaykh is a sublime feeling emanating from the heavenly world above the Divine Throne where the souls originate and meet.

When the Shaykh gives the murid advice or deeds to perform, all the angels and heavenly forces align with the Shaykh's instruction, thus empowering his order with blessings that benefit the murid. If the murid does not act upon the Shaykh's guidance, the instruction becomes void of those blessings and hence the murid will lose out.

The most important adaab with your Shaykh can be summarised in offering service (khidma) for him, in waiting, in patience, in listening more than talking, and in desiring what your Shaykh desires as though it is your own desire. You need to be attentive enough to the personality of your Shaykh in order to understand his mizaj (inner states of mind, moods and inclinations) well and behave in accordance to it.

The murid should always be modest in front of his Shaykh as well as with his fellow companions on the Path. The status of the saints (Awliya) is very dignified in the Divine Presence. At times, they utter or do things that may seem strange to a murid; such things should be viewed in the light of the Divine Love and devotion the Awliya have for Allah Almighty and for you as seeker.

The murid should show complete submission to his Shaykh in whatever he advises him/her regarding any of their affairs, with firm conviction that the Shaykh always knows better and always does and says what is in the interest of the murid. The murid must not object to anything that the Shaykh says or does. A connected Shaykh has reached the level of Muhammadan Authorisation only when Allah has blessed him with protection from sin and error in judgement regarding murids and people in general. Sayyiduna Muhammad, the Messenger of Allah (Salla Allahu 'alaihi wasallam), is fully aware of the murid's external and internal conditions. As the Shaykh is the heir of the holy Messenger in spiritual purification, the Shaykh is endowed with this knowledge about his murids. The scholars say 'A Shaykh among his murids is like the Messenger (pbuh) among his Companions'.

The murid must never reveal the private matters of his/her Shaykh to anyone, not even to the Shaykh's close relatives or friends. Remember the incident between Hadrat Fatima (RA) and Hadrat Aisha (RA) in the presence of the Holy Messenger (pbuh) when he was about to depart this world. If the murid is unsure of whether a matter is private, he should ask permission from his Shaykh first before the murid could reveal it to others. As a seeker of Allah Almighty through your Shaykh, the best etiquette in this regard is to concern yourself with yourself and never try to investigate the Shaykh's personal or private life.

You should consult with your Shaykh before taking action regarding any major matter in your life that may affect your spiritual progress, such going away for a long time, migrating, changing job, moving house, marriage, etc. You should then fully comply with the Shaykh's advice and do your best to apply it. Failing to do this would result in serious setbacks to yourself in relation to the matter in question.

To be in Suhbah (physical company) with the Shaykh is one of the most virtuous adaab, while observing the right etiquette when in the presence of the Shaykh. This is because every moment in the presence of one's Shaykh can eliminate numerous illnesses, obstacles and difficulties that obstruct the murid's Path.

The murid should avoid calling the Shaykh on the phone. If a murid needs to ask the Shaykh a question, it has to be a necessary question and relevant to his/her progress in Tariqah. A murid should use his/her good common sense and good manners at all times. If the murid wants to say something to the Shaykh when in the presence of other people, the murid should not speak openly or loudly. He should go close to the Shaykh and whisper the information to him if it is appropriate.

The murid should never point at, or sit with his feet pointing at, the Shaykh's direction. A murid should not sit higher than the Shaykh. If you need to sit on a chair, you should alert the assistants of the Shaykh so that he may also sit at a similar level in order to protect you from falling into bad manners. This is because the Shaykh is filled with Divine Lights and he manifests Muhammadi Presence or Divine Presence.

In the Shaykh's presence, always sit straight and give him all of your attention even if he is not speaking. A murid should be careful never to lapse into familiarity by joking or leaning back on cushions, etc. Scholars say, "Familiarity breeds contempt; be warned!"

A murid should never take Tariqah instructions from another Shaykh unless you were directed by your own Shaykh to do so. You may learn various religious matters from other scholars but it is harmful to take their instructions on deeds to do for inner purification or their advice about matters that influences your spiritual growth.

ADAAB FOR ATTENDING THE SHAYKH'S GATHERINGS

1. The murid must arrive at the gathering before it starts, and preferably, before the Shaykh takes his seat in the gathering. The murid should have already made ablution (wudu) and prayed the mosque or wudu greeting prayer.

2. The murid should sit properly around the Shaykh in a circle form. He should not leave gaps between him and the other attendees.

3. The murid should observe good physical etiquette, like wearing clean clothes that reflect the Sunnah, such as a long gown or a long shirt and should have his head covered. A male murid should wear a good smelling perfume, such as oud, musk, rose, amber, etc., and should avoid alcohol-based perfumes.

4. The murid should give all his attention to the Shaykh and not be distracted by anything around him or by anything that may happen in the gathering.

5. When the Shaykh starts talking, the murid should look straight at him. When the Shaykh is silent, the murid should put his gaze down, but keep his heart directed to and focused on the presence of the Shaykh always.

6. The murid must keep his hands free from everything extra, such as tasbih beads or counters, etc., unless the Shaykh asks the

murid to use them.

7. Non-Murid adults and the murids' young children (under the age of 12 years) are not permitted to attend the Shaykh's circles of zhikr except by direct permission of the Shaykh.

KHATM KHAWAJAKAN

of Sayyiduna Abdul-khaliq Al-Ghajdawani (RA)

Khatm Khawajakan is a collective form of vocal zhikr, where the murids gather in a halaqa (zhikr circle) led by an authorised leader (the Shaykh or his deputy), to remember Allah Almighty with holy phrases that are useful for seeking Divine Help against all kinds of hardships and calamities and for fulfilling murids' spiritual needs. The Khatm was spiritually instructed to Master Abdul-khaliq Al-Ghajdawani (RA) by the Holy Messenger (pbuh) through an enlightened vision experience, and has ever since become part of the blessed prayers that are recited by the Shaykh or his authorised deputy in a gathering of Naqshabandi seekers.

The main benefit of this Khatm is to attract the Support of Allah Almighty to attain a purer inner self. Moreover, the Khatm is beneficial for solving problems and eradicating difficulties that the murid may be experiencing through his/her spiritual journey.

There are three conditions for holding a gathering for this Khatm. One condition is that the attending murids should be in a state of purity (clean, with wudu). Women who are in impure conditions, such as period and postnatal bleeding, cannot attend the Khatm. The other condition is that the Khatm venue should not be attended by non-murids. The third condition is to have the doors closed and without any interruption.

Khatm Khawajakan:

- Leader and murids repeat the intention: bismi-llahir-raHmanir-raHeem. 'I make this intention to engage in Khatm Khawajakan, only for the sake of Allah Almighty'.

- The murids then follow the leader's instructions, which will include repeating the following prayers:

بِسْمِ اللهِ الرَّحْمَنِ الرَّحِيمِ، اَللَّهُمَّ يَا مُفَتِّحَ الْأَبْوَابِ، وَيَا مُسَبِّبَ الْأَسْبَابِ،
وَيَا مُقَلِّبَ الْقُلُوبِ وَالْأَبْصَارِ، وَيَا دَلِيلَ الْمُتَحَيِّرِينَ، وَيَا غِيَاثَ الْمُسْتَغِيثِينَ،
أَغِثْنِي، تَوَكَّلْتُ عَلَيْكَ يَارَبِّي، وَفَوَّضْتُ أَمْرِي إِلَيْكَ، يَافَتَّاحُ، يَاوَهَّابُ، يَا بَاسِطُ،
وَصلى اللهُ على خَيْرِ خَلْقِهِ سيِّدِنَا محمدٍ وآلِهِ وَصحبِهِ أَجمعِينَ.

- Ash-hadu allaa ilaha illallahu wa ash-hadu anna Muhammadan 'abduhu wa-rasuluh (3 time)
- Astaghfirullah (25 times), followed by the complete istighfar once: "astaghfiru-llahal-'aZeem allazhi laa ilaha illaa huwa alHayyul-qayyumu wa-atoobu ilayhi, yaa arHamar-raaHimeena, ya Allah.

- Leader reads this prayer alone:

Book of Tariqah

اللهم يا مسبب الأسباب، يا مفتح الأبواب، يا مقلب القلوب والأبصار، يا
دليل المتحيرين يا غياث المستغيثين، يا حيُّ يا قيومُ، يا ذا الجلالِ
والإكرامِ، وأفوِّضُ أمري إلى الله. إن الله بصيرٌ بالعباد. يا من لا ملجأ منه إلا
إليه، لا تخيب رجاءنا. يا قديم الإحسان.

- All engage in Rabitah of Shaykh (Connection with the Shaykh)

- Then, all recite together:

  - Surat Fatihah (7 times); Surat Inshirah (7 times); and Surat Ikhlas (11 times)

  - This Salawat (10 times):

  اَللّٰهُمَّ صَلِّ وَسَلِّمْ عَلى سيِّدِنا محمدٍ وآلِ سيِّدِنا محمدٍ.

- Leader reads the ihdaa (prayer of gifting the reward of the above)

- Leader reads this ayah once: fa'lam annahu la ilaha illallah

- Then, leader and murids together repeat: fa'lam annahu la ilaha illallah (100 times)

- Then, repeat together the following:

la ilaha illallah - MuHammadun rasulullah, alaihi Salatullah
la ilaha illallah - MuHammadun Habibullah, alaihi Salatullah
la ilaha illallah - MuHammadun khalilullah, alaihi Salatullah

la ilaha illallah - MuHammadun Safiyyullah, alaihi Salatullah
la ilaha illallah - MuHammadun nabiyyullah, alaihi Salatullah
la ilaha illallah - MuHammadun shafi'ullah, alaihi Salatullah

• Leader reads ihdaa again (prayer of gifting the rewards)
• Leader and murids repeat together the following vocal zhikr:

(Allahu, Allahu, Allah) - 33 times
(hu, hu, hu) - 33 times
(Haqqun, Haqqun, Haqq) - 33 times
(Hayyun, Hayyun, Hayy) - 33 times
(Allahu, Allah Haqq) - 7 times
(Allahu, Allah Hayy) - 7 times
(Allahu Hayyun, Ya qayyum) - 7 times
Ya hu, ya hu, ya daa'im
Allahu, ya hu, ya daa'im
Ya daa'imu, ya daa'imu, ya daa'imu, ya Allah
Ya Haleemu, ya Haleemu, ya Haleemu, ya Allah
Ya HafeeZu, Ya HafeeZu, Ya HafeeZu, ya Allah
Ya laTeefu, ya laTeefu, ya laTeefu, ya Allah
Ya ghaffaru, ya ghaffaru, ya ghaffaru, ya Allah
Ya sattaru, ya sattaru, ya sattaru, ya Allah
Ya fattaHu, ya fattaHu, ya fattaHu, ya Allah
Ya mujeebu, ya mujeebu, ya mujeebu, ya Allah

Book of Tariqah

Ya mu'izzu, ya mu'izzu, ya mu'izzu, ya Allah

Ya mu'eenu, ya mu'eenu, ya mu'eenu, ya Allah

Ya wadudu, ya wadudu, ya wadudu, ya Allah

Ya raHmanu, ya raHmanu, ya raHmanu, ya Allah

Ya raHeemu, Ya raHeemu, ya raHeemu, ya Allah

Ya Hannanu, ya Hannanu, ya Hannanu, ya Allah

Ya mannanu, ya mannanu, ya mannanu, ya Allah

Ya dayyanu, ya dayyanu, ya dayyanu, ya Allah

Ya subHanu, ya subHanu, ya subHanu, ya Allah

Ya sulTanu, ya sulTanu, ya sulTanu, ya Allah

Ya amanu, ya amanu, ya amanu, ya Allah

Ya Allahu, ya Allahu, ya Allahu, ya Allah

Ya arHamar-raHimeena, ya arHamar-raHimeena, ya arHamar-raHimeena, ya Allah

Ya akramal-akrameena, ya akramal akrameena, ya akramal-akrameen, ya Allah

Ya mu'eenal-'ajizeena, ya mu'eenal 'ajizeena, ya mu'eenal-'ajizeena, ya Allah

Hasbunallahu, Rabbunallah; Hasbunallahu, Rabbunallah; Hasbunallahu, Rabbunallah

- Leader reads an ayah from the Holy Quran

- Leader and murids repeat this Salawat 10 times:

اَللّٰهُمَّ صَلِّ على سَيِّدِنا مُحَمَّدٍ وآلِ سَيِّدِنا مُحَمَّدٍ وَسَلِّمْ

Book of Tariqah

- Then, all read this Salawat, followed by Fatiha:

صلِّ يا ربِّ وسَلِّمْ على جميع الأنبياء والمُرسلين وآلِهِم أجمعينَ والحمدُ لله رَبِّ العالمين . على أشرفِ العالمين سيدِنا محمدٍ الصلاةُ والسلامُ، على أفضلِ العالمين سيدِنا محمد الصلاةُ والسلامُ، على أكملِ العالمين سيدِنا محمدٍ الصلاةُ والسلامُ. صلواتُ اللهِ تعالى وملائكتِهِ وأنبيائه ورسله وجميعِ خلقِهِ على محمدٍ وعلى آل محمد عليه وعليهم السلام ورحمة الله تعالى وبركاته، ورضي الله تبارك وتعالى عن ساداتنا أصحاب رسول الله أجمعين وعن التابعين لهم بإحسان وعن الأئمة المجتهدين الماضين، وعن العلماء المتقين وعن الأولياء الصالحين وعن مشايخنا في الطريقة النقشبندية العلية قَدَّسَ اللهُ تعالى أرواحَهُمُ الزَّكِيَّةَ ونوَّرَ اللهُ تعالى أضرِحَتَهم المباركةَ وأعاد اللهُ تعالى علينا من بركاتِهم وفيوضاتِهم دائماً والحمدُ لله ربّ العالمين.

- Leader reads ihdaa (prayer of gifting the reward), followed by Fatiha

- Finally, murids read together with the Shaykh the concluding prayers:

الحمد لله الذي بِنُورِ جماله أضاء قلوبَ العارفين، وبهيبة جلالِهِ أحرقَ أفئِدةَ العاشقين، وبلطائفِ عنايته عمَّرَ سِرَّ الواصلين، والصلاةُ والسلامُ

على خير خلقه سيدنا محمد وعلى آله وصحبه أجمعين. اللهم بلِّغ وأوصل ثوابَ ما قرأناه، ونُوِّرَ ما تلوناه، بعد القَبول منا بالفضل والإحسان، إلى روح سيدنا وطبيب قلوبنا، وقُرّةِ أعيننا محمّدٍ المُصطفى صلى الله عليه وسلم، وإلى أرواح جميع الأنبياء والمُرسلين، صلواتُ الله وسلامُه عليهم أجمعين، وإلى جميع أرواح مشايخ سلاسل الطرق العلية، خصوصاً النقشبنديةِ، والقادريةِ، والكُبرَويّةِ، والسّهرَورَدِيّةِ، والجِشْتِيّةِ، قدَّسَ الله أسرارَهم العليّةُ، وخصوصاً إلى روح القطب الكبير، والعَلَم الشهير، ذي الفيض النوراني، واضع الختمِ مولانا عبدُ الخالقِ الغجدواني، وإلى روح إمام الطريقة، وغوث الخليقة، ذي الفيض الجاري، والنور الساري، السيد الشريف محمد بهاء الدين شاه نقشبند الحَسَني الحُسَيني البخاري، وإلى أستاذنا وأستاذ أستاذنا، وجميع مشايخنا قدس الله تعالى أسرارَهُمُ العَليّةَ. اللهم اجعلنا من المَحسُوبين عليهمُ، ومن المنسُوبين إليهمُ، ووفقنا لما تُحبُّه وترضاهُ، يا أرحم الراحمين. اللهم أجِزنَا من الخواطر النَّفسيّةِ، واحفظنا مِنَ الشَهَواتِ الشَيطانِيّةِ، وطَهِّرنا مِن القاذُورَاتِ البَشَرِيّةِ، وصَفِّنَا بِصَفاء المَحبّة الصِّدِّيقيّةِ، وأرِنَا الحَقَّ حقّاً وارزُقنا اتِّبَاعَهُ، وأرِنَا الباطلَ باطلاً وارزُقنا اجتِنابَهُ، يا أرحمَ الراحمين. اللهم إنا نسألُك أن تُحيِيَ قلوبَنا وأرواحنا وأجسامَنا بنورِ مَعرفتكَ وَوَصلِكَ وتجَلِّيّاتِكَ، دائماً باقياً هادياً يا اللهُ.

- Leader ends the Khatm gathering in the manner the Shaykh has instructed.

End of Khatm Khawajakan

Book of Tariqah

Book of Truth

Book of Truth

The Absolute Truth

IS

ALLAH اللّٰه

GOD OF ALL, THE ONE,
ALL GLORIOUS, ALL COMPASSIONATE

Book of Truth

THE WAY TO THE TRUTH

IS

لا إله إلا الله محمد رسول الله

THERE IS NO DEITY BUT ALLAH,
MUHAMMAD IS THE MESSENGER OF ALLAH

THE ESSENCE OF REALISING THE TRUTH IS IN

THE LOVE OF ALLAH
AND THE LOVE OF HIS MESSENGER,
MUHAMMAD, PEACE BE UPON HIM

ALLAH IS TRUTH

Truth is Allah

There is only one Reality, one Truth. Allah is The Absolute Reality, The Absolute Truth. He has always existed and He never ceases to exist. He is the only Source of any created existence. Through His Perfect Wisdom, He Decided to bring into existence beautiful beings and Made them connected to His Reality; this is why they are part of the True Reality. The first of these beautiful beings is His Beloved, Sayyiduna Muhammad (pbuh), the Messengers of Allah, and his righteous Family and Companions. Then come his luminous brothers and sisters, who are the pure, righteous Saints of Allah from amongst the children of Adam (pbuh).

Now, let us begin with The Absolute Truth, our Lord, Allah Almighty.

"Say: He is Allah, The One and Only God. Allah, the Eternal, the Absolute. He begets not, nor is He begotten; and there is none like unto Him". (Sura Al-ikhlas)

The Absolute Truth is God Almighty: The Indivisible One, The First without a beginning, The Last without an end. He Was and Has always Been. There was nothing but He, and there will be nothing but He. He, The All Glorious, decides who, what and when He brings to existence, and then they exist into relative reality.

He is One, Indivisible, and cannot be multiplied in any form or shape. He is the Source of life and the Source of death; the Source of poverty and wealth; the Source of illness and health. Nothing can escape His Grip. Nothing can hide from His Knowledge and His Awarness. He is The Absolute and Supreme in every Perfection; Free from fault and defect. He is All Magnificent and All Beautiful. He is all Pure and All Good, He accepts from His servants only that which is pure and good.

(وَمَا قَدَرُوا اللَّهَ حَقَّ قَدْرِهِ وَالْأَرْضُ جَمِيعًا قَبْضَتُهُ يَوْمَ الْقِيَامَةِ وَالسَّمَاوَاتُ مَطْوِيَّاتٌ بِيَمِينِهِ سُبْحَانَهُ وَتَعَالَى عَمَّا يُشْرِكُونَ)

"No true understanding have they achieved of God, such as is divinely due to Him: On the Day of Judgment, the whole of the earth will be but in His Grip, and the heavens will be rolled up in His Right Power: Glory to Him! High is He above the partners they attribute to Him!" (Sura Az-zumar: 67)

(سَبَّحَ لِلّٰهِ مَا فِي السَّمَاوَاتِ وَالْأَرْضِ وَهُوَ الْعَزِيزُ الْحَكِيمُ (1) لَهُ مُلْكُ السَّمَاوَاتِ وَالْأَرْضِ يُحْيِي وَيُمِيتُ وَهُوَ عَلَى كُلِّ شَيْءٍ قَدِيرٌ (2) هُوَ الْأَوَّلُ وَالْآخِرُ وَالظَّاهِرُ وَالْبَاطِنُ وَهُوَ بِكُلِّ شَيْءٍ عَلِيمٌ (3) هُوَ الَّذِي خَلَقَ السَّمَاوَاتِ وَالْأَرْضَ فِي سِتَّةِ أَيَّامٍ ثُمَّ اسْتَوَى عَلَى الْعَرْشِ يَعْلَمُ مَا يَلِجُ فِي الْأَرْضِ وَمَا يَخْرُجُ مِنْهَا وَمَا يَنْزِلُ مِنَ السَّمَاءِ وَمَا يَعْرُجُ فِيهَا وَهُوَ مَعَكُمْ أَيْنَ مَا كُنْتُمْ وَاللّٰهُ بِمَا تَعْمَلُونَ بَصِيرٌ (4)

Whatever is in the heavens and on earth declare the Praises and Glory of Allah: for He is The Exalted in Might, The Wise. To Him belongs the dominion of the heavens and the earth: It is He Who gives Life and Death; and He has Power over all things. He is The First and The Last, the Evident and The Immanent: and He has full knowledge of all things. It is He Who Created the heavens and earth in six Days and then Established Himself above the Throne. He knows what goes into the earth and what emerges from it and what descends from the heaven and what ascends therein; and He is with you wherever you are; and Allah is All-Seeing of what you do. (Sura Al-Hadid: 1-4)

Book of Truth

ٱللَّهُ لَا إِلَٰهَ إِلَّا هُوَ ٱلْحَيُّ ٱلْقَيُّومُ لَا تَأْخُذُهُ سِنَةٌ وَلَا نَوْمٌ لَّهُ مَا فِي ٱلسَّمَاوَاتِ وَمَا فِي ٱلْأَرْضِ مَن ذَا ٱلَّذِي يَشْفَعُ عِندَهُ إِلَّا بِإِذْنِهِ يَعْلَمُ مَا بَيْنَ أَيْدِيهِمْ وَمَا خَلْفَهُمْ وَلَا يُحِيطُونَ بِشَيْءٍ مِّنْ عِلْمِهِ إِلَّا بِمَا شَآءَ وَسِعَ كُرْسِيُّهُ ٱلسَّمَاوَاتِ وَٱلْأَرْضَ وَلَا يَئُودُهُ حِفْظُهُمَا وَهُوَ ٱلْعَلِيُّ ٱلْعَظِيمُ ۞

Transliteration and Translation of Ayat Al-Kursi (Verse of 'The Divine Seat'):

Allahu laa ilaaha illaa huwal-Hayyul qayyum; laa ta'khuzhuhu sinatun wa-laa nawm; lahu maa fis-samaawaati wa-maa fil-ard; man zhallazhee yashfa'u 'indahu illaa bi izhnihi; ya'lamu maa bayna aydeehim wa-maa khalfahum; wa-laa yuHeeTuna beshay'im-min 'ilmihee illa bimaa shaa'; wasi'a kursiyyuhus-samaawaati wal-arDa wa-laa ya'uduhu HifZuhumaa; wahuwal 'aliyyul 'aZeem.

"Allah is the One and Only God. There is no god but He - Living, Self-subsisting, Eternal. No slumber nor sleep can seize Him. His are all things in the heavens and the earth. Who is there that can intercede in His Presence except as He Permits? He Knows all what is ahead of them and what is behind them. They shall not compass aught of His Knowledge except as He Wills. His Seat extends high over and around the heavens and the earth, and He gets no fatigue in preserving them, for He is Most High, Supreme in Glory." (Sura Al-Baqarah: 255 Ayat Al-Kursi)

Associated with this only Truth is everyone whom Allah Almighty has Willed to be in His Divine Presence, due to His Love for them and their devout love for Him and total submission to Him. The Master of all such individuals in the Presence of Truth is Sayyiduna Muhammad, peace be upon him, who has always been in Divine Presence, both before and after he manifested in human form.

Abdul-Razzaq narrated, that Jabir ibn Abdullah (RA) asked, "O Messenger of Allah, may my parents be sacrificed for you, tell me about the first thing that Allah created before all other things." He said, "O Jabir! Before everything else, Allah created the Light of your Prophet, which was from His Light. That Light began to revolve by God's Divine Power to wherever Allah wished. At that time, not even the Sacred Tablet nor the Sacred Pen were created; neither Paradise nor Fire, not even angels; neither heavens nor earth; neither the sun nor the moon; neither the spirits nor humankind. When Allah Almighty wanted to create His Creation, He divided that light into four parts. From the first part, He created the Pen; from the second, He created the Sacred Tablet, and from the third, He created the Throne. Then, Allah divided the fourth part of Light into four parts: the first part formed the Bearers of the Throne, the second part became the Divine Seat, and from the third part, He created the rest of the angels. Allah then divided the fourth part into four parts: He created the heavens from the first part, the earths from the second, Paradise and Fire from the third. Then, He divided the fourth part into four parts: the light of the vision of the believers from the first part, the light of their hearts (knowing Allah) from the second and created from the third part the light that gives them their pleasure (which is: la ilaha illa-Allahu, Muhammadun Rasulu-llah).

Another narration by Hadrat Ali ibn Al-Husain (RA), from his father Al-Husain (RA), from his grandfather Ali (RA) that the Messenger (pbuh) said, "I was Light in the Presence of my Lord fourteen thousand years before the creation of Adam."

Also associated with the Truth are the Messenger's immediate Family (Ahlul-Bayt), his Companions (Sahabah) and his Vicegerents (khulafa or awliya) throughout time, Allah be pleased with them all. The Vicegerents (khulafa) of God's Messenger (pbuh) are those men and women who reach perfection (iHsan) in their servitude to God Almighty: they no longer live through their lower self, but through the manifestation of the Presence of the Truth in them. They only see, hear, think and act through the Divine Light and for the Divine Pleasure, satisfied only with Divine Love. In this reference, the Holy Messenger (pbuh) said, "Watch out for the 'deep vision' (or 'prophecy power') of the believer, for he looks through the Light of Allah". (Al-Tirmizi, on the authority of Hadrat Abu Saeed Al-khudri, RA)

In today's world, Muslims have been deceived by movements that make them focus strictly on external behaviour and practice while marginalising the high position of Sayyiduna Muhammad (pbuh) and his Ahlul-Bayt (RaDiya Allahu 'anhum) in the purification of the individual and the community at large. Therefore, the Holy Messenger (pbuh) has kept this Jewel, the Blessed Naqshabandi Tariqah, alive with his love and the love of his Ahlul-Bayt and Vicegerents (khulafa).

In this respect, the Holy Messenger (pbuh) has also deputed me to display the glorious beauty of this Jewel to places that have souls who appreciate it. We need to realise how to place our Masters, Sayyiduna Muhammad, his Ahlul-Bayt and his khulafa in the glorious positions they rightfully deserve. Let us be true Muslims and be deeply grateful to the True Sources of Divine Light.

THE MESSENGER OF ALLAH (PBUH)

Master of Masters, Sayyiduna Muhammad (Salla Allahu 'alaihi wasallam)

Sayyiduna Muhammad (Salla Allahu 'alaihi wasallam) is the Last Messenger of God to the world. Allah Almighty has Sent him to all peoples and to all spirits (jinn) on earth.

Sayyiduna Muhammad (pbuh) was born in Makkah just before the dawn of Monday, 12th of Rabi'ul-awwal, in the Year of the Elephant (c. 570 AD), the year when Allah Almighty destroyed the army with elephants that came to attack the Holy Ka'ba in Makkah. Sayyiduna Muhammad's blessed father, Abdullah (RA), died long before his blessed birth. His blessed mother, Aminah (RA), died when he was six years old. Sayyiduna Muhammad (pbuh) was then raised by his grandfather, Abdul-muttalib, and then, when he passed away, by his uncle, Abu-Talib.

At the age of 25, Sayyiduna Muhammad (pbuh) was employed by Sayyidah Khadija (RA), who was a wealthy widow in Makkah, to do trade for her in the Levant region. On his return (pbuh) from the Levant, and at her indirect proposal, they were married and lived together in a loving, happy relationship for about 24 years.

As Sayyiduna Muhammad (pbuh) was approaching 40 years in his blessed age, Allah put in his heart love for meditation in seclusion (khalwah), and thus Sayyiduna Muhammad (pbuh) started frequenting the Hira Cave in Mount An-noor, at the outskirts of Holy Makkah, contemplating over the Glory of God Almighty.

When he completed 40 years of his blessed age, Sayyiduna Muhammad (pbuh) received his first communication with Archangel Jibril ('alaihis-salam), on a Monday in the month of Ramadan. Jibril (AS) embraced Sayyiduna Muhammad (pbuh) three times and revealed to him the first Divine Speech of Allah Almighty, with holy verses that translate as, "Read! Read in the Name of your Lord, Who created! He created man from a clot of blood. Read, and know that your Lord is the Most Sublime! He Has Taught by the Pen. He Has Taught man what he knew not. (Al-qalam: 1-3) The Divine mission that Sayyiduna Muhammad (pbuh) received was to purify all people's inner selves and hearts from the darkness of immorality and deviated beliefs.

Twelve years later, in the month of Rajab, after much persecution and rejection from the Makkans and the other Arab tribes, Sayyiduna Muhammad (pbuh) was invited by Allah Almighty into His Divine Presence. The Holy Messenger (pbuh) was thus escorted by Jibril (AS) on a miraculous journey to the Holy

Mosque of Jerusalem (Al-Aqsa or Bayt Al-Maqdis) and from there across all the seven heavens until he was ushered into Divine Presence, where there is no where, where creation cease to exist. All this happened in less than one night, called the Night of Isra and Mi'raj (Miraculous Travel and Ascension).

After thirteen years of great effort and sacrifice in inviting people to the Way of Allah, Sayyiduna Muhammad (pbuh) was divinely commanded to migrate with all of his followers to Yathrib, a town over 420 kilometres north of Makkah. This event is celebrated by all Muslims as the Hijrah Sharifah (Blessed Migration), and Yathrib was thus renamed as Al-Madinah Al-Munawarah "the Enlightened City", or Al-Madinah in short, known now in English as Medina.

From Medina, and in a very short time, all Arabia accepted Islam, and within 80 years from the Messenger's mission, Islam reached the Atlantic in one direction and China in the other. The Light of Sayyiduna Muhammad (pbuh) overwhelmed all kinds of people across the globe, and easily penetrated their hearts, and thus saved many from tyranny of unjust rulers in this world and from going to Hellfire in the next.

His Blessed Lineage (pbuh) to Adam (pbuh):

He is Sayyiduna, Master Muhammad (Salla Allahu 'alaihi wasallam) ibn Abdullah ibn Abdul-muttalib (Shaibah) ibn Hashim (Amr) ibn Abdu-Manaf (Al-Mughirah) ibn Qusai ibn Kilab ibn Murrah ibn Ka'b ibn Lu'ayy ibn Ghalib ibn Fihr (Quraish) ibn Malik ibn An-Nadr (Qays) ibn Kinanah ibn Khuzaymah ibn Mudrikah (Amir) ibn Elyas ibn Mudar ibn Nizar ibn Ma'add ibn Adnan ibn Udd ibn Udad ibn Qamisah ibn Qaydar ibn Hamad ibn Nabit ibn Ismael ('alaihis-salam) ibn Ibrahim ('alaihis-salam) ibn Azar (Tarih) ibn Nahur ibn Faligh ibn Abir ibn Arfakhshazh ibn Mattushalakh ibn Sam ibn Nuh (alaihis-salam) ibn Malik ibn Mahla'eal ibn Ya'rub ibn Akhnukh (Idris 'alaihis-salam) ibn Yanush ibn Qainan ibn Sheeth ibn Adam ('alaihis-salam).

• Note: ibn means 'son of'; bint means 'daughter of'

The Holy Messenger's blessed mother is Aminah bint Wahb ibn Abdu-Manaf ibn Zuhra ibn Kilab ibn Murrah (and the rest of her lineage is the same as that of her husband, Abdullah, the father of Sayyiduna Muhammad (pbuh).

On Monday, 12 Rabi'ul-awwal, 10 years after his blessed Migration to Holy Madinah, the Archangel Jibril (AS) and the Angel of Death (AS) visited the Holy Messenger (pbuh) in his chamber with Aisha (RA) and gave him the Divinely gifted choice as to whether he wanted to stay longer in this world or if he would rather go back into Union with his Lord, Allah The Gracious. The Holy Messenger (pbuh) chose to go. When his illuminous soul departed his beautiful physical form (pbuh), his blessed age was exactly 63 lunar years (from 12 Rabi'ul-awwal 53 BH to 12 Rabi'ul-awwal 10 AH)

The Last Messenger of Allah (pbuh) has thus fulfilled his glorious mission, and has left behind devoted luminaries who would carry on the transmission of his Muhammadi Light as they continue to receive it from his universal spiritual existence, all over the world and until the Day of Resurrection.

His Blessed Women:

In the Divine Decree of Allah, lawful cohabitation between men and women comprises of two types, *nikaH* "marriage" (between a free man and a free woman) and *milkul-yameen* "kind possession" (which is a free man owning a slave-woman). The Holy Messenger (pbuh) married 11 free women (whose title is thus the 'Mothers of the Believers'), and had kind possession of two women-slaves. As there was no register of births and deaths at the time, reports of their ages varied widely. Here, I have either put the most historically acceptable age or provided all the reported ages of the blessed wives.

His blessed wives are:

1. Khadijah bint Khuwaylid (RA) - Arab, from Quraish. Her age when marrying the Holy Messenger (pbuh) was 28/35/40

2. Sawdah bint Zamu'ah ibn Qays (RA) - Arab, from Quraish. Her age when marrying the Holy Messenger (pbuh) was 55

3. Aishah bint Abu-Bakr AS-Siddiq (RA) - Arab, from Quraish. Her age when marrying the Holy Messenger (pbuh) was 16-18 (we disregard the single report that her age was nine, as it contradicts the other authentic historical reports about incidents during her life).

4. Hafsah bint Omar ibn Al-khattab (RA) - Arab, from Quraish. Her age when marrying the Holy Messenger (pbuh) was 21

5. Zaynab bint Khuzaymah (RA) - Arab, from Banu Hilal. Her age

when marrying the Holy Messenger (pbuh) was 30/60

6. Um-salamah bint Abi Umayyah (RA) - Arab, from Banu Makhzum. Her age when marrying the Holy Messenger (pbuh) was 27/65

7. Juwayriyah bint Al-Harith (RA) — from the Jewish tribe of Banu Al-Mustaliq; converted to Islam from Judaism. Her age when marrying the Holy Messenger (pbuh) was 35/38

8. Zaynab bint Jahsh (RA) - Arab, from Quraish. Her age when marrying the Holy Messenger (pbuh) was 15/30

9. Um Habibah bint Abi Sufyan (RA) - Arab, from Quraish. Her age when marrying the Holy Messenger (pbuh) was 40/42

10. Maymunah bint Al-Harith (RA) - Arab, from Banu Hilal. Her age when marrying the Holy Messenger (pbuh) was 17

11. Safiyyah bint Huyay ibn Al-akhtab (RA) — from the Jewish tribe of Banu Al-Nadeer; converted to Islam from Judaism. Her age when marrying the Holy Messenger (pbuh) was 26/27

His Blessed Women in 'kind possession':

1. Raihana bint Sham'un, from the Jewish tribe of Banu An-nadeer (RA), converted to Islam from Judaism

2. Mariyah Al-qibtiyah (RA), Coptic Egyptian, converted to Islam from Christianity

His Blessed Offspring:

Sayyiduna Muhammad (pbuh) had blessed sons and daughters, the first of whom was Al-Qasim, and thus the Holy Messenger (pbuh) was nicknamed 'Abul-Qasim'. Al-Qasim passed away when he was still a young child. Then came Zaynab, Ruqayyah, Um-Kulthum, Fatima and Abdullah. There is difference among the scholars as to whether Abdullah was the same person as AT-Tayyib and AT-Tahir, or whether these two were different sons of Sayyiduna Muhammad (pbuh). All his blessed children were born from his first wife, Sayyidah Khadijah (RA). Sayyiduna Muhammad (pbuh) had no children from any other wife (free woman). However, the last to be born to Sayyiduna Muhammad (pbuh) was Ibrahim, from his woman in kind possession, Mariyah Al-qibtiyah (RA), who was gifted to Sayyiduna Muhammad (pbuh) by Muqawqis, the Roman king of Alexandria at the time.

Some of his blessed features:

It is reported that when Sayyiduna Muhammad (pbuh) and his Companion, Sayyiduna Abu-Bakr (RA) were on their blessed journey of migration from Makkah to Madinah, they passed by a tent of a poor family in the desert, and only the woman of the place, Um-Ma'bad, was there. They stayed for some time for the customary provision and then departed. When her husband, Abu-

Ma'bad, returned, he was surprised to find a good amount of milk in his tent. He asked her, "O Um Ma'bad, where did you get this milk from when our goat is so poorly and cannot give milk?" She said to him, "By Allah, a blessed man passed by our way..." and she related to him the miracle that her guest performed right in front of her eyes by making a skinny dying goat produce a lot of milk. Her husband then asked her to describe the guest for him. She said, "He was extremely handsome and of glowing countenance. He was of perfect proportions, with neither a large stomach nor a small head. He has a smart appearance, with balanced features. He has big black eyes and long eyelashes. His voice has a nice coarse tone to it. He has a perfect long neck, a full rounded beard and thick eyebrows that connect slightly. When he is silent, he is stately and composed, and when he speaks, he appears impressive. From a distance, he looks awesome and striking, and from near, he is most beautiful. He is well spoken, clear in what he says. He talks gently, neither too much nor too little. His words flow forth from a mouth that displays teeth like a perfect string of pearls. He is neither too tall nor short. He is a stately man in the company of two other stately men, but he is the most prominent among them and the most revered. His companions surround him, when he speaks they listen attentively to him, and when he orders something, they hasten to fulfil his order. He is neither harsh nor quarrelsome." Abu-Ma'bad then remarked, "By Allah, this is the man Quraish is looking for". (Al-Hakim; Al-Tabarani; Abu Nu'aym)

The blessed life of Sayyiduna Muhammad (pbuh) is so blissful, eventful and glorious that thousands of pages cannot contain its description. I would advise the murids to learn from authentic sources more and more about this Master of Masters, the Beloved of God Almighty. No one day should pass unless you learn something new about Sayyiduna Muhammad (pbuh).

O Allah, Most Gracious! Reward our greatest Master, Sayyiduna Muhammad (pbuh) with the highest of Divine Rewards and grace him with the Praised High Station that he duly deserves.

O Allah, Most Kind and Generous! Grant us the blessings of his company in this life and in the next life; and bless us with beholding his beautiful countenance in wakefulness and in dream.

O Lord of all! Bless us with true knowledge of the reality of Your Beloved, Sayyiduna Muhammad, who is the Guiding Star for all humanity. May Divine Peace and Divine Salutations be upon him forever and ever. Amen.

AHLUL-BAYT

The Blessed Family of the Holy Messenger (pbuh)

Peace be upon them all

(raDiya Allahu 'anhum, 'alayhim assalam)

'Ahlul-Bayt' (or Ahl Al-Bayt) are the noblest Family among humankind. They are the Family of the Master of all Masters, Sayyiduna Muhammad (pbuh). The blessed Family members include various individuals who are directly related to the Holy Messenger (pbuh). They are his blessed children, his blessed wives, his two blessed uncles: Hamza and Al-Abbas, and every believer from the offspring of Abdul-muttalib, the Holy Messenger's paternal grandfather. One common legal characteristic of Ahlul-Bayt is that they are prohibited from taking anything from the people's charities (Zakah and Sadaqah).

Hadrat Zaid ibn Arqam (RA) said, "One day, the Messenger of Allah (pbuh) stood up to deliver a sermon at a water spring known as "Khum", located between Makkah and Madinah. The Messenger (pbuh) praised and glorified Allah, then said, "O people, I am but a human being, I shall soon receive the Messenger (Angel of Death) of my Lord and I shall respond to His Call. I am leaving with you two great things: one is the Book of Allah, in which there is righteous guidance and light; so, hold fast to the Book of Allah and adhere to it". He went on for some time exhorting us to hold fast to the Book of Allah, and then said, "The second great thing I leave behind is my Household (Ahlul-Bayt). I remind you before Allah to take good care of (embrace, follow) my Household". Husain then asked Zaid, "Who are his Household? Are not his wives from his Household? Zaid replied, "Yes, his wives are from his Household, but here (he means) his Household are those who are not allowed to take charity." Husain asked, "And who are they?" Zaid replied, "They are Ali and his offspring, Aqeel and his offspring, Ja'far and his offspring, and Al-Abbas and his offspring." (Muslim).

Hadrat Muttalib ibn Rabi'a (RA) narrated that the Holy Messenger (pbuh) said to Al-Abbas (RA), "By Allah, faith will not enter the heart of a Muslim until he loves you for the sake of Allah and for the sake of your relation to me." (Ahmad, Al-Tirmizi, Al-Nasa'ee, and Al-Hakim).

Book of Truth

In this blessed book, I will present to you only the most immediate of these blessed relatives, who are considered the elite of Ahlul-Bayt and from whom continues the glorious progeny of the Holy Messenger (pbuh) – Sayyidah Fatima, Imam Ali ibn Abi-Talib, Imam Al-Hasan and Imam Al-Husain (raDiya Allahu 'anhum).

SAYYIDAH FATIMA BINT MUHAMMAD

(raDiya Allahu 'anha / 'alaihas-salam)

Daughter of the Holy Messenger, Sayyiduna Muhammad (pbuh)

The pinnacle of Muhammadi love and light. The star in the sky of Divine presence. Our Sayyidah Fatima (RA) was the youngest and most beloved daughter of the Holy Messenger (Salla Allahu 'alaihi wasallam). She occupies one of the most glorious positions in the Divine Presence and the heavenly world.

She was born five years before the beginning of Divine Revelation to her glorious father, Sayyiduna Muhammad (pbuh). In showing her Godly status, the Holy Messenger (pbuh) said, "Fatima is part of me; whoever angers her has angered me; whatever displeases her, displeases me and whatever hurts her hurts me." (Bukhari & Muslim). The Holy Messenger (pbuh) also said, "Fatima is the Leader of the women of Paradise." (Bukhari).

She was married to Sayyiduna Ali ibn Abi-Talib (RA) in the year 2 AH, when she was eighteen years old. Imam Ali (RA) had no wealth whatsoever as he was devoting all his time to the Holy Messenger (pbuh) and his Divine Mission. At this blessed occasion, the Holy Messenger (pbuh) gifted her a simple straw-wooden bed, a basic leather mattress filled with date palm leaves, a bottle of musk, two pottery pots, a silver bracelet, two Yemeni sheets, one blanket, one pillow, one cup, one hand-grinding mill, one bedstead, a small water skin-bag and a leather pitcher.

Lady Fatima (RA) carried out all her daily house chores herself. Her clothes would become dusty and her hands hard from working in that small mud-house. Her soft hands were blistered from constant grinding, and her shoulder became deeply sore from taking out water from the well.

At the departure of her blessed father, Sayyiduna Muhammad (pbuh), she grieved immensely for six months until her day of relief came as she passed away from this world, Allah be pleased with her. The Holy Messenger (pbuh) had already foretold her that she was going to be the first of his family to die after him and the first to join him in heaven.

Hadrat Anas (RA) reported that the Messenger of Allah (pbuh) said, "From amongst the women of this world only four have attained Perfection: Maryam (Mary) the daughter of Imran, Khadijah daughter of Khuwaylid, Fatima daughter of Muhammad, and Asiyah the wife of Fir'aun (Pharao)" (Al-Tirmizi)

Hadrat Anas ibn Malik (RA) narrated that (at a certain time in Madinah) when the Holy Messenger (Salla Allahu 'alaihi wasallam) used to come out for Fajr (dawn) prayer, and passing by the house-door of Fatima (RA), he would call out, "O Ahlul-Bayt (People of my House)! Rise up and perform your prayer," and then he used to recite this verse from the Holy Quran: "Allah Has Purified you and willed to keep away all kinds of impurity from you, Ahlul-Bayt, and to clothe you with Perfect Purity," [Al-Ahzab: 33]. The Holy Messenger continued this practice for six consecutive months. (Al-Tirmizi)

O Allah, Most High! Reward my beloved grandmother with the highest of Divine Stations along with Your Beloved, her blessed father, the Messenger of Allah (pbuh). O Allah! Bless us with Sayyidah Fatima's glorious lights and blessings. Allow us to serve her and be in her company in this life and in the next. You are Most Gracious, Most Kind. Amen.

SAYYIDUNA ALI IBN ABI–TALIB

(raDiya Allahu 'anhu / 'alaihis-salam)

The Fourth Vicegerent of the Holy Messenger (pbuh)
Grand Master of the Naqshabandi Zhahabiyah Chain

The Gateway of Divine Knowledge. The Master of masters on the Path to Allah. An ocean that has no shores. The devoted and beloved cousin of Sayyiduna Muhammad, the Messenger of Allah (pbuh). He is Ali ibn Abi-Talib ibn Abdul-muttalib ibn Hashim ibn Abdu-Manaf. He was the paternal cousin of the Messenger of Allah (pbuh), and the husband of his most beloved daughter, Sayyidah Fatima the Chaste, the Crown of the women of the universe.

Sayyiduna Ali was born inside the Holy Ka'ba, in Makkah, on Friday, 13th of Rajab, thirty years after the Year of the Elephant (c. 570 AD). His blessed mother was Fatima bint Asad ibn Hashim ibn Abdu-Manaf. She was a second mother to the Messenger of Allah (pbuh) as he was brought up in her household after his own blessed mother, Aminah (RA), passed away when he was only six years old (pbuh).

Sayyiduna Ali migrated to Madinah after the migration of the Holy Messenger (pbuh) and Sayyiduna Abu-Bakr (RA), and remained thereafter in the presence of the Holy Messenger (pbuh), learning from him (pbuh) and serving Islam to the highest degree of sacrifice. He remained as a great minister in assistance to all the three Righteous Caliphs before him, Abu-Bakr (RA), Omar (RA) and Othman (RA). Sayyiduna Ali (RA) became the fourth Righteous Caliph in 35 AH after the martyrdom of Sayyiduna Othman (RA).

Some of his wise sayings:

"Hate no one, no matter how much they have wronged you. Live humbly, no matter how wealthy you may be. Think positively, no matter how hard life is. Give plenty even when you are given little. Keep in touch with those who have forgotten you, forgive those who have wronged you, and do not stop praying for those you love."

"The body is purified with water; the ego with tears. The intellect is purified with knowledge; and the soul with love."

"Your remedy is within you, but you do not sense it. Your sickness is from you, but you do not perceive it. You believe you are a small entity, but within you is enfolded the entire universe. You are indeed the evident book, by whose alphabet the hidden becomes the manifest. You therefore have no need to look beyond yourself. What you seek is within you, if you but reflect."

Sayyiduna Ali (RA) was well known for his absolute devotion to Allah and the life hereafter. He was known for his pure heart, generosity, courage, deep knowledge and noble personality. He is an Imam in that he is one of the highest spiritual Vicegerents of the Holy Messenger (pbuh) and was a great leading model for all people to come.

His Blessed Wives and Blessed Children:

Sayyiduna Ali (RA) married nine women and with them he had 14 boys and 17 girls. His blessed offspring, however, continued only from 5 boys: Al-Hasan, Al-Husain, Muhammad ibn Alhanafiyah, Al-Abbas ibn Um-al-baneen and Omar ibn Um-Habibah, Allah be pleased with them all.

Following are the names of his blessed wives:

1. Sayyidah Fatima (RA) bint Muhammad, the Messenger of Allah (pbuh). Sayyiduna Ali did not marry any other woman until Sayyidah Fatima passed away. His children from Sayyidah Fatima are: Al-Hasan, Al-Husain, Al-Muhsen (passed away in childhood), Zainab and Um-Kulthum (who got married to Sayyiduna Omar ibn Alkhattab (RA).

2. Fatima (Um-al-baneen) bint Hizam (RA). Sayyiduna Ali had five sons with her, namely: Abdullah, Ja'far, Abbas, Othman and Omar. All of them were martyred in the Battle of Karbala along

with Sayyiduna Al-Husain ibn Ali, Allah be pleased with them all.

3. Layla bint Mas'ud ibn Al-Yateema (RA). Sayyiduna Ali had two sons with her: Ubaidullah and Abu-Bakr (known as Muhammad Al-Asghar). Both were martyred in Karbala.

4. Asmaa bint Umais (RA). She was the one who washed the blessed body of her second husband, Sayyiduna Abu-Bakr (RA). After him, she married Sayyiduna Ali (RA) and bore two sons from him: Yahya and 'Awn (or Muhammad).

5. Umamah bint Al-'Aas ibn Al-Rabee' (RA). She was the daughter of Sayyidah Zainab bint Sayyiduna Muhammad (pbuh). Sayyiduna Ali had one son with her: Muhammad Al-Awsat.

6. Khaulah bint Ja'far Alhanafiyah (RA). Sayyiduna Ali had one son with her: Muhammad ibn Alhanfiyah (Muhammad Al-Akbar).

7. Al-Sahbaa (Um-Habibah) bint Rabi'ah Al-Taghlibiya (RA). She bore him one son, Omar, and one daughter, Ruqayah.

8. Um-Saeed bint Orwah Al-Thaqafiya (RA). She bore him two daughters: Um-Alhasan and Ramlah.

9. Muhayyah bint Imro-ul-Qays Al-Kalbiyah (RA). She bore him one daughter, Jariyah, who died early in childhood.

After a great and eventful life, Sayyiduna Ali (RA) passed away on Friday, 21st Ramadan, in 40 AH, at the age of 63, two days after he was treacherously attacked with a poisoned sword by the cursed one, Abdurrahman ibn Muljim. That day, Sayyiduna Ali (RA) was fasting; he was in the state of prostration in the Mosque of Kufa, Iraq, when the poisoned sword struck his blessed body. At this moment, Sayyiduna Ali (RA) instantly proclaimed, "By the Lord of the Ka'ba, I have won (gained success)!"

Beloved murid! Be a true seeker for this kind of success that Sayyiduna Ali (RA) meant when he was dying. Know that success is that you leave this transitory life when you are in a state of perfect vision of the Divine Presence and Pleasure.

O Allah, Most High! Grant our Imam Ali ibn Abi-Talib and my grandfather the highest of ranks in Your Divine Presence and bless us with his glorious spiritual flow that You Have Bestowed upon him. You are Most Gracious, Most Kind. Amen.

SAYYIDUNA AL-HASAN IBN ALI

(raDiya Allahu 'anhu / 'alaihis-salam)

About our two Ahlul-Bayt Masters, Al-Hasan and Al-Husain, the Holy Messenger (pbuh) said, "Al-Hasan and Al-Husain are the two best sweet-smelling fragrances of this world for me." (Bukhari). The Holy Messenger (pbuh) also said, "Al-Hasan and Al-Husain are the Masters of the youth of Paradise." (Al-Tirmizi; Al-Hakim).

Sayyiduna Al-Hasan ibn Ali was the elder son of Sayyiduna Ali (RA) with Sayyidah Fatima (RA). He was born in Madinah, on 15th of Ramadan, in the year 3 AH. He held a very dear place in the heart of the Holy Messenger (pbuh) and lived in his holy presence for seven years. Imam Al-Hasan is the father of all the Hasani families of Ahlul-Bayt in the world.

After the martyrdom of his blessed father, Sayyiduna Ali (RA), the people in Hijaz and other Islamic regions, except for the Levant, paid allegiance to Imam Al-Hasan as Commander of the Believers. However, six or eight months later, he abdicated this post to Mu'awiya ibn Abi-Sufyan, to avoid any bloodshed due to the fitna (hidden plots) that were fabricated by the hypocrites in Iraq and other areas. Then, for the rest of his life, Imam Al-Hasan lived in seclusion in Madinah until he passed away by poisoning, at the

Book of Truth

age of 45 or 46. His blessed body was buried in Al-Baqee' Cemetery in Madinah.

His wives and women in 'kind possession' and his blessed children:

Sayyiduna Al-Hasan (RA) married many times as many families were eager to have the honour of marrying into the Holy Family of the Messenger of Allah (pbuh), but, as in accordance with Shari'a, Al-Hasan only had four women in wedlock at one time. However, we only know the names of six of his wives and three of his women in 'kind possession', as follows:

1. Um-Bashir bint Abi Mas'ud: who bore him: Zaid, Um-Alhasan and Um-Alhusain

2. Khawla bint Manzoor ibn Zabban, who bore him: Muhammad Al-Akbar and Alhasan Almuthanna

3. Um-Kulthum bint Al-Fadl ibn Al-Abbas ibn Abdul-Muttalib

4. Um-Is-haq bint Talhah Al-Taimi, who bore him: Husain Al-Athram, Fatima and Talhah

5. Zaynab bint Subai' Albajali

6. Ja'dah bint Al-Ash'ath Al-Kindi

7. Ramlah (Nufailah or Buqailah), a woman in his 'kind possession', who bore him: Alqasim, Amr and Abdullah

8. Saafiyah, a woman in his 'kind possession', who bore him: Abdurrahman

9. Zhamyaa, a woman in his 'kind possession'

The other blessed children of Al-Hasan (RA): Um-Abdullah, Fatima, Ruqayah and Um-Salamah, were from other different wives, Allah bless them all.

Some of his Noble Qualities:

Like the rest of Ahlul-Bayt (RA), Sayyiduna Al-Hasan (RA) was extremely generous and kind. He would give away without looking at what remains for himself. One time, when he was sitting in the Holy Mosque around the Holy Ka'ba, he heard a man nearby praying to Allah to provide him with 10,000 dirhams. Imam Al-Hasan immediately got up, went to his residence and brought with him 10,000 dirhams and gave them to the man.

Another incident was with a slave woman in his own 'kind possession'. Once, when Al-Hasan (RA) was out sitting with other men, she came and greeted him with a bouquet of flowers, so he immediately said to her "You are free (from slavery) for the sake of Allah". When someone asked him why he did this, Al-Hasan (RA) replied, "Allah Almighty taught us noble manners, for He says in the Holy Quran "When you are greeted with a good manner of greeting, respond to it with even a better manner...", and I did not find a better response than setting her free"." (Ibn Al-Atheer: Usdul-ghabah fi-ma'rifat assahabah)

In addition to giving charity continuously, Al-Hasan (RA) offered major charities by giving away exactly all his possessions twice in his lifetime and exactly half of what he owned three times during his lifetime.

His noble nature of forbearance and clemency was of paramount level. Once, as Sayyiduna Al-Hasan (RA) was riding on horseback, an old man started shouting abuses at him. Al-Hasan did not say a word in response nor did he interrupt him. When the old man stopped shouting, Al-Hasan (RA) looked at him with a tender smile and said, "O elder man! I think you are a stranger here! Maybe you mistook me for someone else! Be sure that if you conciliate us, we will surely satisfy you. If you ask us, we will give you all what you ask for. If you seek counsel from us, we will surely guide you. If you need a vehicle to ride, we will carry you with the best of our means. If you are hungry, we will feed you until you are satisfied. If you need clothes, we will clothe you with the best of what we have. If you are in need, we will give you enough wealth. If you are a homeless stranger, we will give you lodging. If you have any request, we shall grant it. It would be good for you if you could bring your luggage and be our guest until the time of your travel, for we have a spacious place, good social position, and great wealth." The old man felt extremely ashamed and remarked, "I bear witness that you are the Vicegerent of Allah on earth; Allah knows where to entrust

His Divine Message. Now, you are more beloved to me than the whole world."

Our Lord, Most High, Most Gracious! Grant our Master, Sayyiduna Al-Hasan ibn Ali the highest of heavenly stations in the company of his blessed Muhammadi Family, peace be upon them all.

O Most Generous Lord! Give me and my murids from the blessings You Have Showered upon our Master, Al-Hasan ibn Ali, so that we too are blessed with the love, light and wisdom You have Poured into his blessed heart. Amen.

SAYYIDUNA AL-HUSAIN IBN ALI

(raDiya Allahu 'anhu / 'alaihis-salam)

Sayyiduna Al-Husain ibn Ali (RA) is the grand Imam in the Golden Chain of this blessed Naqshabandi Tariqah after his father, Hadrat Ali ibn Abi-Talib (RA). He is also my great grandfather, hence, my surname, Al-Husaini.

Imam Al-Husain (RA) was the second grandson of the Holy Messenger (pbuh). He was born on the 3rd of Sha'ban, 4 AH. The Messenger (pbuh) himself recited the calls of azhan and iqamah in his blessed ears, and offered 'aqiqah (birthday sacrifice) for him by sacrificing a goat. Al-Husain (RA) bore the closest physical resemblance to the Holy Messenger (pbuh).

Hadrat Anas (RA) noted that out of all the people in his Household, Al-Hasan and Al-Husain were most beloved to the Holy Messenger (pbuh). He would often go to their house next door to see them and would enjoy watching them play and would lift them up and hold them against his holy chest with affection. The Holy Messenger (pbuh) would often pray for them, "O Allah, I love these two; You, too, love them." (Bukhari). He also used to say, "Whoever loves them, loves me, and whoever dislikes them, in fact dislikes me; Al-Husain is from me and I am from Al-Husain. Whoever loves Al-Husain is loved by Allah." (Musnad Ahmad).

Like his brother, Al-Hasan (RA), Al-Husain (RA) was fortunate to live in the presence of the Holy Messenger (pbuh) for nearly seven years.

As Commanders of the Believers after the departure of the Holy Messenger (pbuh), Sayyiduna Abu-Bakr (RA) and Sayyiduna Omar (RA) looked after Al-Hasan and Al-Husain with great reverence and affection. In the Era of Sayyiduna Othman (RA), Al-Husain (RA) participated in the conquests of Tabristan (Tapuria). During the fitna (tribulation) of the besiegement of Sayyiduna Othman (RA) in Madinah, Al-Hasan and Al-Husain were appointed by their father, Sayyiduna Ali (RA) to guard Sayyiduna Othman (RA) from the rebellious people who were incited by the hypocrites to cause rift and trouble between the Muslims. The two young Imams stayed guarding him until Othman returned them and refused to be guarded by anyone.

After Imam Ali's martyrdom, Al-Husain joined the other Sahabah in pledging allegiance to his brother, Al-Hasan, as Commander of the Believers. When Al-Hasan gave up the position to Mu'awiya, Al-Husain agreed to follow with this new allegiance.

Al-Husain had all the perfect and beautiful qualities that made him shine as a Vicegerent of the Holy Messenger (pbuh) for all the Ummah of Islam. His scholarly knowledge was exemplary and his oratory outstanding. He used to spend his nights in worship and give up his wealth in charity.

Sayyiduna Al-Husain (RA) was wrongly and brutally martyred on the 10th of Muharram, 61 AH, by the oppressive army of Ubaidullah ibn Ziad, governor of Kufa and Basra in Iraq. Al-Husain's blessed head was then severed by the cursed one, Shammar ibn Zul-Jawshan, and was taken to Yazid ibn Mu'awiya, at the seat of government in Damascus. Al-Husain's blessed body was buried in Karbala, Iraq, and his blessed head was consequently buried in Damascus, but was later moved to Asqalan, and from there was finally moved to Cairo, in the Maqam (Tomb) where it now lies, bringing great blessings to Egypt.

His wives and women in 'kind possession' and his blessed children:

1. Hafsah bint Abdurrahman ibn Abu-Bakr AS-Siddiq (RA).
2. Layla bint Urwah ibn Mas'ud Al-Thaqafi, who bore him Ali Al-Akbar.
3. Sulafah (Shah Zanan) bint Yazdajird the Third (last of Persian emperors), who bore him Ali Zainul-'abideen (RA), one of our greatest Naqshabandi Masters.
4. Al-Rubab bint Imro-ul-Qays, who bore him Sukainah and Abdullah Arradee' (Infant, RA), who was martyred in Karbala.

---

5. Um-Is-haq bint Talhah ibn Ubaidullah, who bore him Fatima.
6. Unnamed woman from the tribe of Bila, who bore him Ja'far.

The confirmed children of Sayyiduna Al-Husain (RA) were four boys and two girls, as above. Some scholars, however, reported four other children: Ali Al-Asghar, Muhsen, Ruqayah and Zaynab, Allah bless them all.

Like his blessed brother, Al-Hasan, Al-Husain was well known for his deep knowledge, beautiful manners, courage and generosity. Hadrat Al-Hasan Al-Basri (RA) reported that Sayyiduna Al-Husain (RA) was going once to his farm in Madinah, and as he approached, he saw his slave worker sitting under a tree eating bread and a dog was sitting opposite him. Al-Husain (RA) stopped at a distance and watched. The slave worker was cutting every piece of bread into two pieces; he would give one-half to the dog and would eat the other half. When he finished, he praised Allah for giving him such blessed food. Al-Husain walked to him and enquired of him as to why he was sharing his bread with the dog! The worker replied that he felt ashamed to eat everything he had when the dog was looking at him eating. Sayyiduna Al-Husain immediately set him free and gave him the whole farm as gift.

Some of his wise sayings:

"Two signs of a learned person are, accepting other people's criticism and being knowledgeable in all types and levels of rhetoric and debate."

"If one does not have these five things, there is no good in him: intellect, practice of faith, etiquette, shame and good manners."

"Never will be salvaged the people who gain the pleasure of the creation at the cost of the displeasure of the Creator."

"O Allah! Surely you know that whatever we did was not a competition to gain worldly positions and not for the worthless physical charms of this world. You well know that we only wanted to give rise to the ways of faith and to remove corruption from your land, so that the oppressed can feel secure and free to follow Your Commandments."

O Allah! Bless my grandfather, and our Master and Imam, Al-Husain and his blessed offspring with countless blessings until the Last Day, and please him with continuous Presence in Your Divine Court of Love and Light. O Most Generous! Enlighten our hearts through their glorious lights of guidance and favour us with their company in this life and in the next. You are Most Merciful, Most Kind.

EARLY MASTERS OF TRUTH

Khulafa (Vicegerents) of the Holy Messenger (pbuh)

We owe our knowledge and our inner purification to these masters, the men of Truth, who were directly enlightened by the Messenger of Allah (pbuh). We acknowledge their high stations in the Divine Presence as well as their sacrifice and efforts to allow this knowledge and spiritual enlightenment to reach us.

In addition to the great figures of Ahlul-Bayt mentioned above, we also acknowledge the first three Vicegerents of the Holy Messenger (pbuh) as Men of Truth. They are Sayyiduna Abu-Bakr AS-Siddiq (RA), Sayyiduna Omar ibn Al-khattab (RA) and Sayyiduna Othman ibn Affan (RA).

This is why the murid should know enough about them and seek blessings from their beautifully flowing souls, and should take them as the best role models for his/her life.

May Allah Almighty bless us with their everlasting company in Paradise. Amen.

Our Crown Masters: Muhammad the Messenger of Allah (pbuh), Abu-Bakr AS-Siddiq, Omar ibn Al-khattab, Othman ibn Affan (RA), {Ali ibn Abi-Talib, Fatima Az-zahra, Al-Hasan and Al-Husain (AS)}

SAYYIDUNA ABU-BAKR AS-SIDDIQ

(raDiya Allahu 'anhu)

First Vicegerent of the Holy Messenger (pbuh)

Grand Master of the Siddiqiyah Chain

His first name is Abdullah, ibn Othman ibn Aamir ibn Amr ibn Ka'b ibn Sa'd ibn Taym ibn Murrah ibn Ka'b ibn Lu'ai. He joins with the blessed lineage of Sayyiduna Muhammad (pbuh) in their sixth grandfather, Murrah ibn Ka'b. He was born in Holy Makkah around 573 CE and passed away in 634 CE in Holy Madinah. He became the first man to accept Sayyiduna Muhammad as the Messenger of Allah, and he is the father of the Messenger's wife, Aisha Siddiqah (RA).

Sayyiduna Abu-Bakr's personality is a Perfect personality and his Islamic record is full of magnificent deeds and sacrifices. It is enough credit to Sayyiduna Abu-Bakr (RA) in Islam that he spent literally all of his wealth and earnings on the Messenger of Allah (pbuh) and on his holy mission of calling people to Allah. It reached to a point that he did not leave any money at all for his wife and children as he took everything to the Holy Messenger (pbuh), who asked Abu-Bakr "And what did you leave for your family, O Abu-Bakr?", and to this remark Abu-Bakr (RA) says "I left for them Allah and His Messenger". What a total devotion! What a perfect sacrifice! Who can reach Abu-Bakr and his heavenly station? Allah bless him.

Not only that, but Abu-Bakr (RA) was the only companion who joined the Holy Messenger (pbuh) in the most illustrious event in Islamic history, the Hijrah, Blessed Journey of Migration from Makkah to Madinah. He was thus the only companion who spent three consecutive days alone with the Holy Messenger (pbuh) in a cave outside Makkah during this glorious Journey.

Hadrat Ibn Abbas (RA) reported that the Messenger of Allah (pbuh) said (to the other Companions), "Abu-Bakr is my Close (Special) Friend and my companion in the Cave; all of you should acknowledge these virtues for him. If I were to take a khalil (one's only spiritual companion), I would take Abu-Bakr." (Abdullah ibn Ahmed, Al-Daylami and others).

Hadrat Aisha (RA) reported that the Messenger of Allah (pbuh) said, "Abu-Bakr is from me and I am from him. Abu-Bakr is my brother in this world and in the Hereafter." (Al-Daylami) Hadrat Aisha (RA) reported that the Messenger of Allah (pbuh) said, "Allah has confirmed for Abu-Bakr his salvation from Hellfire." (Abu Nu'aym).

Hadrat Abu Hurairah (RA) narrated that the Messenger of Allah (pbuh) said, "Jibril came to me and took me by the hand then showed me the door of Paradise from which my nation will enter." Abu-Bakr said, "How would I have loved to be with you when you saw it!" He replied, "As for you, Abu-Bakr, surely you will be the first of my nation to enter Paradise." (Abu Dawood and others)

Hadrat Ali (RA) narrated that the Messenger of Allah (pbuh) said, 'Jibril came to me and I asked him, "Who should I take as companion in migration (to Madinah)?" He said to me, "Take Abu-Bakr; he will lead your nation after you, and he is the best of your nation.' (Al-Daylami)

Hadrat Jabir ibn Abdullah (RA) narrated, 'Once, we were in the presence of the Holy Messenger (pbuh) when he said, "Now, a man will appear to you who is the best and noblest person Allah has created after me, and his intercession is equal to the intercession of God's Prophets." Thus, appeared Abu-Bakr AS-Siddiq, then the Holy Messenger (pbuh) stood up, kissed him and embraced him.' (Alhafiz Al-khatib Al-baghdadi)

For Master Abu-Bakr, I only pray that Allah Almighty give me and my murids enough love and respect for him, and bless us with his company when Master Abu-Bakr enters Paradise from all of its eight magnificent gates! O Allah, we seek Divine Light from Sayyiduna Abu-Bakr as we seek Divine Light from Sayyiduna Ali ibn Abi Talib, Allah be pleased with them and their Vicegerents until the Last Day, for You Have Favoured them with Your Divine Secret. Amen.

SAYYIDUNA OMAR IBN AL-KHATTAB

(raDiya Allahu 'anhu)

The Second Vicegerent of the Holy Messenger (pbuh)

Sayyiduna Omar ibn Al-khattab was born in Holy Makkah around 583 CE and passed away in 644 CE in Holy Madinah. He is the father of the Holy Messenger's wife, Hafsah (RA).

One day, in the early stage of Islam in Makkah, the Messenger of Allah (pbuh) invoked Allah Almighty, "O Allah, give glory to Islam through the one you love of these two men: Amr ibn Hisham or Omar ibn Al-khattab." In response to this prayer, Allah Almighty chose Omar ibn Al-khattab and thus he embraced Islam. (Sunan Ibn Hibban) Ibn Hajar wrote, "Among the things that attracted Omar to Islam was the recitation of the Holy Quran he heard in the house of his sister, Fatima." (Fat-hul Bari)

Sa'eed ibn Abi Waqqas (RA) said, 'Once, Omar ibn Al-khattab sought permission to enter in the presence of the Holy Messenger (pbuh) and there were some Quraishi women with him asking him questions and their voices were loud. When Omar entered, they went quiet and rushed to veil themselves from him. The Messenger of Allah (pbuh) started smiling. Upon this, Omar remarked, "May Allah continue to make you happy!"

The Holy Messenger (pbuh) said, "I am amazed at these women here! When they heard your voice, they rushed to veil themselves." Omar said, "But O Messenger of Allah, you are more worthy to be feared." Then, Omar turned to the women and said, "O enemies of yourselves! Do you fear me and not fear the Messenger of Allah?" They replied, "Yes, we do. You are harsher and more difficult than the Messenger of Allah." The Holy Messenger then said, "O Ibn Al-Khattab! By Allah, the One Who Holds my soul, whenever Satan finds you taking a way, he would rush to take a way other than yours."' (Bukhari)

Ibn Abbas (RA) said, 'When Omar was placed on his bed (after being stabbed), I was among the people who gathered around him to pray for him before he would pass away. Suddenly, a man took hold of my shoulder. He was Ali ibn Abi-Talib, who then started praying for Omar and said, "You have not left behind anyone I would prefer to meet Allah with his deeds other than you. By Allah, I always believed that Allah would place you at the end with your two companions. I often heard the Messenger of Allah (pbuh) say, 'I, Abu-Bakr and Omar went to...', and 'I, Abu-Bakr and Omar entered...' and 'I, Abu-Bakr and Omar left...'"' (Bukhari)

Abu Huraira (RA) narrated that the Holy Messenger (pbuh) said, "Among the people of Bani Israel before you there were men who were divinely spoken to though they were not prophets. If there are any such people in my followers, he is Omar (i.e., one of them)." (Bukhari). Muhammad ibn Al-Hanafiya (RA), son of Ali ibn Abi-Talib (RA) said, 'I asked my father, "Who was the best of people after the Holy Messenger?" He said, "Abu-Bakr". I asked him, "Who is the best of people after Abu-Bakr?" He replied, "Omar."' (Bukhari)

Abdullah Ibn Mas'ud (RA) said, "If the knowledge of Omar were to be put on one side of a scale, and the knowledge of all other people on the other side of the scale, Omar's knowledge would outweigh their knowledge." (Al-Mustadrak) Ibn Abbas (RA) narrated that the Messenger of Allah (pbuh) said, "The likeness of Abu-Bakr and Omar in this religion is like hearing and seeing in the head." (Al-khatib).

Sayyiduna Omar (RA) led a life so close to his beloved Master, the Holy Messenger (pbuh) that he was even buried in the same Holy Chamber of the Prophet (pbuh) and his closest Friend, Abu-Bakr AS-Siddiq (RA). For over 14 centuries, Muslims going to visit the Holy Messenger (pbuh), they also visit Abu-Bakr and Omar with him, Allah be pleased with them all.

The virtues of our Master Omar ibn Al-khattab (RA) are endless. I would encourage my murids to learn more about him as well as about all the other Masters of Truth.

Our Crown Masters: Muhammad the Messenger of Allah (pbuh), Abu-Bakr AS-Siddiq, Omar ibn Al-khattab,
Othman ibn Affan (RA), {Ali ibn Abi-Talib, Fatima Az-zahra, Al-Hasan and Al-Husain (AS)}

I sincerely pray to my Lord, Allah Almighty, to reward Sayyiduna Omar with the perfect Light and the highest station in His Divine Presence and in Paradise.

I pray to Allah, The Most Beneficent, to bless me and my murids with the Faith and Strength on the Truth that Hadrat Omar and the other Vicegerents of the Holy Messenger (pbuh) have, and to bless me and my murids with their Divine Love and Light. Amen.

SAYYIDUNA OTHMAN IBN AFFAN

(raDiya Allahu 'anhu)

The Third Vicegerent of the Holy Messenger (pbuh)

Sayyiduna Othman (RA) embraced Islam very early, due to the invitation to Islam by Sayyiduna Abu-Bakr AS-Siddiq (RA). Othman was born in Holy Makkah (or Taif) in the year 47 before Hijra Sharifa. He was from the Banu Umayyah clan of Quraish.

The Holy Messenger (pbuh) gave to Othman his daughter, Ruqayyah (RA), in marriage and when she died, gave him his other daughter, Um-Kulthum (RA); hence his nickname, Zhun-nurayn (one with 'the two lights'). The scholars noted that Othman is the only man in history who married two daughters of a messenger of Allah. Othman is one of the infamous ten men who were given by the Holy Messenger (pbuh) confirmed glad tidings of being of the dwellers of Paradise, known as "Al-'asharah al-mubashareen bil-jannah".

Abdur-Rahman ibn Othman Al-qurashi narrated that the Messenger of Allah (pbuh) once entered his daughter's house when she was washing the head of her husband, Othman, and thus he (pbuh) remarked "O my daughter, take good care of Abu Abdullah, for he is the closest of my companions to me in attitude." (Al-Tabarani)

Othman (RA) migrated twice for the sake of Allah, the first time to Abyssinia with his wife, Ruqayyah, and the second to Madinah. He made great sacrifices for the Holy Messenger and Islam. He equipped the Army of Hardship all by himself. He bought the most expensive sweet-water Well of Rumah in Madinah and gave it out in charity for all the Muslims. He expanded the Holy Messenger's Mosque in Madinah. He collected all the scattered writings of the Holy Quran and made them into one single book for the first time since Holy Revelation. He supplied from his own money the Expedition of Tabuk with 940 camels and 60 horses. He gave the Holy Messenger (pbuh) ten thousand dinars to equip its army. As he placed the money before the Messenger of Allah (pbuh), the Holy Messenger (pbuh) began turning the money over with his blessed hands and repeated twice, "Nothing can disadvantage Otham after today, no matter what he does."

Othman (RA) recited the entire Holy Quran to the Messenger of Allah (pbuh) before he passed away. Othman used to say, "Three things in this world have been made dear to me: feeding the hungry, clothing the naked and reciting the Holy Quran."

In relation to the holy verse "Can one who is devoutly obedient during the night, prostrating and standing [in prayer], observing the Hereafter and hoping for the mercy of his Lord, (be like one who is not in this condition?) (Al-Zumar: 9), Ibn Umar

(RA) remarked, "Such was Othman ibn Affan"; and in relation to this holy verse "... can this man be equal to one who enjoins justice and remains steadfast on the Straight Path?" (Al-Nahl: 76), Ibn Abbas (RA) remarked, "That was Othman ibn Affan." (Ibn-Katheer)

O Allah, Most Glorious! How beautiful Your Friends are! O Most High Lord! Bless them further and further with the most glorious of Your Heavenly Blessings, and grace us with their blessed company forever. Amen.

Beloved murid! These are your Masters of true guidance to the Pleasure and Presence of God Almighty. These are your role models – know them, understand them, love them and follow them in every quality and in every way.

Ibn Omar (RA) used to say, "We (the Companions in Madinah) used to make preference between the people, so we used to put Abu-Bakr first, then Omar, then Othman, Allah be pleased with them." (Al-Bukhari). Abdullah ibn Buraida (RA) reported from his father that the Holy Messenger (pbuh) said, "Anyone of my Companions dies in any land, he will be resurrected as the leader and guiding light of its people on the Day of Resurrection." (Al-Tirmizi, Al-Bukhari, Al-Bazzar, Abu-Nu'aim, Ibn Mindah, Ibn Asakir)

There are many other men and women of Truth among the Sahabah (Companions) who were raised and perfected by the Holy Messenger (pbuh), and whom the murid should devote his/her life to learn about. Rediscover your real and genuine role models.

Other prominent Men and Women of Truth from the first blessed generation are:

Talhah ibn Ubaidullah; Sa'd ibn Abi Waqqas; Abu Ubaidah ibn Aljarrah; Azzubair ibn Al'awwam; Abdurrahman ibn Awf; Sa'eed ibn Zaid ibn Amr; Zayd ibn Harithah; Osamah ibn Zayd; Bilal ibn Rabah, Mu'azh ibn Jabal; Asmaa bint Abu-Bakr; Sumayya bint Alkhayyat; Fatima bint Alkhattab; Arqam ibn Abil-arqam; Mus'ab ibn Umair; Abu Zhar Alghifari; Abdullah ibn Mas'ud; and many more whose souls are shining stars in the dark skies.

Ibn Mas'ud (RA) says, "In this Ummah, the Companions were the purest at heart, the deepest in (Divine) Knowledge, the least in pretence and affectation, the most straight on the Way, and the most beautiful in internal and external states. Loving them is Sunnah, praying for them is a means of nearness to Allah, taking them as guides is a means to the Pleasure of Allah, and following their footsteps is a great virtue."

The other saints (awliya) of Allah who followed the Sahabah very closely and took Divine Knowledge from the two Grand Masters, Abu-Bakr (RA) and Ali (RA), are also our role models, who even explained the Way to us more clearly. You find many of them in our blessed Naqshabandi Chains, may Allah bless you with their spiritual flow of Light and Love.

O Allah, enlighten our hearts to see their glory and benefit from their glorious light. May Allah grant us their blessed company here and in the Everlasting Abode. Amen.

Book of Truth

Book of Prayers

Book of Prayers

INTRODUCTION TO BOOK OF PRAYERS

Beloved seeker! To pray to your Lord is a true confession from you that Allah is your Creator and your Sustainer. Where can you go from Him? The state of being murid is the state of complete submission to Allah and of complete conviction that only He is the Supreme Deity; this is why the Holy Quran and the Holy Messenger (pbuh) continue to direct us to supplicate to Allah and show our weakness before His Greatness and our poverty before His Power.

Abu Hurairah (RA) reported, the Messenger of Allah (pbuh) said, "The supplication of every one of you will be granted as long as he does not become impatient and say 'I called upon my Lord but my prayer has not been granted'." (Al-Bukhari, Muslim). The narration by Imam Muslim says, "The supplication of a servant of Allah continues to be granted as long as he does not pray for a sinful matter or for something that would cut off the ties of kinship, and as long as he does not grow impatient." Someone asked: "O Messenger of Allah! What does growing impatient mean?" He (pbuh) replied, "It means when one says, 'I prayed again and again but my prayer was not answered!', so he would become frustrated and give up supplication altogether."

In order to become steadfast on your occasion-related supplications throughout the year, you need to be aware of the Hijri months and to base most of your important affairs on this Calendar. I would encourage you to convert your dates of birth and other important events into the Hijri Calendar, and to count your age and occasions accordingly. The Hijri Calendar is a lunar calendar of 12 months that begin and end according to the cycle of the moon. Allah Almighty has connected many of the blessed occasions with the days of the lunar month, like mid-Sha'ban, Ramadan, Blessed Mawlid in Rabi'ul-awwal, Ashura, Hajj, etc.

Months of the Hijri Calendar are:

(1) Muharram, (2) Safar, (3) Rabi'ul-awwal,

(4) Rabi'ul-thani, (5) Jumadal-awwal, (6) Jumadal-thani,

(7) Rajab, (8) Sha'ban, (9) Ramadan, (10) Shawwal,

(11) Zul-Qi'dah, and (12) Zul-Hijjah.

CALENDAR OF BLESSED ANNUAL OCCASIONS

Hijri date	Event
1st Muharram	Hijrah Sharifah & the First Ten Days of Muharram
10th Muharram	Ashura
14th Muharram	Milad of Imam of Tariqah: Blessed Birth of Sayyiduna Muhammad Baha-uddin Shah Naqshaband Al-Husaini (RA)
12th Rabi'ul-awwal	Mawlid An-Nabi (pbuh): Blessed Birth of the Holy Messenger, Sayyiduna Muhammad (Salla Allahu 'alaihi wasallam)
27th Rajab	Isra and Mi'raj Miraculous Journey
14th Sha'ban	Laylatul-bara'ah / Night of Salvation
15th Sha'ban	Mid-Shaban Day
29/30 Sha'ban	Entry of blessed Ramadan
17th Ramadan	Great Expedition of Badr
20-29 Ramadan	Laylatul-Qadr
1st Shawwal	Eidul-Fitr
1-10 Zhul-Hijjah	First 10 days of Zul-Hijjah
10th Zhul-Hijjah	Eidul-Adha

Book of Prayers

This Calendar of Blessed Occasions includes important events in the Hijri Calendar that murids should celebrate collectively, first, to gain heavenly rewards, and secondly, to maintain strong ties with their Islamic roots and keep their God-related identity. When the community of murids around you organises an event for any of these occasions, always invite others to join you in these celebrations so they too can acquire and enjoy this blessed identity – that is, to become a true and sincere servant of Allah, on the Path of His last Messenger, Sayyiduna Muhammad (pbuh).

NEW YEAR'S PRAYER

On the 1ˢᵗ of Muharram

Recite this dua (prayer) during Fajr time, whether before or after Fajr Salah, on the first day of Muharram:

بِسْمِ اللهِ الرَّحْمَنِ الرَّحِيمِ، وَصَلَّى اللهُ عَلَى سَيِّدِنَا مُحَمَّدٍ وَعَلَى آلِهِ وَصَحْبِهِ وَسَلَّمَ، اَللَّهُمَّ أَنْتَ الْأَبَدِيُّ الْقَدِيمُ الْأَوَّلُ، وَعَلَى فَضْلِكَ الْعَظِيمِ وَجُودِكَ الْمُعَوَّلُ، وَهَذَا عَامٌ جَدِيدٌ قَدْ أَقْبَلَ، نَسْأَلُكَ الْعِصْمَةَ فِيهِ مِنَ الشَّيْطَانِ الرَّجِيمِ وَأَوْلِيَائِهِ وَجُنُودِهِ وَأَعْوَانِهِ، وَنَسْأَلُكَ الْعَوْنَ عَلَى هَذِهِ النَّفْسِ الْأَمَّارَةِ بِالسُّوءِ، وَالاشْتِغَالَ بِمَا يُقَرِّبُنِي إِلَيْكَ زُلْفَى، يَا ذَا الْجَلَالِ وَالْإِكْرَامِ.

bismillahirraH-manirraheem, wa-Salla Allahu 'ala sayyidina muHammadin wa'ala alihi wa-SaHbihi wa-sallam, allahumma antal-abadiyyul-qadeemul-awwal, wa'ala faDlikal-'aZeemil-mu'awwal, wa-hazha 'amun jadeedun qad aqbal, nas'alukal-'Smata fihi minashayTanir-rajeemi wa-awliya'ihi wa-junudihi wa-a'wanihi, wa-nas'alukal'awna 'ala hazhin-nafsil-ammarati bissu'I, wal-ishtighali bima yuqarribuni ilayka zulfa, ya zhal-jalali wal-ikram.

Then, send any number of Salawat to Sayyiduna Muhammad (Salla Allahu 'alaihi wasallam).

Book of Prayers

Through the blessings of this prayer, Allah will appoint for you protective angels whose task is to protect you from the Devil's influence throughout the year.

END OF YEAR PRAYER

You can read the Prayer below 3 times on the last day, 29th or 30th, of the month of Zul-Hijjah. You may read either the Arabic prayer, if you can, or my English translation as below.

بِسْمِ اللهِ الرَّحْمَنِ الرَّحِيْمِ، وَصَلَّى اللّهُ عَلَى سَيِّدِنَا مُحَمَّدٍ وَعَلَى آلِهِ وَصَحْبِهِ وَسَلَّمَ، اَللّهُمَّ إِنَّكَ عَفُوٌّ كَرِيْمٌ تُحِبُّ الْعَفْوَ فَاعْفُ عَنِّي، أَسْتَغْفِرُكَ اللّهُمَّ فَاغْفِرْ لِيْ مَا فَعَلْتُهُ فِيْ هَذِهِ السَّنَةِ مِمَّا نَهَيْتَنِيْ عَنْهُ وَلَمْ تَرْضَهُ، اَللّهُمَّ إِنِّيْ أَعْلَمُ قُدْرَتَكَ عَلَى عُقُوْبَتِيْ، وَأَعْلَمُ دَعْوَتَكَ لِيْ إِلَى التَّوْبَةِ مِنْ بَعْدِ جُرْأَتِيْ عَلَى مَعْصِيَتِكَ، فَتَقَبَّلْ تَوْبَتِيْ، وَأَسْأَلُكَ اللّهُمَّ يَا كَرِيْمُ يَا تَوَّابُ يَا ذَا الْجَلَالِ وَالْإِكْرَامِ أَنْ تَتَقَبَّلَ مِنِّيْ، وَلَا تَقْطَعْ رَجَائِيْ مِنْكَ، وَصَلَّى اللّهُ عَلَى سَيِّدِنَا مُحَمَّدٍ وَعَلَى آلِهِ وَصَحْبِهِ وَسَلَّمَ.

English translation of 'End of Year Prayer':

In the name of Allah, Most Gracious, Most Merciful. Peace and blessings be upon our Master, Muhammad, and upon his noble Family and Companions. O Allah! You are All Forgiving, Most Generous; You love to forgive, and I beg You to forgive me. I beg You to pardon me for all that I have done during this past year which You had forbidden me from doing. O Allah! I realise Your Might over me and Your Power to punish me, and I am aware of

Your Call for me to repent after I have transgressed by disobeying You. O Allah! Please accept my repentance to You. O Allah, Most Generous, Most High! I beg You to accept me and not to deprive me from my hope in Your Mercy. My Lord, send Your prayers and blessings unto Your Messenger, Sayyiduna Muhammad, and unto his noble Family and Companions.

PRAYER ON THE DAY OF ASHURA

On 10th of Muharram

حَسْبُنَا اللهُ وَنِعْمَ الْوَكِيلُ، نِعْمَ الْمَوْلَى وَنِعْمَ النَّصِيرُ

Read the above ayat 70 times, then read the Prayer below once:

سُبْحَانَ اللهِ مِلْءَ الْمِيْزَانِ، وَمُنْتَهَى الْعِلْمِ، وَمَبْلَغَ الرِّضَا، وَزِنَةَ الْعَرْشِ، لَا
مَلْجَأَ وَلَا مَنْجَا مِنَ اللهِ إِلَّا إِلَيْهِ، سُبْحَانَ اللهِ عَدَدَ الشَّفْعِ وَالْوَتْرِ، وَعَدَدَ كَلِمَاتِ
رَبِّنَا التَّامَّاتِ كُلِّهَا. أَسْأَلُكَ السَّلَامَةَ بِرَحْمَتِكَ يَا أَرْحَمَ الرَّاحِمِيْنَ، وَلَا حَوْلَ وَلَا
قُوَّةَ إِلَّا بِاللهِ الْعَلِيِّ الْعَظِيْمِ، وَهُوَ حَسْبِي وَنِعْمَ الْوَكِيلُ، نِعْمَ الْمَوْلَى وَنِعْمَ
النَّصِيرُ، وَصَلَّى اللهُ عَلَى سَيِّدِنَا مُحَمَّدٍ وَعَلَى آلِهِ وَصَحْبِهِ أَجْمَعِيْنَ.

subHanallahi mil'al-mizan, wa-muntahal-'ilmi, wa-mablaghar-riDa, wa-zinatal-'arsh, la malja'a minallahi illa ilaihi, subHanallahi 'adadashf'I wal-watri, wa-'adada kalimati rabbina attaammaati kulliha, as'alukas-salamat biraHmatika ya arHamar-raahimin, wa-la Hawla wa-laa quwwata illa billahil-'aliyyil-'aZeem, wahuwa Hasbi wa-ni'mal-wakeel, ni'mal-mawla wa-ni'mannaseer, wa-Salla Allahu 'ala siyyidina muHammadin wa'ala aalihi wa-SaHbihi ajma'een.

LAYLATUL BARA'AH: NIGHT OF SALVATION

Or Night of Mid-Sha'ban

The 14th night of Sha'ban is a very blessed night. According to Hadith Sharif, its name in Arabic is niSf sha'ban, which means mid-Sha'ban, referring to the night preceding the 15th day of Sha'ban.

This Night is the night of seeking total pardon and of repenting unto Allah, The All-Merciful. Remember your negligence and past sins and make sincere intention never to commit sins again. Laylatul Bara'ah is known in Persian and Urdu as 'Shabbe Baraat', in English, we may use the name 'Night of Salvation'.

About this blessed night, Sayyiduna Muhammad (pbuh) said, "Verily! Almighty Allah directs His Special Grace to the world during this Night; He forgives more of my Ummah than the amount of hair on the goats of Banu Kalb". The Holy Messenger (pbuh) also said, "On this Night, Almighty Allah forgives all the Muslims except the fortune tellers, the magicians, the alcoholics, those who are bad to their parents and those engaged in fornication".

How to welcome the Night of Salvation:

During such a glorious night, try to observe these blessed deeds to gain immense Divine Lights, Blessings and Mercy.

First, between Maghrib and Isha on the 14th day of Sha'ban: Read Surat Yasin 3 times, and each time begin with a different intention, and after the recitation supplicate to Allah with the Prayer as below.

- Intention of the first reading: for 'a long life spent in obedience to Allah Almighty'

- Intention of the second reading: for 'protection from calamities'

- Intention of the third reading: for 'becoming absolutely needless of others'

After each recitation of Surat Yasin, read the following prayer, or its translation, once.

Prayer of the Night of Salvation:

بِسْمِ اللهِ الرَّحْمَنِ الرَّحِيمِ. اَللّهُمَّ يَا ذَا الْمَنِّ وَلَا يُمَنُّ عَلَيْهِ، يَا ذَا الْجَلَالِ
وَالْإِكْرَامِ يَا ذَا الطَّوْلِ وَالْإِنْعَامِ. لَا إِلَهَ إِلَّا أَنْتَ، ظَهَرَ اللَّاجِئِيْنَ، وَجَارَ
الْمُسْتَجِيرِينَ، وَأَمَانَ الْخَائِفِينَ، اَللّهُمَّ إِنْ كُنْتَ كَتَبْتَنِي عِنْدَكَ فِي أُمِّ الْكِتَابِ
شَقِيًّا أَوْ مَحْرُومًا أَوْ مَطْرُودًا أَوْ مُقَتَّرًا عَلَيَّ فِي الرِّزْقِ، فَامْحُ اللّهُمَّ بِفَضْلِكَ
شَقَاوَتِي وَحِرْمَانِي وَطَرْدِي وَإِقْتَارَ رِزْقِي، وَاكْتُبْنِي عِنْدَكَ فِي أُمِّ الْكِتَابِ سَعِيدًا
مَرْزُوقًا مُوَفَّقًا لِلْخَيْرَاتِ، إِنَّكَ عَلَى كُلِّ شَيْءٍ قَدِيرٌ. اَللّهُمَّ إِنَّكَ قُلْتَ وَقَوْلُكَ
الْحَقُّ فِي كِتَابِكَ الْمُنْزَلِ عَلَى لِسَانِ نَبِيِّكَ الْمُرْسَلِ "يَمْحُو اللهُ مَا يَشَاءُ وَيُثْبِتُ
وَعِنْدَهُ أُمُّ الْكِتَابِ". إِلَهِي بِالتَّجَلِّي الْأَعْظَمِ. فِي لَيْلَةِ النِّصْفِ مِنْ شَعْبَانَ
الْمُكَرَّمِ. اَلَّتِي يُفْرَقُ فِيهَا كُلُّ أَمْرٍ حَكِيمٍ وَيُبْرَمُ، أَنْ تَكْشِفَ عَنَّا مِنَ الْبَلَاءِ مَا
نَعْلَمُ وَمَا لَا نَعْلَمُ، وَمَا أَنْتَ بِهِ مِنَّا أَعْلَمُ. إِنَّكَ أَنْتَ الْأَعَزُّ الْأَكْرَمُ، وَصَلَّى اللهُ
عَلَى سَيِّدِنَا مُحَمَّدٍ وَعَلَى آلِهِ وَصَحْبِهِ وَسَلَّمَ.

English Translation of the 'Night of Salvation Prayer'

"O Allah! You Bestow numerous favours upon everyone and no one can do You any favour. O Possessor of All Majesty and All Honour, Distributor of bounties and rewards! There is no one worthy of being worshipped but You. You Help the fallen, Provide refuge to the refugees and Bring peace to those who are in fear. O Allah! If in the Master-of-All-Books that is with You, You have written me as doubtful in achieving salvation, or deprived, or rejected, or with insufficient sustenance, then, O Allah, with Your Glorious Grace, remove from me all of these misfortunes. In the Master-of-All-Books that is with You, please write me as someone who is blessed, one with abundant provision and with charitable good deeds. Indeed, what You have Revealed in The Book that You Have Sent on the tongue of Your Blessed Prophet is all truth: "Allah changes and establishes whatever He wants, and with Him is the Master-of-All-Books." My Lord! With Your Divine Manifestation in this Night of the blessed mid-Sha'ban, in which You Bring forth every Wise and Irrevocable Decree, hold away from us all calamities and hardships, those that we know and those that we do not know, for You Know all things. Truly, You are Most Powerful, Most Gracious. O Allah, The Exalted, send Your Blessings and Peace upon our Master, Muhammad, and upon his Family and Companions. All praise is for Allah, Lord of the worlds.

Good deeds during the Night of Salvation:

1. Visit the Muslim cemetery in your area and pray for the deceased there. Hadrat Aisha (RA) reported: "One night, which was the mid-Sha'ban Night, I did not find the Messenger of Allah (pbuh) next to me, so I went outside in search for him.

I found him in the Baqee' Cemetery praying for the deceased there and seeking forgiveness for them ..." (Baihaqi).

2. Recite Surat Al-Dukhan.

3. Do heart zhikr, as taught to you by your Shaykh.

4. Read in the Holy Quran, do abundant Salawat (darud sharif), do Istighfar and recite the Blessed Word (la ilaha illallah).

5. Eat Sahur (Sehri) pre-dawn meal, with the intention to fast the following day (15th of Sha'ban).

6. Fast the 15th of Sha'ban, taking good care to keep all your senses free from sin and your heart from forgetting Allah Almighty.

The Messenger of Allah (pbuh) said, "When the Night of mid-Sha'ban arrives, spend the night awake in devotions and keep fast of the following day". Hadrat Abu Hurairah (RA) reported that the Holy Messenger (pbuh) often said in his sermons, "O people! Refresh and cleanse your bodies by way of fasting during Sha'ban, so that it becomes easy for you to fast Ramadan. Whoever fasts for three days during Sha'ban, all his past sins are forgiven". (Baihaqi).

Beloved murid, I would also recommend for you to fast the 14th, 15th and 16th days of Sha'ban, being the days of the Bright Nights, to which the Holy Messenger (pbuh) has attributed great virtues. May Allah accept you amongst His devout servants and shower you with His Magnificent Mercy. Amen.

PRAYERS FOR THE FIRST TEN DAYS OF ZHUL-HIJJAH

Hadrat Ibn Abbas (RA) narrated that the Holy Messenger (pbuh) said, "There are no other days in which righteous deeds are more loved by Allah than these days (the first ten days of Zul-Hijjah)". The Companions (RA) asked, "O, Messenger of Allah, not even Jihad in the cause of Allah?" He said, "Not even Jihad in the cause of Allah, except for a man who goes out for the sake of Allah offering his own soul and his wealth and does not return with any of them (i.e., dies in the Cause of Allah)." (Bukhari).

Beloved murid! I would advise you to read the following prayers daily throughout the first 10 days of Zul-Hijjah:

لَا إِلَهَ إِلَّا اللهُ عَدَدَ اللَّيَالِي وَالدُّهُورِ، لَا إِلَهَ إِلَّا اللهُ عَدَدَ الْأَيَّامِ وَالشُّهُورِ. لَا إِلَهَ إِلَّا اللهُ عَدَدَ أَمْوَاجِ الْبُحُورِ، لَا إِلَهَ إِلَّا اللهُ عَدَدَ أَضْعَافِ الْأُجُورِ. لَا إِلَهَ إِلَّا اللهُ عَدَدَ الرِّيَاحِ فِي الْبَرَارِي وَالصُّخُورِ. لَا إِلَهَ إِلَّا اللهُ عَدَدَ أَوْرَاقِ الشَّجَرِ، لَا إِلَهَ إِلَّا اللهُ عَدَدَ الشَّعْرِ وَالْوَبَرِ، لَا إِلَهَ إِلَّا اللهُ عَدَدَ الرَّمْلِ وَالْحَجَرِ. لَا إِلَهَ إِلَّا اللهُ عَدَدَ الزَّهْرِ وَالثَّمَرِ، لَا إِلَهَ إِلَّا اللهُ عَدَدَ أَنْفَاسِ الْبَشَرِ. لَا إِلَهَ إِلَّا اللهُ عَدَدَ لَمْحِ الْعُيُونِ، لَا إِلَهَ إِلَّا اللهُ عَدَدَ مَا كَانَ وَمَا يَكُونُ. لَا إِلَهَ إِلَّا اللهُ تَعَالَى عَمَّا يُشْرِكُونَ، لَا إِلَهَ إِلَّا اللهُ خَيْرٌ مِمَّا يَجْمَعُونَ. لَا إِلَهَ إِلَّا اللهُ فِي اللَّيْلِ إِذَا عَسْعَسَ، لَا إِلَهَ إِلَّا اللهُ

Book of Prayers

فِي الصُّبْحِ إِذَا تَنَفَّسَ. لَا إِلَهَ إِلَّا اللهُ عَدَدَ خَلْقِهِ أَجْمَعِينَ. لَا إِلَهَ إِلَّا اللهُ مِنْ يَوْمِنَا هَذَا إِلَى يَوْمِ الدِّينِ.

Also, read the Prayer below 10 times, at any time, on each day of these Ten Blessed Days:

اَللَّهُمَّ فَرَجَكَ الْقَرِيبُ، اَللَّهُمَّ سِتْرَكَ الْحَصِينَ، اَللَّهُمَّ مَعْرُوفَكَ الْقَدِيمُ، اَللَّهُمَّ عَوَائِدَكَ الْحَسَنَةُ. اَللَّهُمَّ عَطَاءَكَ الْحَسَنَ الْجَمِيلُ، يَا قَدِيمَ الْإِحْسَانِ إِحْسَانَكَ الْقَدِيمُ، يَا دَائِمَ الْمَعْرُوفِ مَعْرُوفَكَ الدَّائِمُ. حَسْبِيَ اللهُ وَكَفَى، سَمِعَ اللهُ لِمَنْ دَعَا. لَيْسَ وَرَاءَهُ مُنْتَهَى، مَنْ تَوَكَّلَ عَلَى اللهِ كُفِيَ، وَمَنِ اعْتَصَمَ بِاللهِ نَجَا.

You should also observe the Sunnah in doing loud zhikr on these ten days, by reciting the zhikr below in a loud manner. It is recommended that men recite it in public places, like streets and markets, while women recite it within their homes:

اللهُ أَكْبَرُ، اللهُ أَكْبَرُ، لَا إِلَهَ إِلَّا اللهُ

وَاللهُ أَكْبَرُ، اللهُ أَكْبَرُ، وَلِلّهِ الْحَمْدُ

Allahu-akbaru, Allahu-akbar, la-ilaha-illallah
wallahu-akbaru, Allahu-akbar, wa-lillahil-Hamd

Our Crown Masters: Muhammad the Messenger of Allah (pbuh), Abu-Bakr AS-Siddiq, Omar ibn Al-khattab, Othman ibn Affan (RA), {Ali ibn Abi-Talib, Fatima Az-zahra, Al-Hasan and Al-Husain (AS)}

Ibn Omar (RA) narrated that the Holy Messenger (pbuh) said, "...so do abundant zhikr of tahleel (la-ilaha illallah), takbeer (Allahu-akbar) and taHmeed (alHamdu-lillah) during these ten days." (Musnad Ahmad). Ibn Omar and Abu Hurairah (RA) used to go out to the market place during these ten days and repeat loudly 'Allahu-akbar' and the people there would repeat loudly after them." (Bukhari)

The resident murid (who is not on Hajj) should also fast the Day of Arafah. Hadrat Abu Qatadah (RA) narrated that Holy Messenger (pbuh) said, "The one who fasts the Day of Arafah, will be forgiven for his sins of the previous year and the following year." (Muslim)

PRAYER FOR YOUR SHAYKH

Al-Sharif ibn-Hashim Abdullah Al-Husaini Al-Madani

Your Shaykh is your guide on the most blessed path to the most glorious of destinations. The Shaykh is your gateway to knowing and pleasing your Lord, Allah Almighty. The more you pray for your Shaykh, the more you get enlightened with the great spiritual flow that the Shaykh has and is permitted to give.

You can pray for your Shaykh at any time and with any good words you know, in any language you know, but it is recommended that you read the prayer below, or its translation, for your Shaykh at least once a week. Remember, gratefulness is one of the best qualities Allah loves.

اَللَّهُمَّ لَكَ الْحَمْدُ وَالثَّنَاءُ كَمَا أَنْتَ أَهْلُهُ مِنْ حَمْدٍ وَثَنَاءٍ، أَنْتَ كَمَا أَثْنَيْتَ عَلَى نَفْسِكَ، أَسْأَلُكَ أَنْ تُصَلِّيَ وَتُسَلِّمَ عَلَى نَبِيِّكَ الْكَرِيمِ وَرَسُولِكَ الْعَظِيمِ، سَيِّدِنَا مُحَمَّدٍ، وَعَلَى آلِهِ وَصَحْبِهِ أَجْمَعِينَ، أَدْعُوكَ يَا كَامِلَ الإِحْسَانُ أَنْ تُكْرِمَ شَيْخَنَا، عَبْدَكَ الْفَقِيرَ إِلَيْكَ، سَيِّدَنَا اَلشَّرِيفَ ابْنَ هَاشِمْ عَبْدَاللهِ اَلْحُسَيْنِيّ الْمَدَنِيّ، بِمَا عَهِدَهُ عِنْدَكَ النَّبِيُّونَ وَالصَّالِحُونَ مِنْ كَرَمٍ وَإِحْسَانٍ، فِي الرُّوحِ وَالْقَلْبِ وَالْعَقْلِ وَالنَّفْسِ وَالْجَسَدِ، وَفِي الأَهْلِ وَالْمَالِ وَالْوَلَدِ.

Book of Prayers

اَللَّهُمَّ تَمِّمْ لَهُ كَرِيمَ إِحْسَانِكَ، وَاجْزِلْ لَهُ عَظِيمَ عَطَائِكَ، وَاجْعَلْهُ مِنَ الْآمِنِينَ فِي الدُّنْيَا وَالْآخِرَةِ وَمَا بَيْنَهُمَا. اَللَّهُمَّ سَلِّمْهُ مِنَ الْكُرَبِ وَالْمَعَاصِي وَالْبَلَايَا وَالْأَمْرَاضِ وَالْفِتَنِ، مَا ظَهَرَ مِنْهَا وَمَا بَطَنَ، وَاحْفَظْهُ يَا رَبَّنَا مِنْ شُرُورِ خَلْقِكَ. اَللَّهُمَّ لَا تُرِهِ مَكْرُوهاً فِي نَفْسِهِ وَلَا فِي أَهْلِهِ وَذُرِّيَتِهِ، وَلَا فِي مُرِيدِيهِ وَأَحْبَابِهِ، يَا رَبَّ الْعَالَمِينَ وَرَبَّ الْمُسْتَضْعَفِينَ.

اَللَّهُمَّ افْتَحْ عَلَى شَيْخِيَ الشَّرِيفِ الْحُسَيْنِيِّ الْمَدَنِيِّ فُتُوحَ الْعَارِفِينَ وَنَوِّرْ قَلْبَهُ بِحَقِيقَةِ مُحَبَّتِكَ وَمَعْرِفَتِكَ، وَا كْشِفْ لَهُ الْحُجُبَ حَتَّى يَرَاكَ وَيَسْعَدَ بِبَهَائِكَ وَجَمَالِكَ، وَارْزُقْهُ أَعْلَى مَرَاتِبِ الْإِحْسَانِ لَدَيْكَ، وَأَقْرَبَ مَنَازِلِ الْمُكْرَمِينَ بَيْنَ يَدَيْكَ، وَانْفَعْنِي بِمَا تَفْتَحُ عَلَيْهِ يَا فَتَّاحُ يَا عَلِيمُ. اَللَّهُمَّ ارْضَ عَنْهُ كَامِلَ الرِّضَا، وَبَشِّرْهُ اللَّهُمَّ عِنْدَ فِرَاقِهِ لِخَلْقِكَ وَإِقْبَالِهِ عَلَى جُودِكَ بِأَعْظَمِ بِشَارَةٍ تُهْدِيهَا لِأَحْبَابِكَ وَأَصْفِيَائِكَ. وَابْعَثْهُ اللَّهُمَّ فِي صُحْبَةِ تَاجِ الْمُحِبِّينَ سَيِّدِنَا مُحَمَّدٍ صَلَّى اللهُ عَلَيْهِ وَآلِهِ وَسَلَّمَ، وَأَدْخِلْنِي مَعَ شَيْخِيَ الشَّرِيفِ فِي جَنَّةِ الْخُلْدِ أَوَّلَ الدَّاخِلِينَ مَعَ السَّابِقِينَ الْأَوَّلِينَ مِنَ الْمُهَاجِرِينَ وَالْأَنْصَارِ، بِلُطْفِكَ وَمَنِّكَ يَا عَزِيزُ يَا غَفَّارُ، وَالصَّلَاةُ وَالسَّلَامُ عَلَى رَسُولِكَ الْأَعْظَمِ، وَصَفِيِّكَ الْأَكْرَمِ، حَبِيبِنَا وَسَيِّدِنَا مُحَمَّدٍ وَعَلَى آلِهِ وَأَزْوَاجِهِ وَذُرِّيَتِهِ وَأَصْحَابِهِ وَمَنْ تَبِعَهُمْ بِإِحْسَانٍ، يَا حَنَّانُ يَا مَنَّانُ، وَالْحَمْدُ لِلَّهِ رَبِّ الْعَالَمِينَ.

TRANSLATION OF 'PRAYER FOR YOUR SHAYKH'

O Allah, All praise be to You as You deserve to be praised. You are as You Have Praised Yourself. We are so grateful to You and we cannot thank You enough. O Most Kind, send your blessings and greetings unto Your Noble Prophet and Greatest Messenger, our Master Muhammad, and unto his Family and Companions.

My Lord, I beseech You to bestow Your Grace unto Your poor slave, my Shaykh Al-Sharif ibn Hashim Abdullah Al-Husaini, as You Have Bestowed unto Your Prophets and righteous servants. Bless him with Your magnanimous generosity and benevolence in his soul, mind, heart, inner self and body, and so bless those whom he loves of his family, his offspring and his murids.

O Allah, shower my Shaykh, Al-Sharif, with Your Perfect endowment and give him in abundance from Your great gifts that raise his ranks. Make him from those who are safe from all calamities in this life and in the next life and in that which is between them.

O Allah, protect my Shaykh, Al-Sharif, from difficulties, disasters, sins, illnesses, and all tribulations, the apparent and hidden. Protect him from all that veils You from him, O Most

Generous. O Allah, do not show him anything that he may dislike in his family, children, murids and loved ones, O Lord of the worlds, You are the Lord of the poor ones.

O Allah, give our Shaykh, Al-Sharif, the spiritual openings of those who truly know You, and enlighten his heart with the Reality of Your Divine Love and Knowledge. Remove all the veils so that he may see You and please him with the countenance of Your Glorious Beauty. Lord, Most Knowledgeable, grant my Master Al-Sharif the highest ranks of Perfection in Your Divine Presence and the closest of stations to the ennobled ones, and grant me the blessings of the openings You bestow upon him.

O Allah, be completely pleased with our Shaykh, Al-Sharif, forever and ever. O Allah, grant him glad tidings when he is about to leave this created world. Bless him from Your Grace with the greatest of glad tidings that You give to Your beloved and chosen ones, and resurrect him in the company of The Crown of All Lovers, our Master, Muhammad, peace and blessings be upon him.

O Allah, grace us with eternal dwelling in Paradise in the company of our Shaykh and the company of our beloved Messenger, Sayyiduna Muhammad, peace and blessings be upon him. O Kind Forgiver, all praise be to You, for You Are our only Lord. Let Peace

---

Our Crown Masters: Muhammad the Messenger of Allah (pbuh), Abu-Bakr AS-Siddiq, Omar ibn Al-khattab, Othman ibn Affan (RA), {Ali ibn Abi-Talib, Fatima Az-zahra, Al-Hasan and Al-Husain (AS)}

and Blessings be unto Your Greatest Messenger, Your Chosen One, Your Beloved, Sayyiduna Muhammad, and unto his noble Family, Descendants, and Companions and unto those who follow him in sincerity to the end of time. With the blessings of Al-Fatihah... (Read Surat Al-Fatihah and send its blessings to your Shaykh).

End of Prayer

BEGGING FOR DIVINE HELP

O You Who See and Hear all what is in my heart

You are the only One I can count on to save me

You are the only One I seek in all my difficulties

You are the only One I tell of my distress

O You Who Rules over all treasures and kingdoms

Come to my help, for all good is in Your Hands

I have no other door to stand at and knock on

If You do not open Your Door for me,

which other door can I turn to?

I came to You with nothing better than

my poverty and need for You

I can only use my need for You as means

to turn away my poverty.

Whose name may I call upon other than Your Name

If I am ever denied Your Grace and Favour!

I am certain Your Glory is High and Sublime

It does not befit You to leave Your sinner slave abandoned.

Here I stand at Your Door in humility,

Knowing well that humility at Your Door is beneficial.

Here I am, my Lord, putting all my reliance on You

Stretching my hands begging for Your Favours.

I beseech You, for the sake of Muhammad,

the one You Love most dearly, Your greatest Messenger,

to give me relief from all my trials and fulfil all of my needs.

O Allah! I beg You to bless me with all kinds of favours

through the blessings of Your Prayers upon my Master

Muhammad and his Noble Family,

For he is the best of Your creation and he is the greatest

Intercessor in Your Divine Presence.

✳✳✳

These blessed supplications are my translation of the Arabic poem written by Imam Muhammad Idris Al-Shafi'ee (RA). I would encourage the English speaking murid to supplicate often in these beautiful words, especially when feeling down.

For more prayers and Salawat in English, see my other book, "The English Muslim's Companion".

Book of Prayers

Book of Prayers

Book of Salawat

Book of Salawat

INTRODUCTION TO THE JEWEL OF SALAWAT

إِنَّ اللَّهَ وَمَلَائِكَتَهُ يُصَلُّونَ عَلَى النَّبِيِّ ۚ يَا أَيُّهَا الَّذِينَ آمَنُوا صَلُّوا عَلَيْهِ وَسَلِّمُوا تَسْلِيمًا

"Allah and His Angels Send Prayers (Blessings) upon the Prophet! O Believers! Send your prayers upon him and salute him often with the greatest of salutations" (Sura Al-Ahzab: 56)

Sayyiduna Muhammad, Al-Makki Al-Madani (pbuh), is not just any other man! He is not just any other creation of Allah! He is not just any Friend of Allah! Muhammad (pbuh) is the Beloved of Allah and His purest and most submissive servant. So much he is in union with The Truth that The Truth Himself prays upon him and greets him. This glorious action is called Salawat!

For you as a believer, Salawat come to your salvation in many occasions, when you need them the most. They come to save you from hardships and difficulties while you are still in this world. They come to your salvation from the great horror of death if you were to be terrified by death due to some of your bad deeds. Salawat will come to unite you with the Holy Messenger (pbuh) when all the billions of people are gathered for Judgement. Salawat come to save you at the time of Judgement when your scales indicate that you are a loser. Salawat come to your salvation when you are on the thin bridge of SiraT over Hellfire and you are about to fall off. Salawat will come to your assistance when you enter Paradise and they will take you higher degrees in closeness to the Holy Messenger, Sayyiduna Muhammad (pbuh). Moreover, the Holy Messenger (pbuh) has so many glorious favours upon us that we need to show gratefulness at least by sending him Salawat.

To send Salawat to the Holy Messenger (pbuh), we invoke Allah Almighty to do this on our behalf. When the holy verse 56 in Sura Al-Ahzab as above was revealed, the Companions (RA) asked, 'O Prophet of Allah! We know how to greet you (offer salam to you), but how do we pray upon you? The Holy Messenger (pbuh) replied: "Say it this way: 'O Allah, (Salli 'ala) Send Your Prayers upon Muhammad and upon his Family as You have Sent Your Prayers upon Ibrahim and upon his Family; verily, You are The Praiseworthy, The Glorious. O Allah, Bless Muhammad and his Family as You have Blessed Ibrahim and his Family; verily, You are The Praiseworthy, The Glorious'."

In his book, *al-qawlul-badee'*, Imam Al-sakhawi (RA) says, "One of the reasons why we are ordered to say 'O Allah, send Your Blessings and Prayers upon Muhammad (pbuh)' instead of saying, 'I send my prayers and blessings upon Muhammad (pbuh)' is that we are imperfect and sinful while the Holy Prophet (pbuh) is perfect and pure. The blessings and praises of a sinner are blemished, thus we need a perfect being to send him Salawat on our behalf. The only possible way, therefore, is to request Allah Almighty Himself to send His choicest and Perfect Blessings and prayers upon the Holy Prophet (pbuh). This is a request for the blessings from the One who is All-Pure upon such a person who is Virtuous and Modest."

Here, I will present to you here only a few of the numerous virtues and benefits of praying Salawat upon the Holy Messenger, Sayyiduna Muhammad (pbuh).

1. Sending Salawat is an action that Allah Almighty Himself is constantly doing, so it is a great virtue for the servant of Allah to be practicing a Divine action.

2. One receives ten holy blessings from Allah Almighty for each one Salat a person prays, and receives the rewards of ten good deeds, while ten of his/her bad deeds are erased from his/her deeds' Register.

3. The dua (prayer) that a person makes is answered when it is invoked between Salawat that are made at the beginning and at the end of the dua.

4. Salawat attract the intercession of the Holy Messenger (pbuh) on the Day of Judgement.

5. Salawat are a great means for getting increased halal provision and for having one's needs fulfilled.

6. Salawat attract the blessed attention of the Holy Messenger (pbuh) to purify the heart of the person who practices them abundantly.

7. Salawat increase one's love for the Holy Messenger (pbuh) as well as the Messenger's love for the person.

8. Salawat attract to you abundance of Divine Mercy.

SALAWAT OF AL-SHARIF AL-HUSAINI

The following are blessed Salawat that Allah Almighty has opened for me and has blessed me with accepting them to be taught to others. I would recommend that you take one or more of these Salawat and pray them on a daily or a weekly basis in multiple of 10 times each. This means you can increase the number of times you repeat these Salawat to 20, 30, 40, etc. Always remember to pray for this poor slave for being the means to bless you with great Salawat. May Allah accept you a lover of His beloved Muhammad (peace be upon him).

Salawat (1)

يَا مَالِكَ الْمَلَكُوتِ، يَا رَبَّ النَّاسُوتِ، الْمُتَفَرِّدَ بِاللَّاهُوتِ، صَلِّ عَلَى جَوْهَرِ الْيَاقُوتِ، مُحَمَّدٍ الْمُحِبِّ الْمَحْبُوبِ، الْمَمْدُوحِ فِي عَوَالِمِ اللَّاهُوتِ وَالْمَلَكُوتِ وَالْجَبَرُوتِ، الَّذِي هُوَ بِكَامِلِ الْمَحَامِدِ مَنْعُوتٌ، وَعَلَى آلِهِ سَادَاتِ الْبُيُوتِ، وَسَلِّمْ تَسْلِيماً كَثِيراً.

Salawat (2)

رَبِّ أَنْتَ الْعَزِيزُ، وَأَنَا الذَّلِيلُ، رَبِّ أَنْتَ الْقَوِيُّ، وَأَنَا الضَّعِيفُ، أَدْعُوكَ بِعِزَّتِكَ وَذُلِّي، وَبِقُوَّتِكَ وَضَعْفِي، أَنْ تُدِيمَ الصَّلَاةَ وَالسَّلَامَ، عَلَى النُّورِ التَّمَامِ، سَيِّدِنَا مُحَمَّدٍ، تَاجِ الْعَالَمِينَ، نِبْرَاسِ الْأَوَّلِينَ وَالْآخِرِينَ، وَعَلَى آلِ بَيْتِهِ الْأَكْرَمِينَ.

Salawat (3)

نُورُ الْهُدَى تَجَلَّى، رَآهُ الْعَالَمُ فَتَحَلَّى، فَمَا أَجْمَلَ الصَّلَاةِ عَلَيْهِ وَأَحْلَى،
اَللّهُمَّ يَا مُنْشِئَ هَذَا النُّورِ الْبَاهِرِ، صَلِّ عَلَيْهِ صَلَاةَ جَلَالٍ، وَسَلِّمْ
عَلَيْهِ سَلَامَ جَمَالٍ، وَعَلَى كُلِّ مَنْ أَحَبَّهُ، مِنْ أَهْلِ بَيْتِهِ وَأَصْحَابِهِ
وَإِخْوَانِهِ، الَّذِينَ تَجَمَّلُوا بِجَمَالِهِ، وَتَنَوَّرُوا بِأَنْوَارِهِ.

Salawat (4)

أَلْفُ أَلْفِ صَلَاةٍ، مَعَ أَلْفِ أَلْفِ سَلَامٍ، عَلَيْكَ يَا سَيِّدِي، يَا رَسُولَ اللهِ،
نَظْرَةً يَا سَيِّدِي، إِلَيَّ وَإِلَى شَيْخِيَ الشَّرِيفِ الْحُسَيْنِي.

أَلْفُ أَلْفِ صَلَاةٍ، مَعَ أَلْفِ أَلْفِ سَلَامٍ، عَلَيْكَ يَا سَيِّدِي، يَا نَبِيَّ اللهِ،
نَظْرَةً يَا سَيِّدِي، إِلَيَّ وَإِلَى شَيْخِيَ الشَّرِيفِ الْحُسَيْنِي.

أَلْفُ أَلْفِ صَلَاةٍ، مَعَ أَلْفِ أَلْفِ سَلَامٍ، عَلَيْكَ يَا سَيِّدِي، يَا حَبِيبَ اللهِ،
نَظْرَةً يَا سَيِّدِي، إِلَيَّ وَإِلَى شَيْخِيَ الشَّرِيفِ الْحُسَيْنِي.

Salawat (5)

اَللّٰهُمَّ صَلِّ عَلَى أَرْحَمِ الْخَلْقِ بِالْخَلْقِ، وَسَلِّمْ عَلَيْهِ وَعَلَى آلِهِ، اَللّٰهُمَّ
صَلِّ عَلَى أَشْفَقِ الْخَلْقِ بِالْخَلْقِ، وَسَلِّمْ عَلَيْهِ وَعَلَى آلِهِ.

Salawat (6)

أَلْفُ صَلَاةٍ عَلَيْكَ يَا مَبْدَأَ الْخَلْقِ، وَأَلْفُ سَلَامٍ. يَا تَاجَ رَأْسِي اسْمَعْ لِمَا
أَقُولُ: إِنِّي لَأَرْجُو شَفَاعَةَ الرَّسُولِ، فِي وَقْتِ الصُّدُورِ، مِنْ بَيْنِ الْقُبُورِ،
فَأَلْفُ صَلَاةٍ عَلَيْكَ يَا مَبْدَأَ الْعَالَمِ مَعَ أَلْفِ سَلَامٍ.

Salawat (7)

يَا حَمِيدُ، صَلِّ عَلَى الْحَامِدِ، وَسَلِّمْ عَلَيْهِ وَآلِهِ، يَا مَجِيدُ، صَلِّ عَلَى
الْمَاجِدِ، وَسَلِّمْ عَلَيْهِ وَآلِهِ، يَا حَبِيبُ، صَلِّ عَلَى الْمَحْبُوبِ، وَسَلِّمْ
عَلَيْهِ وَآلِهِ، يَا رَحِيمُ، صَلِّ عَلَى الرَّحِيمِ بِالْمُؤْمِنِينَ، وَسَلِّمْ عَلَيْهِ
وَآلِهِ، يَا رَؤُوفُ، صَلِّ عَلَى الرَّؤُوفِ بِالْمُؤْمِنِينَ، وَسَلِّمْ عَلَيْهِ وَآلِهِ.

AL-SALAWAT AL-MADANIYYAH

These blessed Salawat were Divinely opened for my late Shaykh, Sayyiduna Uwais ibn Abdullah Al-Husaini, may Allah bless his soul and raise his station to the highest in Heaven. These Salawat are called 'Madaniyyah' because they were inspired to Sayyidi Shaykh Uwais (RA) when he was in Holy Madinah.

I have made some humble editing and additions to these Salawat to maximize their benefits for the reciter. The murid is recommended to read these Salawat at least once a week, preferably on Friday or Thursday night. These Salawat should also be recited in congregation in our Thursday evening gatherings of Salawat wherever there are three or more murids in one town.

When you are about to recite Salawat, visualise the reverence of Sayyiduna Muhammad (pbuh) and his glorious favours over you. Be as humble as a servant before his most noble and generous Master. Also, remember to pray in gratefulness for the Shaykh of these Salawat, Sayyiduna Uwais Al-Husaini, and to this poor slave who taught them to you.

Our Crown Masters: Muhammad the Messenger of Allah (pbuh), Abu-Bakr AS-Siddiq, Omar ibn Al-khattab, Othman ibn Affan (RA), {Ali ibn Abi-Talib, Fatima Az-zahra, Al-Hasan and Al-Husain (AS)}

Al-Salawat Al-Madaniyyah

بِسْمِ اللهِ الرَّحْمَنِ الرَّحِيمِ ، إِنَّ اللهَ وَمَلَائِكَتَهُ يُصَلُّونَ عَلَى النَّبِيِّ ، يَا أَيُّهَا الَّذِينَ آمَنُوا صَلُّوا عَلَيْهِ وَسَلِّمُوا تَسْلِيمًا.

أَلْفُ أَلْفِ صَلَاةٍ مَعَ أَلْفِ أَلْفِ سَلَامٍ عَلَيْكَ يَا سَيِّدِي يَا رَسُولَ اللهِ.

أَلْفُ أَلْفِ صَلَاةٍ مَعَ أَلْفِ أَلْفِ سَلَامٍ عَلَيْكَ يَا سَيِّدِي يَا نَبِيَّ اللهِ.

أَلْفُ أَلْفِ صَلَاةٍ مَعَ أَلْفِ أَلْفِ سَلَامٍ عَلَيْكَ يَا سَيِّدِي يَا حَبِيبَ اللهِ.

اللَّهُمَّ صَلِّ عَلَى مُحَمَّدٍ وَعَلَى آلِ مُحَمَّدٍ، كَمَا صَلَّيْتَ عَلَى إِبْرَاهِيمَ وَعَلَى آلِ إِبْرَاهِيمَ، إِنَّكَ حَمِيدٌ مَجِيدٌ، اللَّهُمَّ بَارِكْ عَلَى مُحَمَّدٍ وَعَلَى آلِ مُحَمَّدٍ، كَمَا بَارَكْتَ عَلَى إِبْرَاهِيمَ وَعَلَى آلِ إِبْرَاهِيمَ، إِنَّكَ حَمِيدٌ مَجِيدٌ.

اللَّهُمَّ صَلِّ عَلَى سَيِّدِنَا مُحَمَّدٍ وَعَلَى آلِهِ وَأَصْحَابِهِ، بِاسْمِكَ الْمَكْنُونِ الْمَخْزُونِ، صَلَاةً تَغْفِرُ بِهَا لِأُمَّةِ سَيِّدِنَا مُحَمَّدٍ مَا كَانَ مِنْ ذُنُوبٍ وَمَا يَكُونُ، وَبَارِكْ وَسَلِّمْ.

اللَّهُمَّ يَا عَظِيمُ صَلِّ عَلَى سَيِّدِنَا مُحَمَّدٍ، الَّذِي هُوَ بِالْمُؤْمِنِينَ رَؤُوفٌ رَحِيمٌ، صَلَاةً تَغْفِرُ بِهَا لِأُمَّةِ سَيِّدِنَا مُحَمَّدٍ مَا كَانَ مِنْ ذُنُوبٍ عَلَى هَذَا الْأَدِيمِ، وَبَارِكْ وَسَلِّمْ.

اللَّهُمَّ صَلِّ عَلَى سَيِّدِنَا مُحَمَّدٍ وَعَلَى آلِهِ وَصَحْبِهِ، زِنَةَ مَا خَرَجَ مِنَ النُّونِ، وَعَدَدَ مَا سَطَرَ قَلَمُكَ وَمَا يَسْطُرُونَ، وَعَدَدَ مَا خَلَقْتَ وَمَا أَنْتَ خَالِقٌ بِالْكَافِ وَالنُّونِ، وَبَارِكْ وَسَلِّمْ.

اللَّهُمَّ يَا غَفَّارُ صَلِّ عَلَى سَيِّدِنَا مُحَمَّدٍ وَعَلَى آلِهِ وَصَحْبِهِ، صَلَاةً تَغْفِرُ بِهَا لِأُمَّةِ سَيِّدِنَا مُحَمَّدٍ كُلَّ ذَنْبٍ يُوجِبُ عَذَابَ النَّارِ، وَبَارِكْ وَسَلِّمْ.

اللَّهُمَّ صَلِّ عَلَى سَيِّدِنَا مُحَمَّدٍ الْمُخْتَارِ وَعَلَى آلِهِ وَصَحْبِهِ، صَلَاةً تَغْفِرُ بِهَا لِأُمَّةِ سَيِّدِنَا مُحَمَّدٍ كُلَّ ذُنُوبِ اللَّيْلِ وَالنَّهَارِ، وَبَارِكْ وَسَلِّمْ.

اللَّهُمَّ صَلِّ عَلَى سَيِّدِنَا مُحَمَّدٍ عَدَدَ حُرُوفِ الْقُرْآنِ حَرْفاً حَرْفاً، وَعَدَدَ كُلِّ حَرْفٍ أَلْفاً أَلْفاً، وَعَلَى آلِهِ وَصَحْبِهِ، وَبَارِكْ وَسَلِّمْ.

اللّٰهُمَّ صَلِّ عَلَى سَيِّدِنَا مُحَمَّدٍ عَدَدَ الْأَفْرَاحِ، وَعَدَدَ الْأَحْزَانِ، وَعَدَدَ الْأَنْفَاسِ، وَعَدَدَ أَلْحَاظِ الْمَلَائِكَةِ وَالْإِنْسِ وَالْجَانِّ، وَجَمِيعِ مَا خَلَقْتَ يَا رَحْمَانُ، وَبَارِكْ وَسَلِّمْ.

اللّٰهُمَّ صَلِّ عَلَى سَيِّدِنَا مُحَمَّدٍ مِلْءَ الدُّهُورِ وَالْأَزْمَانِ، وَعَدَدَ مَا خَلَقْتَ فِيهَا مِنْ حَرَكَاتٍ وَسَكَنَاتِ الْمَلَائِكَةِ وَالْإِنْسِ وَالْجَانِّ، وَعَلَى آلِهِ وَصَحْبِهِ، وَبَارِكْ وَسَلِّمْ.

اللّٰهُمَّ صَلِّ عَلَى سَيِّدِنَا مُحَمَّدٍ صَلَاةً يَتَضَاعَفُ بِهَا حُبُورُهُ، وَيُشْرِقُ بِهَا عَلَى لَطَائِفِنَا نُورُهُ، وَعَلَى آلِهِ وَصَحْبِهِ، وَبَارِكْ وَسَلِّمْ.

اللّٰهُمَّ يَا مُيَسِّرُ أَسْأَلُكَ بِأَنَّ لَكَ الْحَمْدَ وَالشُّكْرَ أَنْ تُصَلِّيَ عَلَى سَيِّدِنَا مُحَمَّدٍ صَلَاةً تُيَسِّرُ بِهَا عَلَيْنَا بِالْيُسْرِ الَّذِي يَسَّرْتَ بِهِ عَلَى كَثِيرٍ مِنْ عِبَادِكَ وَعَلَى آلِهِ وَصَحْبِهِ، وَبَارِكْ وَسَلِّمْ.

اللّٰهُمَّ صَلِّ عَلَى سَيِّدِنَا آدَمَ وَأُمِّنَا حَوَّاءَ، وَسَيِّدِنَا نُوحٍ وَسَيِّدِنَا إِبْرَاهِيمَ وَسَيِّدِنَا مُوسَى وَسَيِّدِنَا هُودٍ وَسَيِّدِنَا عِيسَى وَسَيِّدِنَا مُحَمَّدٍ، وَمَا بَيْنَهُمْ مِنَ الْأَنْبِيَاءِ وَالْمُرْسَلِينَ، وَآلِهِمْ

وَصَحْبِهِمْ، وَبَارِكْ وَسَلِّمْ، عَدَدَ الْعَدَدِ، وَمَدَدَ الْمَدَدِ، صَلَاةً لَا انْقِطَاعَ
لَهَا أَبَدَ الْأَبَدِ، تَكْتُبُ لَنَا بِهَا نُورًا وَحُبًّا وَرِضًا لَا يَزِيدُ عَلَيْنَا فِيهِ
أَحَدٌ، وَبَارِكْ وَسَلِّمْ.

اللَّهُمَّ صَلِّ عَلَى سَيِّدِنَا مُحَمَّدٍ الْحَبِيبِ الْكَامِلِ، وَافْتَحْ لَنَا بِجَاهِهِ
أَبْوَابَ الْمَحَبَّةِ وَحُبَّ النَّوَافِلِ، وَبِحُبِّكَ وَحُبِّهِ اطْوِ لَنَا الْمَقَامَاتِ
وَالْمَنَازِلَ، وَعَلَى آلِهِ وَصَحْبِهِ، وَبَارِكْ وَسَلِّمْ.

اللَّهُمَّ صَلِّ عَلَى سَيِّدِنَا مُحَمَّدٍ كَرِيمِ النَّسَبِ، وَيَسِّرْ لَنَا بِحُبِّكَ وَحُبِّهِ
كُلَّ سَبَبٍ، وَبَارِكْ وَسَلِّمْ.

اللَّهُمَّ صَلِّ عَلَى سَيِّدِنَا وَمَوْلَانَا مُحَمَّدٍ أَفْضَلِ إِنْسَانٍ، صَلَاةً تَهَبُنَا بِهَا
حِفْظَ الْقُرْآنِ وَالْعَمَلَ بِالْقُرْآنِ وَعَلَى آلِهِ وَصَحْبِهِ، وَبَارِكْ وَسَلِّمْ.

اللَّهُمَّ صَلِّ عَلَى سَيِّدِنَا مُحَمَّدٍ نُورِ سِرَاجِ الرَّحْمَنِ، صَلَاةً تَكْفِنَا بِهَا
وَسَاوِسَ النَّفْسِ وَالْإِنْسِ وَالشَّيْطَانِ وَعَلَى آلِهِ وَصَحْبِهِ، وَبَارِكْ
وَسَلِّمْ.

اللّٰهُمَّ صَلِّ وَسَلِّمْ عَلَى سَيِّدِنَا مُحَمَّدٍ الْمُبَيِّنِ لِلْقُرْآنِ، صَلَاةً تَهَبُنَا بِهَا عِلْمًا وَفَهْمًا وَكَشْفًا لَا لَبْسَ فِيهِ وَلَا خِذْلَانَ، وَبَارِكْ وَسَلِّمْ.

اللّٰهُمَّ صَلِّ وَسَلِّمْ عَلَى سَيِّدِنَا مُحَمَّدٍ النَّبِيِّ الْأَعْظَمِ سَيِّدِ الْعَرَبِ وَالْعَجَمِ الْكَاشِفِ بِدُعَائِهِ الْغَمَّ، وَعَلَى آلِهِ وَصَحْبِهِ وَبَارِكْ وَسَلِّمْ.

اللّٰهُمَّ صَلِّ وَسَلِّمْ عَلَى سَيِّدِنَا مُحَمَّدٍ النَّبِيِّ الْحَبِيبِ صَلَاةً تُيَسِّرُ بِهَا مَطْلُوبَنَا فِي وَقْتٍ قَرِيبٍ، وَعَلَى آلِهِ وَصَحْبِهِ وَبَارِكْ وَسَلِّمْ.

اللّٰهُمَّ صَلِّ وَسَلِّمْ عَلَى سَيِّدِنَا مُحَمَّدٍ صَلَاةَ عَبْدٍ ضَجَّ مِنْ ضِيقٍ وَحَرَجٍ، فَاسْتَغَاثَ بِاللهِ وَتَوَسَّلَ بِرَسُولِهِ فَأَتَاهُ الْعَوْنُ وَالْمَطْلُوبُ وَالْفَرَجُ، وَبَارِكْ وَسَلِّمْ.

اللّٰهُمَّ يَا مُنَزِّلَ الْقُرْآنِ، وَيَا مُعَلِّمَ الْبَيَانِ، يَسِّرْ لِي حِفْظَ الْقُرْآنِ وَفَهْمَ الْقُرْآنِ، بِحُبِّ حَبِيبِكَ مِنْ وَلَدِ عَدْنَانَ، صَلَّى اللهُ عَلَيْهِ وَعَلَى آلِهِ وَبَارَكَ وَسَلَّمَ.

اللَّهُمَّ يَا رَبَّ سَيِّدِنَا مُحَمَّدٍ، يَا حَبِيبَ سَيِّدِنَا مُحَمَّدٍ، زِدْنِي حُبًّا فِي
سَيِّدِنَا مُحَمَّدٍ، وَآلِ سَيِّدِنَا مُحَمَّدٍ، وَأَصْحَابِ سَيِّدِنَا مُحَمَّدٍ، وَأَزْوَاجِ
سَيِّدِنَا مُحَمَّدٍ، صَلَّى اللهُ عَلَيْهِ وَعَلَى آلِهِ وَصَحْبِهِ، وَبَارَكَ وَسَلَّمَ.

اللَّهُمَّ صَلِّ وَسَلِّمْ عَلَى سَيِّدِنَا مُحَمَّدٍ بِقَدْرِ مَشِيئَتِكَ مِنْ دَوَامِ
صَلَاتِكَ عَلَيْهِ، صَلَاةً تَغْفِرُ بِهَا ذُنُوبَنَا وَتَسْتُرُ بِهَا عُيُوبَنَا، وَتُفَرِّجُ
بِهَا كُرُوبَنَا، وَتَرْحَمُ بِهَا مَوْتَانَا، وَتُعَافِي بِهَا مُبْتَلَانَا، وَتَكْتُبُ بِهَا
بِفَضْلِكَ فِي الدَّارَيْنِ غِنَانَا، وَعَلَى آلِهِ وَصَحْبِهِ، وَبَارِكْ وَسَلِّمْ.

اللَّهُمَّ صَلِّ عَلَى سَيِّدِنَا مُحَمَّدٍ صَلَاةً تُلْهِمُنَا بِهَا ذِكْرَكَ
وَشُكْرَكَ، وَتَكْتُبُنَا بِهَا مِنْ أَهْلِ قُرْبِكَ، وَعَلَى آلِهِ وَصَحْبِهِ وَبَارِكْ
وَسَلِّمْ.

اللَّهُمَّ صَلِّ عَلَى سَيِّدِنَا مُحَمَّدٍ الْحَبِيبِ الْمَحْبُوبِ، صَلَاةً تَكْشِفُ بِهَا
لَنَا بِخَيْرٍ كُلَّ مَحْجُوبٍ، يَا اَللهُ يَا عَلَّامَ الْغُيُوبِ، وَعَلَى آلِهِ وَصَحْبِهِ
وَبَارِكْ وَسَلِّمْ.

اللّٰهُمَّ صَلِّ عَلَى سَيِّدِنَا مُحَمَّدٍ النَّاصِرِ بِكَ، صَلَاةً تَنْصُرُنَا بِهَا عَلَى عَدُوِّنَا وَعَدُوِّكَ، وَعَلَى آلِهِ وَصَحْبِهِ وَبَارِكْ وَسَلِّمْ.

اللّٰهُمَّ صَلِّ عَلَى سَيِّدِنَا مُحَمَّدٍ صَلَاةً تُلْهِمُنَا بِهَا سِرَّ سِرِّكَ مِنِ اسْمِكَ الَّذِي خَصَصْتَ بِهِ الْمُقَرَّبِينَ مِنْ خَلْقِكَ، وَعَلَى آلِهِ وَصَحْبِهِ وَبَارِكْ وَسَلِّمْ.

اللّٰهُمَّ صَلِّ عَلَى سَيِّدِنَا مُحَمَّدٍ الَّذِي مَنَنْتَ بِهِ عَلَيْنَا أَعْظَمَ الْمِنَّةِ. صَلَاةً تَفْتَحُ لَنَا بِهَا أَبْوَابَ الْجَنَّةِ، وَعَلَى آلِهِ وَصَحْبِهِ وَبَارِكْ وَسَلِّمْ.

اللّٰهُمَّ صَلِّ عَلَى سَيِّدِنَا مُحَمَّدٍ الَّذِي مَدَدْتَ بِهِ الْأَوْلِيَاءَ وَالْأَنْبِيَاءَ وَالْمُرْسَلِينَ، صَلَاةً تَعْدِلُ صَلَاةَ الْأَوَّلِينَ وَالْآخِرِينَ، وَعَلَى آلِهِ وَصَحْبِهِ وَبَارِكْ وَسَلِّمْ.

اللّٰهُمَّ صَلِّ عَلَى سَيِّدِنَا مُحَمَّدٍ صَاحِبِ الْفَتْحِ الْمُبِينِ، صَلَاةً تَفْتَحُ لَنَا بِهَا فُتُوحَ الْعَارِفِينَ، وَتُبَلِّغُنَا فِيهَا مَقَامَ التَّمْكِينِ، وَعَلَى آلِهِ وَصَحْبِهِ وَبَارِكْ وَسَلِّمْ.

اللَّهُمَّ صَلِّ وَسَلِّمْ وَبَارِكْ عَلَى خَيْرِ الْبَرِيَّةِ، صَلَاةً تُبَارِكُ لَنَا فِي

الذُّرِّيَّةِ، وَتَحْفَظُنَا وَإِيَّاهُمْ بِهَا مِنْ كُلِّ أَذِيَّةٍ، وَتَصْرِفُ بِهَا عَنَّا وَعَنْهُمْ

كُلَّ فِتْنَةٍ وَبَلِيَّةٍ، وَتَجْعَلُنَا بِهَا وَإِيَّاهُمْ عِنْدَكَ مِنَ السَّابِقِينَ أَهْلِ

الْأَوَّلِيَّةِ، وَعَلَى آلِهِ وَصَحْبِهِ وَبَارِكْ وَسَلِّمْ.

اللَّهُمَّ صَلِّ عَلَى سَيِّدِنَا مُحَمَّدٍ الَّذِي أَيَّدْتَهُ بِالْمَلَائِكَةِ ذَوِي

الْقُوَّةِ، صَلَاةً نَبْرَأُ بِهَا مِنْ حَوْلِنَا وَالْقُوَّةِ، وَنَلْجَأُ بِهَا إِلَى حَوْلِكَ

وَطَوْلِكَ، وَتَهَبُنَا بِهَا الْعَوْنَ عَلَى طَاعَتِكَ وَالْقُوَّةَ، وَعَلَى آلِهِ وَصَحْبِهِ

وَبَارِكْ وَسَلِّمْ.

لَا إله إِلَّا أَنْتَ سُبْحَانَكَ يَا رَحْمَنُ يَا رَحِيمُ، يَا هَادِي يَا وَدُودُ، يَا حَيُّ

يَا قَيُّومُ، يَا عَزِيزُ يَا حَكِيمُ.

اللَّهُمَّ صَلِّ عَلَى سَيِّدِنَا مُحَمَّدٍ، رَفِيعِ الدَّرَجِ، صَلَاةً تُؤْتِينَا بِهَا الْيُسْرَ

وَالْفَرَجَ، وَتُذْهِبُ بِهَا عَنَّا الضِّيقَ وَالْحَرَجَ، وَعَلَى آلِهِ وَصَحْبِهِ وَبَارِكْ

وَسَلِّمْ.

اللّٰهُمَّ يَا نُورَ النُّورِ، صَلِّ عَلَى سَيِّدِنَا مُحَمَّدٍ كَامِلِ النُّورِ، عَدَدَ الْأَزْمِنَةِ وَالدُّهُورِ، صَلَاةً تَدْفَعُ بِهَا عَنَّا جَمِيعَ الْآثَامِ وَالشُّرُورِ، وَتَهَبُنَا بِهَا نُورًا عَلَى نُورٍ، وَعَلَى آلِهِ وَأَزْوَاجِهِ وَأَصْحَابِهِ الْبُدُورِ، وَبَارِكْ وَسَلِّمْ.

اللّٰهُمَّ صَلِّ عَلَى حَبِيبِكَ عَيْنِ إِنْسَانِ الْوُجُودِ، بِلِسَانِ الْأَبَدِيَّةِ وَالْخُلُودِ، صَلَاةً يُرَدِّدُهَا كُلُّ مَخْلُوقٍ وَمَوْلُودٍ، صَلَاةً تَهَبُنَا بِهَا سَعْدَ السُّعُودِ، وَعَلَى آلِهِ وَأَزْوَاجِهِ وَأَصْحَابِهِ وَبَارِكْ وَسَلِّمْ.

اللّٰهُمَّ صَلِّ وَسَلِّمْ عَلَى سَيِّدِ أَهْلِ وِدَادِكَ، قَاسِمِ إِمْدَادِكَ بَيْنَ عِبَادِكَ، مِفْتَاحِ الْيَسَارَيْنِ فِي الدَّارَيْنِ، وَعَلَى آلِهِ وَصَحْبِهِ وَبَارِكْ وَسَلِّمْ.

اللّٰهُمَّ صَلِّ وَسَلِّمْ عَلَى شَمْسِ نُورِ الْهِدَايَةِ، اَلْهَادِي إِلَى رَبِّهِ مِنَ الْبِدَايَةِ إِلَى مَا لَا نِهَايَةٍ، مُحَقِّقِ غَرَضِ الْوُجُودِ، وَإِنْسَانِ عَيْنِ الْوُجُودِ، مَعْدِنِ الْكَرَمِ وَالْجُودِ، مِنْ مُفِيضِ الْجُودِ وَالْوُجُودِ، قَائِدِ حَقِيقَةِ الْعَبْدِيَّةِ وَالْعُبُودِيَّةِ لِلذَّاتِ الْإِلَهِيَّةِ، صَاحِبِ الْعُبُودِيَّةِ الْأَوْفَى وَالْمَحَبَّةِ وَالْمَحْبِيَّةِ الْأَصْفَى، مَنْ جَعَلْتَهُ هِدَايَةً

لِلضَّآلِّينَ، وَرَحْمَةً لِلْعَالَمِينَ، سَبَبَ رَفْعِ أَعْمَالِ الْأَنَامِ، بِذِكْرِهِ فِي الْبِدَايَةِ وَالْوَسَطِ وَالتَّمَامِ، إِحَاطَةِ الْعِنَايَةِ وَالرِّعَايَةِ، لِمَنْ كَتَبَ اللهُ لَهُ الْوُقُوفَ تَحْتَ الرَّايَةِ، وَعَلَى آلِهِ وَصَحْبِهِ وَبَارِكْ وَسَلِّمْ.

الصَّلَاةُ وَالسَّلَامُ عَلَيْكَ يَا كَنْزَ الْوَرَى، الصَّلَاةُ وَالسَّلَامُ عَلَيْكَ يَا نُورَ الْهُدَى، الصَّلَاةُ وَالسَّلَامُ عَلَيْكَ مِلْءَ الْأَرْضِ وَالسَّمَاءِ، الصَّلَاةُ وَالسَّلَامُ عَلَيْكَ عَدَدَ التَّهْلِيلِ وَالتَّسْبِيحِ وَالذِّكْرِ وَالدُّعَاءِ، مَا كَانَ وَيَكُونُ مِنْ خَلْقِ اللهِ فِي الْأَرْضِ وَالسَّمَاءِ، الصَّلَاةُ وَالسَّلَامُ عَلَيْكَ يَا سَيِّدَ ذَوِي الْحِجَا وَالنُّهَى، الصَّلَاةُ وَالسَّلَامُ عَلَيْكَ صَلَاةً نَخْرُجُ بِهَا مِنَ الظُّلُمَاتِ إِلَى الْهُدَى، وَعَلَى آلِكَ وَأَزْوَاجِكَ وَأَصْحَابِكَ.

اللَّهُمَّ صَلِّ وَسَلِّمْ عَلَى الْمُحَمَّدِ، اللَّهُمَّ صَلِّ وَسَلِّمْ عَلَى الْأَحْمَدِ، اللَّهُمَّ صَلِّ وَسَلِّمْ عَلَى الْحَامِدِ، اللَّهُمَّ صَلِّ وَسَلِّمْ عَلَى الْمَحْمُودِ، أَعْظَمِ مَظَاهِرِ رَحْمَتِكَ وَكَرَمِكَ وَالْجُودِ، الْعَبْدِ الْكَامِلِ الْهَادِي لِرَبِّهِ الْوَاحِدِ الْمَعْبُودِ، مُنْذُ بَدْءِ الْوُجُودِ، السَّابِقِ الْخَاتِمِ، سَيِّدِ كُلِّ حَامِدٍ وَذَاكِرٍ وَسَاجِدٍ وَرَاكِعٍ وَقَائِمٍ،

مَنْ شَهِدَتْ بِفَضْلِهِ الْأَفْلَاكُ وَالْأَمْلَاكُ، حَبِيبِكَ الْأَعْظَمِ، مُجْتَبَاكَ
الْمُكَرَّمِ، وَعَلَى آلِهِ وَأَزْوَاجِهِ، وَبَارِكْ وَسَلِّمْ.

اللَّهُمَّ صَلِّ وَسَلِّمْ عَلَى سَيِّدِنَا مُحَمَّدٍ خِيَرَتِكَ مِنْ خَلْقِكَ فِي الْأَرْضِينَ
وَالسَّمَاوَاتِ الْعُلَى، إِمَامِ أَهْلِ الْأَرْضِ وَالْبَرْزَخِ وَالسَّمَاءِ، عَلَامَةِ
وَبِشَارَةِ الْأَوَّلِينَ، إِمَامِ وَمُرْشِدِ الْآخِرِينَ، رَسُولِ رَبِّ الْعَالَمِينَ، مَنِ
اصْطَفَيْتَهُ اصْطِفَاءً، وَجَعَلْتَهُ أَكْثَرَ خَلْقِكَ بِرًّا وَرَحْمَةً وَرَأْفَةً وَوَفَاءً،
مَا مِنْ مَقَامٍ إِلَّا جَعَلْتَ مِنْهُ الْمُفِيضَ، وَجَعَلْتَ حُبَّهُ سَبَبًا لِلْمَزِيدِ، لَا
يَكْمُلُ إِلَّا بِحُبِّهِ الْإِيمَانُ، وَإِذَا تَضَلَّعَ بِحُبِّهِ الْجَنَانُ وَالْوِجْدَانُ، عَيْنِ
عُيُونِ دَوَائِرِ الْإِمْكَانِ، مَا أَخْلَيْتَ مِنْ ذِكْرِهِ وَالصَّلَاةِ عَلَيْهِ
زَمَانٌ، خَلَعْتَ عَلَيْهِ حُلَّةَ الْمَحَبَّةِ فَقُلْتَ لَهُ كُنْ حَبِيبِي فَكَانَ، فَأَفِضْ
عَلَيْنَا مِمَّا أَفَضْتَ عَلَيْهِ حَتَّى نَبْلُغَ الدَّرَجَاتِ الْعُلَا مِنَ الْعُبُودِيَّةِ
وَالْمَحَبَّةِ وَالْمَحْبُوبِيَّةِ وَالرِّضْوَانِ، وَعَلَى آلِهِ وَصَحْبِهِ وَبَارِكْ وَسَلِّمْ.

اللَّهُمَّ صَلِّ عَلَى سَيِّدِنَا مُحَمَّدٍ الْأَوَّلِ فِي الْخَلْقِ، وَالْآخِرِ فِي
الْبَعْثِ، وَالظَّاهِرِ فِي الرِّسَالَةِ، وَالْبَاطِنِ بِالرَّحْمَةِ لِلْعَالَمِينَ، مَنْ تَعَلَّقَ
بِهِ اهْتَدَى وَنَجَا، وَعَلَى آلِهِ وَصَحْبِهِ وَبَارِكْ وَسَلِّمْ.

اللّٰهُمَّ يَا كَافِي صَلِّ عَلَى سَيِّدِنَا مُحَمَّدٍ، ٱلْأَمِينِ الْمُؤْتَمَنِ، صَلَاةً تَكْفِنَا بِهَا صُرُوفَ الزَّمَنِ وَشُرُورَ الْفِتَنِ، مَا ظَهَرَ مِنْهَا وَمَا بَطَنَ، وَتُؤَمِّنَّا بِهَا فِي الْحِلِّ وَالتِّرْحَالِ وَالْوَطَنِ، وَعَلَى آلِهِ وَصَحْبِهِ وَبَارِكْ وَسَلِّمْ.

اللّٰهُمَّ إِنَّا نَسْأَلُكَ الْهِدَايَةَ فَاهْدِنَا، وَنَسْأَلُكَ الِاسْتِقَامَةَ، عَلَى كِتَابِكَ الْمُنْزَلِ، وَسُنَّةِ نَبِيِّكَ الْمُرْسَلِ، وَعَلَى الطَّرِيقَةِ الْمُوصِلَةِ، إِلَى ذَلِكَ، وَإِلَى حَقِيقَةِ مَعْرِفَتِكَ وَمَحَبَّتِكَ، إِلَهِي أَنْتَ مَقْصُودِي وَرِضَاكَ مَطْلُوبِي، أَسْأَلُكَ الْفَرَجَ، مِنْ كُلِّ هَمٍّ وَغَمٍّ وَكَرْبٍ، إِنَّكَ أَنْتَ الْأَعَزُّ الْأَكْرَمُ.

اللّٰهُمَّ فَصَلِّ عَلَى مُحَمَّدٍ وَعَلَى آلِ مُحَمَّدٍ، كَمَا صَلَّيْتَ عَلَى إِبْرَاهِيمَ وَعَلَى آلِ إِبْرَاهِيمَ، إِنَّكَ حَمِيدٌ مَجِيدٌ، اللّٰهُمَّ بَارِكْ عَلَى مُحَمَّدٍ وَعَلَى آلِ مُحَمَّدٍ، كَمَا بَارَكْتَ عَلَى إِبْرَاهِيمَ وَعَلَى آلِ إِبْرَاهِيمَ، إِنَّكَ حَمِيدٌ مَجِيدٌ. بِرَحْمَتِكَ يَا أَرْحَمَ الرَّاحِمِينَ. وَبِسِرِّ أَسْرَارِ الْفَاتِحَةِ.

AL-SHARIF'S SELECTION OF DALA-EL ALKHAYRAT

of Imam Muhammad Al-Jazuli (RA)

These Salawat, from the famous Salawat book *dala-el alkhayrat*, are selected and edited by this poor slave to be used by our Naqshabandi murids, especially during our Thursday evening Salawat gatherings.

At the completion of the recitation of these Salawat, murids should make a prayer for the author, Imam Al-Jazuli (RA) and for their Shaykh:

'O Allah! Please accept these Salawat from us and gift them on our behalf to our Master, Sayyiduna Muhammad (pbuh) and to his blessed Family. O Allah, reward Sayyiduna Imam Muhammad Al-Jazouli and reward our Shaykh, Sayyiduna Al-Sharif Abdullah Al-Husaini, with the best of rewards and with the highest of heavenly stations for the great and beautiful Salawat they have taught us; You are Most Magnificent, Most Gracious. Amen.'

اللّٰهُمَّ صَلِّ عَلَى مُحَمَّدٍ النَّبِي الزَّاهِدِ، رَسُولِ الْمَلِكِ الصَّمَدِ الْوَاحِدِ، صَلَاةً دَائِمَةً إِلَى مُنْتَهَى الْأَبَدِ بِلَا انْقِطَاعٍ وَلَا نَفَادٍ، صَلَاةً تُنَجِّينَا بِهَا مِنْ حَرِّ جَهَنَّمَ وَبِئْسَ الْمِهَادُ. اللّٰهُمَّ صَلِّ عَلَى مُحَمَّدٍ النَّبِيِّ الْأُمِّيِّ وَعَلَى آلِهِ وَسَلِّمْ، صَلَاةً لَّا يُحْصَى لَهَا عَدَدٌ وَلَا يُعَدُّ لَهَا مَدَدٌ.

اللّٰهُمَّ صَلِّ عَلَى مُحَمَّدٍ صَلَاةً تُكْرِمُ بِهَا مَثْوَاهُ، وَتُبَلِّغُ بِهَا يَوْمَ الْقِيَامَةِ مِنَ الشَّفَاعَةِ رِضَاهُ. اللّٰهُمَّ صَلِّ عَلَى مُحَمَّدٍ النَّبِيِّ الْأَصِيلِ السَّيِّدِ النَّبِيلِ، الَّذِي جَاءَ بِالْوَحْيِ وَالتَّنْزِيلِ، وَأَوْضَحَ بَيَانَ التَّأْوِيلِ، وَجَاءَهُ الْأَمِينُ جِبْرِيلُ عَلَيْهِ السَّلَامُ بِالْكَرَامَةِ وَالتَّفْضِيلِ، وَأَسْرَى بِهِ الْمَلِكُ الْجَلِيلُ فِي اللَّيْلِ الْبَهِيمِ الطَّوِيلِ، فَكَشَفَ لَهُ عَنْ أَعْلَى الْمَلَكُوتِ وَأَرَاهُ سَنَاءَ الْجَبَرُوتِ، وَنَظَرَ إِلَى قُدْرَةِ الْحَيِّ الدَّائِمِ الْبَاقِي الَّذِي لَا يَمُوتُ، ﷺ صَلَاةً مَقْرُونَةً بِالْجَمَالِ، وَالْحُسْنِ وَالْكَمَالِ، وَالْخَيْرِ وَالْإِفْضَالِ.

اللّٰهُمَّ صَلِّ عَلَى مُحَمَّدٍ وَعَلَى آلِ مُحَمَّدٍ عَدَدَ الْأَقْطَارِ، وَصَلِّ عَلَى مُحَمَّدٍ وَعَلَى آلِ مُحَمَّدٍ عَدَدَ وَرَقِ الْأَشْجَارِ، وَصَلِّ عَلَى مُحَمَّدٍ وَعَلَى آلِ

مُحَمَّدٍ عَدَدَ زَبَدِ الْبِحَارِ، وَصَلِّ عَلَى مُحَمَّدٍ وَعَلَى آلِ مُحَمَّدٍ عَدَدَ

الْأَنْهَارِ. وَاللَّهُمَّ صَلِّ عَلَى مُحَمَّدٍ وَعَلَى آلِ مُحَمَّدٍ عَدَدَ رَمْلِ

الصَّحَارِي وَالْقِفَارِ. وَاللَّهُمَّ صَلِّ عَلَى مُحَمَّدٍ وَعَلَى آلِ مُحَمَّدٍ عَدَدَ

ثِقَلِ الْجِبَالِ وَالْأَحْجَارِ. وَاللَّهُمَّ صَلِّ عَلَى مُحَمَّدٍ وَعَلَى آلِ مُحَمَّدٍ عَدَدَ

أَهْلِ الْجَنَّةِ وَأَهْلِ النَّارِ، وَصَلِّ عَلَى مُحَمَّدٍ وَعَلَى آلِ مُحَمَّدٍ عَدَدَ

الْأَبْرَارِ وَالْفُجَّارِ، وَصَلِّ عَلَى مُحَمَّدٍ وَعَلَى آلِ مُحَمَّدٍ عَدَدَ مَا يَخْتَلِفُ

بِهِ اللَّيْلُ وَالنَّهَارُ، وَاجْعَلِ اللَّهُمَّ صَلَاتَنَا عَلَيْهِ حِجَابًا مِنْ عَذَابِ

النَّارِ، وَسَبَبًا لِإِبَاحَةِ دَارِ الْقَرَارِ، إِنَّكَ أَنْتَ الْعَزِيزُ الْغَفَّارُ، وَصَلَّى اللَّهُ

عَلَى سَيِّدِنَا مُحَمَّدٍ وَعَلَى آلِهِ الطَّيِّبِينَ وَذُرِّيَّتِهِ الْمُبَارَكِينَ، وَصَحَابَتِهِ

الْأَكْرَمِينَ، وَأَزْوَاجِهِ أُمَّهَاتِ الْمُؤْمِنِينَ، صَلَاةً مَوْصُولَةً تَتَرَدَّدُ إِلَى يَوْمِ

الدِّينِ.

اللَّهُمَّ صَلِّ عَلَى سَيِّدِ الْأَبْرَارِ، وَزَيْنِ الْمُرْسَلِينَ الْأَخْيَارِ، وَأَكْرَمِ مَنْ

أَظْلَمَ عَلَيْهِ اللَّيْلُ وَأَشْرَقَ عَلَيْهِ النَّهَارُ.

اللَّهُمَّ يَا ذَا الْمَنِّ الَّذِي لاَ يُكَافَى امْتِنَانُهُ، وَالطَّوْلِ الَّذِي لاَ يُجَازَى

إِنْعَامُهُ وَإِحْسَانُهُ، نَسْأَلُكَ بِكَ وَلاَ نَسْأَلُكَ بِأَحَدٍ غَيْرِكَ أَنْ تُطْلِقَ

أَلْسِنَتَنَا عِنْدَ السُّؤَالِ وَتُوَفِّقَنَا لِصَالِحِ الْأَعْمَالِ، وَتَجْعَلَنَا مِنَ

الْآمِنِينَ يَوْمَ الرَّجْفِ وَالزِّلْزَالِ، يَا ذَا الْعِزَّةِ وَالْجَلَالِ، أَسْأَلُكَ يَا نُورَ

النُّورِ، قَبْلَ الْأَزْمِنَةِ وَالدُّهُورِ، أَنْتَ الْبَاقِي بِلاَ زَوَالٍ، الْغَنِيُّ بِلاَ مِثَالٍ،

الْقُدُّوسُ الظَّاهِرُ الْعَلِيُّ الْقَاهِرُ، الَّذِي لاَ يُحِيطُ بِهِ مَكَانٌ وَلاَ يَشْتَمِلُ

عَلَيْهِ زَمَانٌ،

أَسْأَلُكَ بِأَسْمَائِكَ الْحُسْنَى كُلِّهَا، وَبِأَعْظَمِ أَسْمَائِكَ إِلَيْكَ وَأَشْرَفِهَا

عِنْدَكَ مَنْزِلَةً وَأَجْزَلِهَا عِنْدَكَ ثَوَابًا، وَأَسْرَعِهَا مِنْكَ إِجَابَةً، وَبِاسْمِكَ

الْمَخْزُونِ الْمَكْنُونِ الْجَلِيلِ الْأَجَلِّ الْكَبِيرِ الْأَكْبَرِ الْعَظِيمِ الْأَعْظَمِ،

الَّذِي تُحِبُّهُ وَتَرْضَى عَمَّنْ دَعَاكَ بِهِ وَتَسْتَجِيبُ لَهُ دُعَاءَهُ. أَسْأَلُكَ

اللَّهُمَّ بِلاَ إِلَهَ إِلَّا أَنْتَ الْحَنَّانُ الْمَنَّانُ، بَدِيعُ السَّمَوَاتِ وَالْأَرْضِ، ذُو

الْجَلَالِ وَالْإِكْرَامِ، عَالِمُ الْغَيْبِ وَالشَّهَادَةِ الْكَبِيرُ الْمُتَعَالِ، وَأَسْأَلُكَ

بِاسْمِكَ الْعَظِيمِ الْأَعْظَمِ الَّذِي إِذَا دُعِيتَ بِهِ أَجَبْتَ، وَإِذَا سُئِلْتَ بِهِ

أَعْطَيْتَ، وَأَسْأَلُكَ بِاسْمِكَ الَّذِي يَذِلُّ لِعَظَمَتِهِ الْعُظَمَاءُ وَالْمُلُوكُ

وَالسِّبَاعُ وَالْهَوَامُّ، وَكُلُّ شَيْءٍ خَلَقْتَهُ يَا اللَّهُ، يَا رَبِّ اسْتَجِبْ دَعْوَتِي،

يَا مَنْ لَهُ الْعِزَّةُ وَالْجَبَرُوتُ، يَا ذَا الْمُلْكِ وَالْمَلَكُوتِ،

يَا مَنْ هُوَ حَيٌّ لَا يَمُوتُ، سُبْحَانَكَ رَبِّي مَا أَعْظَمَ شَأْنَكَ، وَأَرْفَعَ مَكَانَكَ،

أَنْتَ رَبِّي، يَا مُتَقَدِّسًا فِي جَبَرُوتِهِ، إِلَيْكَ أَرْغَبُ وَإِيَّاكَ أَرْهَبُ، يَا عَظِيمُ

يَا كَبِيرُ، يَا جَبَّارُ، يَا قَادِرُ، يَا قَوِيُّ، تَبَارَكْتَ يَا عَظِيمُ، تَعَالَيْتَ يَا

عَلِيمُ، سُبْحَانَكَ يَا عَظِيمُ، سُبْحَانَكَ يَا جَلِيلُ، أَسْأَلُكَ بِاسْمِكَ

الْعَظِيمِ التَّامِّ الْكَبِيرِ، أَنْ لَا تُسَلِّطَ عَلَيْنَا جَبَّارًا عَنِيدًا، وَلَا شَيْطَانًا

مَرِيدًا، وَلَا إِنْسَانًا حَسُودًا، وَلَا ضَعِيفًا مِنْ خَلْقِكَ وَلَا شَدِيدًا، وَلَا

بَارًّا وَلَا فَاجِرًا، وَلَا عَبِيدًا وَلَا عَنِيدًا.

اللَّهُمَّ إِنِّي أَسْأَلُكَ، فَإِنِّي أَشْهَدُ أَنَّكَ أَنْتَ اللَّهُ الَّذِي لاَ إِلَهَ إِلَّا أَنْتَ

الْوَاحِدُ الْأَحَدُ الصَّمَدُ، الَّذِي لَمْ يَلِدْ وَلَمْ يُولَدْ وَلَمْ يَكُنْ لَهُ كُفُوًا

أَحَدٌ. يَا هُوَ، يَا مَنْ لَا هُوَ إِلَّا هُوَ، يَا مَنْ لَا إِلَهَ إِلَّا هُوَ، يَا أَزَلِيُّ، يَا أَبَدِيُّ،

يَا دَهْرِيُّ، يَا دَيْمُومِيُّ، يَا مَنْ هُوَ الْحَيُّ الَّذِي لَا يَمُوتُ، يَا إِلَهَنَا وَإِلَهَ

كُلِّ شَيْءٍ، إِلَهاً وَاحِداً لَا إِلَهَ إِلَّا أَنْتَ . اللَّهُمَّ فَاطِرَ السَّمَوَاتِ وَالْأَرْضِ

عَالِمَ الْغَيْبِ وَالشَّهَادَةِ، الرَّحْمَنُ الرَّحِيمُ الْحَيُّ الْقَيُّومُ، الدَّيَّانُ

الْحَنَّانُ الْمَنَّانُ، الْبَاعِثُ الْوَارِثُ، يَا ذَا الْجَلَالِ وَالْإِكْرَامِ، قُلُوبُ

الْخَلَائِقِ بِيَدِكَ، نَوَاصِيهِمْ إِلَيْكَ، فَأَنْتَ تَزْرَعُ الْخَيْرَ فِي قُلُوبِهِمْ،

وَتَمْحُو الشَّرَّ إِذَا شِئْتَ مِنْهُمْ، فَأَسْأَلُكَ اللَّهُمَّ أَنْ تَمْحُوَ مِنْ قَلْبِي كُلَّ

شَيْءٍ تَكْرَهُهُ، وَأَنْ تَحْشُوَ قَلْبِي مِنْ خَشْيَتِكَ وَمَعْرِفَتِكَ وَرَهْبَتِكَ،

وَالرَّغْبَةِ فِيمَا عِنْدَكَ، وَالْأَمْنِ وَالْعَافِيَةِ، وَاعْطِفْ عَلَيْنَا بِالرَّحْمَةِ

وَالْبَرَكَةِ مِنْكَ، وَأَلْهِمْنَا الصَّوَابَ وَالْحِكْمَةَ، فَأَسْأَلُكَ اللَّهُمَّ عِلْمَ

الْخَائِفِينَ وَإِنَابَةَ الْمُخْبِتِينَ، وَإِخْلَاصَ الْمُوقِنِينَ، وَشُكْرَ

الصَّابِرِينَ، وَتَوْبَةَ الصِّدِّيقِينَ، وَنَسْأَلُكَ اللَّهُمَّ بِنُورِ وَجْهِكَ الَّذِي

مَلَأَ أَرْكَانَ عَرْشِكَ أَنْ تَزْرَعَ فِي قَلْبِي مَعْرِفَتَكَ حَتَّى أَعْرِفَكَ حَقَّ

مَعْرِفَتِكَ كَمَا يَنْبَغِي أَنْ تُعْرَفَ بِهِ. وَصَلَّى اللهُ عَلَى سَيِّدِنَا مُحَمَّدٍ

خَاتَمِ النَّبِيِّينَ وَإِمَامِ الْمُرْسَلِينَ، وَعَلَى آلِهِ وَصَحْبِهِ وَسَلَّمَ تَسْلِيمًا،

وَالْحَمْدُ لِلَّهِ رَبِّ الْعَالَمِينَ .

اللَّهُمَّ صَلِّ عَلَى سَيِّدِنَا مُحَمَّدٍ عَبْدِكَ وَرَسُولِكَ النَّبِيِّ الأُمِّيِّ وَعَلَى آلِ مُحَمَّدٍ.

اللَّهُمَّ صَلِّ عَلَى مُحَمَّدٍ وَعَلَى آلِ مُحَمَّدٍ صَلَاةً تَكُونُ لَكَ رِضَاءً، وَلَهُ جَزَاءً، وَلِحَقِّهِ أَدَاءً، وَأَعْطِهِ الْوَسِيلَةَ وَالْفَضِيلَةَ وَالْمَقَامَ الْمَحْمُودَ الَّذِي وَعَدْتَهُ، وَاجْزِهِ عَنَّا مَا هُوَ أَهْلُهُ، وَاجْزِهِ أَفْضَلَ مَا جَزَيْتَ نَبِيّاً عَنْ قَوْمِهِ، وَرَسُولاً عَنْ أُمَّتِهِ، وَصَلِّ عَلَى جَمِيعِ إِخْوَانِهِ مِنَ النَّبِيِّينَ وَالصَّالِحِينَ يَا أَرْحَمَ الرَّاحِمِينَ . اللَّهُمَّ اجْعَلْ فَضَائِلَ صَلَوَاتِكَ، وَشَرَائِفَ زَكَوَاتِكَ، وَنَوَامِي بَرَكَاتِكَ، وَعَوَاطِفَ رَأْفَتِكَ وَرَحْمَتِكَ وَتَحِيَّتِكَ وَفَضَائِلَ آلَائِكَ عَلَى مُحَمَّدٍ سَيِّدِ الْمُرْسَلِينَ، وَرَسُولِ رَبِّ الْعَالَمِينَ، قَائِدِ الْخَيْرِ وَفَاتِحِ الْبِرِّ وَنَبِيِّ الرَّحْمَةِ، وَسَيِّدِ الْأُمَّةِ.

اللَّهُمَّ ابْعَثْهُ مَقَامًا مَحْمُودًا تُزْلِفُ بِهِ قُرْبَهُ، وَتُقِرُّ بِهِ عَيْنَهُ يَغْبِطُهُ بِهِ الْأَوَّلُونَ وَالْآخِرُونَ . اللَّهُمَّ أَعْطِهِ الْفَضْلَ وَالْفَضِيلَةَ، وَالشَّرَفَ وَالْوَسِيلَةَ وَالدَّرَجَةَ الرَّفِيعَةَ، وَالْمَنْزِلَةَ الشَّامِخَةَ. اللَّهُمَّ أَعْطِ مُحَمَّداً الْوَسِيلَةَ، وَبَلِّغْهُ مَأْمُولَهُ، وَاجْعَلْهُ أَوَّلَ شَافِعٍ، وَأَوَّلَ مُشَفَّعٍ.

اللَّهُمَّ عَظِّمْ بُرْهَانَهُ، وَثَقِّلْ مِيزَانَهُ، وَأَبْلِجْ حُجَّتَهُ وَارْفَعْ فِي أَهْلِ

عِلِّيِّينَ دَرَجَتَهُ، وَفِي أَعْلَى الْمُقَرَّبِينَ مَنْزِلَتَهُ. اللَّهُمَّ أَحْيِنَا عَلَى سُنَّتِهِ،

وَتَوَفَّنَا عَلَى مِلَّتِهِ، وَاجْعَلْنَا مِنْ أَهْلِ شَفَاعَتِهِ، وَاحْشُرْنَا فِي زُمْرَتِهِ،

وَأَوْرِدْنَا حَوْضَهُ وَاسْقِنَا مِنْ كَأْسِهِ غَيْرَ خَزَايَا، وَلَا نَادِمِينَ وَلَا

شَاكِّينَ، وَلَا مُبَدِّلِينَ وَلَا مُغَيِّرِينَ وَلَا فَاتِنِينَ وَلَا مَفْتُونِينَ، آمِينَ

يَا رَبَّ الْعَالَمِينَ . اللَّهُمَّ صَلِّ عَلَى مُحَمَّدٍ، وَعَلَى آلِ مُحَمَّدٍ وَأَعْطِهِ

الْوَسِيلَةَ وَالْفَضِيلَةَ وَالدَّرَجَةَ الرَّفِيعَةَ وَابْعَثْهُ الْمَقَامَ الْمَحْمُودَ الَّذِي

وَعَدْتَهُ مَعَ إِخْوَانِهِ النَّبِيِّينَ.

صَلَّى اللَّهُ عَلَى مُحَمَّدٍ نَبِيِّ الرَّحْمَةِ، وَسَيِّدِ الْأُمَّةِ وَعَلَى أَبِينَا آدَمَ،

وَأُمِّنَا حَوَّاءَ، وَمَنْ وَلَدَا مِنَ النَّبِيِّينَ وَالصِّدِّيقِينَ وَالشُّهَدَاءِ

وَالصَّالِحِينَ، وَصَلِّ عَلَى مَلَائِكَتِكَ أَجْمَعِينَ، مِنْ أَهْلِ السَّمَوَاتِ

وَالْأَرَضِينَ، وَعَلَيْنَا مَعَهُمْ يَا أَرْحَمَ الرَّاحِمِينَ. اللَّهُمَّ اغْفِرْ لِي ذُنُوبِي،

وَلِوَالِدَيَّ وَارْحَمْهُمَا كَمَا رَبَّيَانِي صَغِيراً، وَلِجَمِيعِ الْمُؤْمِنِينَ

وَالْمُؤْمِنَاتِ، وَالْمُسْلِمِينَ وَالْمُسْلِمَاتِ، الْأَحْيَاءِ مِنْهُمْ وَالْأَمْوَاتِ،

وَتَابِعْ بَيْنَنَا وَبَيْنَهُمْ بِالْخَيْرَاتِ. رَبِّ اغْفِرْ وَارْحَمْ وَأَنْتَ خَيْرُ الرَّاحِمِيْنَ، وَلَا حَوْلَ وَلَا قُوَّةَ إِلَّا بِا اللهِ الْعَلِيِّ الْعَظِيْمِ.

اللّٰهُمَّ صَلِّ عَلَى مُحَمَّدٍ، نُوْرِ الْأَنْوَارِ، وَسِرِّ الْأَسْرَارِ، وَسَيِّدِ الْأَبْرَارِ، وَزَيْنِ الْمُرْسَلِيْنَ الْأَخْيَارِ، وَأَكْرَمِ مَنْ أَظْلَمَ عَلَيْهِ اللَّيْلُ وَأَشْرَقَ عَلَيْهِ النَّهَارُ، وَعَدَدَ مَا نَزَلَ مِنْ أَوَّلِ الدُّنْيَا إِلَى آخِرِهَا مِنْ قَطْرِ الْأَمْطَارِ، وَعَدَدَ مَا نَبَتَ مِنْ أَوَّلِ الدُّنْيَا إِلَى آخِرِهَا مِنَ النَّبَاتِ وَالْأَشْجَارِ، صَلَاةً دَائِمَةً بِدَوَامِ مُلْكِ اللَّهِ الْوَاحِدِ الْقَهَّارِ.

اللّٰهُمَّ صَلِّ عَلَى سَيِّدِنَا مُحَمَّدٍ صَلَاةً تُكْرِمُ بِهَا مَثْوَاهُ، وَتُشَرِّفُ بِهَا عُقْبَاهُ، وَتُبَلِّغُ بِهَا يَوْمَ الْقِيَامَةِ مُنَاهُ وَرِضَاهُ، هٰذِهِ الصَّلَاةُ تَعْظِيْماً لِحَقِّكَ يَا مُحَمَّدُ.

اللّٰهُمَّ صَلِّ عَلَى مُحَمَّدٍ، حَاءِ الرَّحْمَةِ، وَمِيمِي الْمُلْكِ، وَدَالِ الدَّوَامِ، السَّيِّدِ الْكَامِلِ الْفَاتِحِ الْخَاتِمِ، عَدَدَ مَا فِي عِلْمِكَ كَائِنٌ أَوْ قَدْ كَانَ، كُلَّمَا ذَكَرَكَ وَذَكَرَهُ الذَّاكِرُوْنَ، وَكُلَّمَا غَفَلَ عَنْ ذِكْرِكَ وَذِكْرِهِ الْغَافِلُوْنَ،

صَلَاةً دَائِمَةً بِدَوَامِكَ بَاقِيَةً بِبَقَائِكَ، لَا مُنْتَهَى لَهَا دُونَ عِلْمِكَ، إِنَّكَ عَلَى كُلِّ شَيْءٍ قَدِيرٌ.

اللَّهُمَّ صَلِّ عَلَى مُحَمَّدٍ النَّبِيِّ الأُمِّيِّ، وَعَلَى آلِ مُحَمَّدٍ الَّذِي هُوَ أَبْهَى شُمُوسِ الْهُدَى نُورًا وَأَبْهَرُهَا، وَأَسْيَرُ الْأَنْبِيَاءِ فَخْرًا وَأَشْهَرُهَا، وَنُورُهُ أَزْهَرُ أَنْوَارِ الْأَنْبِيَاءِ وَأَشْرَقُهَا وَأَوْضَحُهَا، وَأَزْكَى الْخَلِيقَةِ أَخْلَاقاً وَأَطْهَرُهَا وَأَكْرَمُهَا خَلْقاً وَأَعْدَلُهَا. اللَّهُمَّ صَلِّ عَلَى مُحَمَّدٍ النَّبِيِّ الأُمِّيِّ وَعَلَى آلِ مُحَمَّدٍ الَّذِي هُوَ أَبْهَى مِنَ الْقَمَرِ التَّامِّ، وَأَكْرَمُ مِنَ السَّحَابِ الْمُرْسَلَةِ وَالْبَحْرِ الْخِضَمِّ. اللَّهُمَّ صَلِّ عَلَى سَيِّدِنَا مُحَمَّدٍ النَّبِيِّ الأُمِّيِّ، وَعَلَى آلِ مُحَمَّدٍ الَّذِي قُرِنَتِ الْبَرَكَةُ بِذَاتِهِ وَمُحَيَّاهُ، وَتَعَطَّرَتِ الْعَوَالِمُ بِطِيبِ ذِكْرِهِ وَرَيَّاهُ.

اللَّهُمَّ صَلِّ عَلَى سَيِّدِنَا مُحَمَّدٍ، وَعَلَى آلِهِ وَسَلِّمْ. اللَّهُمَّ صَلِّ عَلَى مُحَمَّدٍ، وَعَلَى آلِ مُحَمَّدٍ، وَبَارِكْ عَلَى مُحَمَّدٍ وَعَلَى آلِ مُحَمَّدٍ، وَارْحَمْ مُحَمَّداً وَآلَ مُحَمَّدٍ، كَمَا صَلَّيْتَ وَبَارَكْتَ وَتَرَحَّمْتَ عَلَى إِبْرَاهِيمَ، وَعَلَى آلِ إِبْرَاهِيمَ. إِنَّكَ حَمِيدٌ مَجِيدٌ. اللَّهُمَّ صَلِّ عَلَى مُحَمَّدٍ عَبْدِكَ

وَنَبِيِّكَ وَرَسُولِكَ النَّبِيِّ الْأُمِّيِّ وَعَلَى آلِ مُحَمَّدٍ. اللَّهُمَّ صَلِّ عَلَى
مُحَمَّدٍ، وَعَلَى آلِ مُحَمَّدٍ، مِلْءَ الدُّنْيَا وَمِلْءَ الْآخِرَةِ، وَبَارِكْ عَلَى
مُحَمَّدٍ، وَعَلَى آلِ مُحَمَّدٍ، مِلْءَ الدُّنْيَا وَمِلْءَ الْآخِرَةِ، وَارْحَمْ مُحَمَّداً
وَآلَ مُحَمَّدٍ مِلْءَ الدُّنْيَا وَمِلْءَ الْآخِرَةِ، وَاجْزِ مُحَمَّداً وَآلَ مُحَمَّدٍ
مِلْءَ الدُّنْيَا وَمِلْءَ الْآخِرَةِ، وَسَلِّمْ عَلَى مُحَمَّدٍ وَعَلَى آلِ مُحَمَّدٍ، مِلْءَ
الدُّنْيَا وَمِلْءَ الْآخِرَةِ.

اللَّهُمَّ صَلِّ عَلَى مُحَمَّدٍ كَمَا أَمَرْتَنَا أَنْ نُصَلِّيَ عَلَيْهِ، وَصَلِّ عَلَيْهِ كَمَا
يَنْبَغِي أَنْ يُصَلَّى عَلَيْهِ. اللَّهُمَّ صَلِّ عَلَى نَبِيِّكَ الْمُصْطَفَى، وَرَسُولِكَ
الْمُرْتَضَى، وَوَلِيِّكَ الْمُجْتَبَى، وَأَمِينِكَ عَلَى وَحْيِ السَّمَاءِ. اللَّهُمَّ صَلِّ
عَلَى مُحَمَّدٍ، أَكْرَمِ الْأَسْلَافِ، الْقَائِمِ بِالْعَدْلِ وَالْإِنْصَافِ، الْمَنْعُوتِ
فِي سُورَةِ الْأَعْرَافِ، الْمُنْتَخَبِ مِنْ أَصْلَابِ الشِّرَافِ، وَالْبُطُونِ
الظِّرَافِ، الْمُصَفَّى مِنْ مُصَاصِ عَبْدِ الْمُطَّلِبِ بْنِ عَبْدِ مَنَافٍ، الَّذِي
هَدَيْتَ بِهِ مِنَ الْخِلَافِ وَبَيَّنْتَ بِهِ سَبِيلَ الْعَفَافِ.

اللَّهُمَّ إِنِّي أَسْأَلُكَ بِأَفْضَلِ مَسْأَلَتِكَ، وَبِأَحَبِّ أَسْمَائِكَ إِلَيْكَ وَأَكْرَمِهَا

عَلَيْكَ، وَبِمَا مَنَنْتَ عَلَيْنَا بِمُحَمَّدٍ نَبِيِّنَا ﷺ فَاسْتَنْقَذْتَنَا بِهِ مِنَ

الضَّلَالَةِ، وَأَمَرْتَنَا بِالصَّلَاةِ عَلَيْهِ وَجَعَلْتَ صَلَاتَنَا عَلَيْهِ دَرَجَةً،

وَكَفَّارَةً وَلُطْفًا وَمَنًّا مِنْ إِعْطَائِكَ فَأَدْعُوكَ تَعْظِيمًا لِأَمْرِكَ، وَاتِّبَاعًا

لِوَصِيَّتِكَ وَمُنْتَجِزًا لِمَوْعُودِكَ لِمَا يَجِبُ لِنَبِيِّنَا ﷺ فِي أَدَاءِ حَقِّهِ

قِبَلَنَا إِذْ آمَنَّا بِهِ وَصَدَّقْنَاهُ، وَاتَّبَعْنَا النُّورَ الَّذِي أُنْزِلَ مَعَهُ، وَقُلْتَ

"إِنَّ اللَّهَ وَمَلَائِكَتَهُ يُصَلُّونَ عَلَى النَّبِيِّ يَا أَيُّهَا الَّذِينَ آمَنُوا صَلُّوا

عَلَيْهِ وَسَلِّمُوا تَسْلِيمًا"، وَأَمَرْتَ الْعِبَادَ بِالصَّلَاةِ عَلَى نَبِيِّهِمْ فَرِيضَةً

افْتَرَضْتَهَا وَأَمَرْتَهُمْ بِهَا، فَنَسْأَلُكَ بِجَلَالِ وَجْهِكَ وَنُورِ عَظَمَتِكَ،

وَبِمَا أَوْجَبْتَ عَلَى نَفْسِكَ لِلْمُحْسِنِينَ، أَنْ تُصَلِّيَ أَنْتَ وَمَلَائِكَتُكَ عَلَى

مُحَمَّدٍ عَبْدِكَ وَرَسُولِكَ وَنَبِيِّكَ وَصَفِيِّكَ وَخِيَرَتِكَ مِنْ خَلْقِكَ، أَفْضَلَ

مَا صَلَّيْتَ عَلَى أَحَدٍ مِنْ خَلْقِكَ إِنَّكَ حَمِيدٌ مَجِيدٌ.

اللَّهُمَّ ارْفَعْ دَرَجَتَهُ وَأَكْرِمْ مَقَامَهُ، وَثَقِّلْ مِيزَانَهُ، وَأَبْلِجْ حُجَّتَهُ،

وَأَظْهِرْ مِلَّتَهُ، وَأَجْزِلْ ثَوَابَهُ، وَأَضِئْ نُورَهُ، وَأَدِمْ كَرَامَتَهُ، وَأَلْحِقْ بِهِ

مِنْ ذُرِّيَّتِهِ وَأَهْلِ بَيْتِهِ مَا تَقَرُّ بِهِ عَيْنُهُ، وَعَظِّمْهُ فِي النَّبِيِّينَ الَّذِينَ خَلَوْا قَبْلَهُ. اللَّهُمَّ اجْعَلْ مُحَمَّداً أَكْثَرَ النَّبِيِّينَ تَبَعًا وَأَكْثَرَهُمْ أُزَرَاءَ، وَأَفْضَلَهُمْ كَرَامَةً وَنُورًا، وَأَعْلَاهُمْ دَرَجَةً، وَأَفْسَحَهُمْ فِي الْجَنَّةِ مَنْزِلاً . اللَّهُمَّ اجْعَلْ فِي السَّابِقِينَ غَايَتَهُ وَفِي الْمُنْتَخَبِينَ مَنْزِلَهُ، وَفِي الْمُقَرَّبِينَ دَارَهُ وَفِي الْمُصْطَفَيْنَ مَنْزِلَهُ.

اللَّهُمَّ اجْعَلْهُ أَكْرَمَ الْأَكْرَمِينَ عِنْدَكَ مَنْزِلاً وَأَفْضَلَهُمْ ثَوَاباً، وَأَقْرَبَهُمْ مَجْلِساً، وَأَثْبَتَهُمْ مَقَاماً، وَأَصْوَبَهُمْ كَلَاماً، وَأَنْجَحَهُمْ مَسْأَلَةً، وَأَفْضَلَهُمْ لَدَيْكَ نَصِيباً، وَأَعْظَمَهُمْ فِيمَا عِنْدَكَ رَغْبَةً، وَأَنْزِلْهُ فِي غُرُفَاتِ الْفِرْدَوْسِ مِنَ الدَّرَجَاتِ الْعُلَى الَّتِي لَا دَرَجَةَ فَوْقَهَا. اللَّهُمَّ اجْعَلْ مُحَمَّداً أَصْدَقَ قَائِلٍ وَأَنْجَحَ سَائِلٍ، وَأَوَّلَ شَافِعٍ، وَأَفْضَلَ مُشَفَّعٍ، وَشَفِّعْهُ فِي أُمَّتِهِ بِشَفَاعَةٍ يَغْبِطُهُ بِهَا الْأَوَّلُونَ وَالْآخِرُونَ، وَإِذَا مَيَّزْتَ عِبَادَكَ بِفَضْلِ قَضَائِكَ، فَاجْعَلْ مُحَمَّداً فِي الْأَصْدَقِينَ قِيلاً، وَالْأَحْسَنِينَ عَمَلاً، وَفِي الْمَهْدِيِّينَ سَبِيلاً .

اللَّهُمَّ اجْعَلْ نَبِيَّنَا لَنَا فَرَطاً، وَاجْعَلْ حَوْضَهُ لَنَا مَوْعِداً، لِأَوَّلِنَا

وَآخِرِنَا. اللَّهُمَّ احْشُرْنَا فِي زُمْرَتِهِ وَاسْتَعْمِلْنَا فِي سُنَّتِهِ، وَتَوَفَّنَا عَلَى

مِلَّتِهِ، وَعَرِّفْنَا وَجْهَهُ، وَاجْعَلْنَا فِي زُمْرَتِهِ وَحِزْبِهِ. اللَّهُمَّ اجْمَعْ بَيْنَنَا

وَبَيْنَهُ كَمَا آمَنَّا بِهِ وَلَمْ نَرَهُ، وَلَا تُفَرِّقْ بَيْنَنَا وَبَيْنَهُ حَتَّى تُدْخِلَنَا

مُدْخَلَهُ، وَتُورِدَنَا حَوْضَهُ، وَتَجْعَلَنَا مِنْ رُفَقَائِهِ مَعَ الْمُنْعَمِ عَلَيْهِمْ

مِنَ النَّبِيِّينَ وَالصِّدِّيقِينَ وَالشُّهَدَاءِ وَالصَّالِحِينَ وَحَسُنَ أُوْلَئِكَ

رَفِيقاً، 69 وَالْحَمْدُ لِلَّهِ رَبِّ الْعَالَمِينَ.

أَلْفُ أَلْفِ صَلاةٍ مَعَ أَلْفِ أَلْفِ سَلامٍ عَلَيْكَ يَا سَيِّدِي يَا رَسُولَ الله.

أَلْفُ أَلْفِ صَلاةٍ مَعَ أَلْفِ أَلْفِ سَلامٍ عَلَيْكَ يَا سَيِّدِي يَا نَبِيَّ الله.

أَلْفُ أَلْفِ صَلاةٍ مَعَ أَلْفِ أَلْفِ سَلامٍ عَلَيْكَ يَا سَيِّدِي يَا حَبِيبَ الله.

اَللَّهُمَّ صَلِّ وَسَلِّمْ وَبَارِكْ عَلَيْهِ وَعَلَى آلِهِ، بِسِرِّ أَسْرَارِ الْفَاتِحَةُ...

Book of Salawat

Book of Safety

INTRODUCTION TO BOOK OF SAFETY

In Book of Safety, I want to help you save yourself from the miserable destruction of your happiness. True happiness is to experience Perfect Pleasure through living in the magnificence of Divine faith, which will result in passing away to the Next Life with certainty of faith in God Almighty, Glory be to Him.

Beloved murid! Please awaken! Take my advice with utmost vigilance and give your greatest attention to what I say here and everywhere you are in my Suhbah (companionship). Safeguard yourself from all the enemies of your Faith: from Satan, the Thief of Faith, from dark tribulations (fitan) and from extreme grief and distress. All of these negative forces disturb you deep inside; they ruin the clarity of your inner vision and the purity of your heart, which will ultimately disturb your growth on the Way to the Divine. If you lose all your Faith (iman), you have lost all happiness, forever.

The first thing you need to do is save others from your own harm, and this will help you be safe from their harm. Know that the worst harm that can ever happen to you is the loss of your faith in Allah Almighty. Always be vigilant! Be careful in every step and every breath you take! Never hide away from your Shaykh; look for his Suhbah in every way possible. Never go astray from the crowd of truthful believers, even if it is a small crowd. Allah Almighty has

Book of Safety

already ordered you with the clear order to keep you safe from loss of faith and from tribulations by commanding you as such: "O believers! Fear Allah and remain in the company of the Truthful people" (Tawbah: 119)

{يَا أَيُّهَا الَّذِينَ آمَنُوا اتَّقُوا اللَّهَ وَكُونُوا مَعَ الصَّادِقِينَ} (التوبة: 119)

Hadrat Abu Hurairah (RA) reported that the Holy Messenger (pbuh) said, "A Muslim is one from whom other Muslims are safe, both from his hand (bad actions) and from his tongue (bad speech); and a mu'min (believer) is one from whose harm the property and life of others are safe." (Ahmad)

SAFETY FROM LOSS OF FAITH

Loss of Faith (iman) is the worst catastrophe that can ever befall a believer in God Almighty. With loss of faith, you lose the Pleasure and Presence of God and hence lose entry into Paradise, thus losing your eternal happiness.

There are many thieves who can steal your Faith. The first of them is Satan the cursed, who made a promise before Allah Almighty that he will use all of his powers to rob the believers in God off their faith in God.

Allah Almighty says, "He (Satan) then said, 'Now, that You have disclosed my defect (taken me out of Your Presence), verily I shall lurk in ambush for them on Your Straight Path. I shall come upon them from before them and from behind them and from their right side and from their left side, and You will not find many of them grateful to You'." (Surat Al-a'raf: 17)

Allah also says, "He (Satan) said: 'Then, I swear by Your Glory, I surely will beguile every one of them, save Your chosen slaves among them'." (Surat Saad: 81, 82)

Another thief of faith is the combined quality of hate and anger against your Muslim relatives or any Muslim brother or sister. Hadrat Abu Hurairah (RA) reported that the Holy Messenger (pbuh) said, "You shall not enter Paradise unless you become believers, and you will not become believers unless you love one another; spread peace amongst yourselves and you will gain love for one another. Beware! I strongly warn you from hate between you, for hate is the shaving tool; I do not say it shaves hair, but it shaves (eradicates) faith." (Al-Tirmizi)

Hadrat Abu Hurairah (RA) also reported that the Holy Messenger (pbuh) said, "Do not have ill-will against one another; do not be jealous from one another; do not turn your backs to one another. O servants of Allah! Be brothers (and sisters) to each other - it is not permissible for a Muslim to cut relations with another Muslim for more than three days." (Al-Bukhari)

Another thief of faith is the combined quality of craving wealth and social status among the people.

Hadrat Ka'b ibn Malik Al-Ansari (RA) reported that the Holy Messenger (pbuh) said, "Two hungry wolves let loose on a herd of sheep are not more harmful than one's cravings for wealth and status to his faith." (Al-Tirmizi)

Hadrat Jabir (RA) reported that the Holy Messenger (pbuh) said, "Two ravenous wolves that spend the night amongst sheep whose shepherd is absent will not cause more damage than will the love of status and wealth cause to a believer's faith." (Al-Tirmizi)

Also, beware of arrogance and haughtiness. Treat your heart with the medicine of Tazkiya (purification) on our blessed Naqshabandi Tariqah so that you become cured from these evils before they destroy your faith.

Allah Almighty says: "That Abode in the Hereafter (Paradise), We shall assign to those who seek neither haughtiness nor any corruption on earth. The Good End is certainly for the righteous ones." (Surat Al-Qasas: 83)

Not only protect your faith from loss, but you must also do all you can to earn more faith. Let us reflect on these holy verses of the Holy Quran:

"And when His Signs (verses of Holy Quran) are recited unto them, they cause their faith to increase." (Al-anfal: 2)

"... As for those who believe, every revelation of the Quran increased them in faith and caused them to rejoice (at receiving these good favours in Allah)." (Surat Al-tawbah: 124)

The Ark of Safety:

Beloved seeker! No one can do it by himself. The Muhammadi-connected Path to Allah is the Ark of Safety. In our time, this Blessed Naqshabandi Tariqah is the best means of safety from the biggest thief of faith, Satan, who wants you to leave this world with zero faith in God so that you end up in Hellfire. Our Madani Branch of this Blessed Naqshabandi Tariqah is one of the best cradles of safety from the dark tribulations, in this most difficult of times, that continuously shake and attempt to destroy your faith. We adhere strongly to the Pure Source and avoid innovations that disturb the Principles of the Blessed Tariqah. We adhere to silent zhikr with holy Rabitah Sharifa, to the Naqshabandi Supplications and to Islamic adaab and Sunnah.

In our Blessed Naqshabandi Tariqah, the Master of salvation who enlightens our hearts and minds is Sayyiduna Muhammad (pbuh), who is the last Messenger of Allah to all humankind. When he (pbuh) left this world, he did not leave us lost and disconnected from him (pbuh) and his God-Given Light and Powers of Guidance and Salvation. He has left us with Vicegerents (khulafa) who continue to connect us with him (pbuh), no matter how far we are in place or in time from the Holy Messenger's physical presence.

We, therefore, have special gratitude for the Holy Messenger (pbuh) and his blessed Vicegerents: the Leaders of Ahlul-Bayt, Sayyiduna Abu-Bakr AS-Siddiq, Sayyiduna Omar ibn Al-khattab, Sayyiduna Othman ibn Affan, and other Muhammadi Companions and the saints (awliya) who received Divine enlightenment from them, such as our Masters in the Naqshabandi Chains of Saints. From these glorious friends of God, we receive the light of guidance and strong currents of inner purification, no matter how dark the tribulations may be.

Hadrat Malik ibn Anas (RA) reported that the Holy Messenger (pbuh) said, "I leave with you two major things, that as long as you hold on firmly to them you will never go astray - the Book of Allah and my Sunnah (my Wisdom and Way of Life)." (Al-Muwatta'; Al-Hakim from Ibn Abbas).

In another Hadith, we find even a third major element of safety, which is as vital for our faith and salvation as the other two holy elements. Hadrat Zaid ibn Al-Arqam (RA) reported, the Holy Messenger (pbuh) said, "... I am leaving with you two major things. The first is the Book of Allah (Holy Quran): in it is the true guidance and light; hold on firmly to it." The Holy Messenger spoke in length prompting the believers to adhere to the Book of Allah; he then said, "And my Household (Ahlul-Bayt). I remind you with an oath by Allah to (honour and hold on to) my Household. I remind you with an oath by Allah to (honour and hold on to) my

Household. I remind you with an oath by Allah to (honour and hold on to) my Household." (Muslim; Ahmad; Al-Darimi)

Therefore, every murid should seek internal as well as external knowledge from, and attachment to, these three major elements of safety: the Holy Quran, the Sunnah (Wisdom and Way of Life) of the Holy Messenger (pbuh) and Ahlul-Bayt (RA): through their love and their guidance. Internal knowledge comes directly from devotion to Tariqah, and external knowledge can be sought from the Shaykh of the Tariqah as well as from other devout Sunni scholars. Any scholar who has hate or arrogance, or runs after wealth, is not a safe scholar to learn from. Take your knowledge from humble scholars who do not crave to be in the spotlight.

May Allah protect our iman from loss, and may He increase His Faith in our hearts and souls so that we may never go astray. O Allah! Protect my iman and the iman of my murids and bless them to die with perfect faith in You, You are our only God, Most Kind.

SAFETY FROM FITAN (TRIBULATIONS)

May Allah save us from the dark fitnah. May Allah save us from the dark fitnah. O Allah, if you do not save us, we would be utterly ruined!

My beloved murid!

The matter is extremely serious and dangerous! When a fitnah (tribulation) befalls a community, even wise people fail to see the truth. The tribulation would be too dark for the human intellect to see due to intense confusion. Everybody is brainwashing and manipulating everybody. There is no purity nor clarity. There is no inner light to enable reasoning to be sound and to be able to make sound judgements.

The only thing that saves you from making the wrong choices during a fitnah is the Light you gain from perfect faith in Allah Almighty. Such Light enters the heart that is blessed with holy connection with the Source of Light, Sayyiduna Muhammad (pbuh). His glorious Light comes from being in total submission and perfect spiritual awareness in the Divine Presence.

In this blessed Madani Naqshabandi Tariqah, the murid is connected with the Blessed Source of Light (pbuh) through this poor slave authorised Guide/Master in the Path. This is because the murid is holding strong onto the same spiritual chain that ends in the hands of his/her Shaykh. One of the benefits of this blessed

Tariqah is that it enables the seeker to have awareness of the knowledge that our Master Muhammad (pbuh) revealed to us about the dark tribulations that the Muslims would live through in various periods.

Our time is the darkest of all times. It is the time of the dark deception, the Dajjal, the cleverest deceiver and magician. You will understand the Messenger's revelations only when you become connected with the Messenger's glorious light. In this sense, the blessed Tariqah is not a luxury or something extra to worship. Our Tariqah is your boat of salvation.

I want you to use whatever light you have been given in Tariqah to try to understand the revelations in the Messenger's traditions below. Those who have been more in Suhbah (companionship) with me will understand more than others will. Suhbah changes your life because your awareness becomes wider in scope and greater in depth. Knowledge that changes your life to the better is true knowledge. Other forms of knowledge only increase your darkness, and hence, your confusion.

The fitnah of Dajjal (Antichrist) is not restricted to the presence of an individual man. You should broaden your mind to see the deceitful Dajjal way of life around you, at all levels without exception. Dajjal is mainly the material-based lifestyle that started around 1799 AD with the summit of the French Revolution, accompanied later with the Industrial Revolution in Europe in the

Book of Safety

18th century and afterwards. The lust of materialism took over the spirit of man, and the people began to be disinterested in the Path of the Truth, Allah Almighty.

Let us look at these blessed Hadiths and contemplate on their true prophecies and wisdom.

(Narrated by Bukhari/Muslim):

Hadrat Huzhaifah ibn Al-Yaman (RA) said, "People used to ask the Messenger of Allah (pbuh) about the good things, while I used to ask him about the bad things, fearing that I would live long to see them. I said, 'O Messenger of Allah, we were in a state of ignorance and evil before, then Allah sent us this good (Islam); will there be any evil after this good?' He said, 'Yes.' I said, 'Will there be any good after that evil?' He said, 'Yes, but tainted.' I said, 'How will it be tainted?' He said, '(There will be) some people who will lead others in a way that is not according to my guidance. One may approve of some of their deeds and disapprove others.' I said, 'Will there be any evil after that good?' He said, 'Yes, there will be people calling others at the gates of Hell, and they will throw in Hell whoever responds to their call.' I said, 'O Messenger of Allah, describe them to us.' He said, 'They will be from among our own people, speaking our language.' I said, 'What do you command me to do if I live to witness such a situation?' He said, 'Stay with the

---

community of Muslims and their Imam (leader).' I asked, 'What if there is no unified community and no leader?' He said, 'Then, keep away from all of those groups, even if you have to bite at the roots of a tree until death overtakes you whilst you are in this condition."

Hadrat Abu Zaid Amr ibn Akhtab (RA) reported, "Once, the Messenger of Allah (pbuh) led us in the Fajr prayer and then mounted the pulpit and addressed us all the way until the time of Zuhur prayer. He then came down the pulpit and led us in the prayer, then again mounted the pulpit and again addressed us until it was time for Asr prayer. He then came down and led the Asr prayer, then again mounted the pulpit and addressed us until the sun was set. In that address, he informed us of everything that happened in the past as well as what lies ahead in the future. So the one amongst us who knows most about these matters is the one who had better memory."

Hadrat Huzhaifah Al-Ghifari (RA) reported that one day the Messenger of Allah (pbuh) passed by us when we were talking. He said, 'What are you talking about?' We said, 'We are talking about the Last Hour.' Thereupon he (pbuh) said, 'It will not strike until you see ten signs before it.' He mentioned the Great Smoke, the Dajjal, the Beast, the sun rising from the West, the descent of Jesus (son of Mary, pbuh), Gog and Magog, and three major destructions by landslides: one in the East, one in the West and one in the Arabian Peninsula. These will be followed by a great Fire that will burn forth from Yemen, driving people to the Place of their Assembly (for the Day of Judgement).

Hadrat An-Nawwas ibn Sam'an (RA) reported that the Messenger of Allah (pbuh) mentioned Dajjal one day in the morning in so much detail that we felt as if Dajjal were among our date-palm trees. Later in the evening, when we went to the Holy Messenger (pbuh), he noticed the sign of fear in our faces, so he asked us, 'What is the matter with you?' We said, 'O Messenger of Allah! You made mention of Dajjal morning so much in detail that we began to feel as if he were present in some of our farms.' Thereupon he (pbuh) said, 'In fact, I harbour fear about you in other things besides Dajjal. If he comes forth while I am here with you, I shall contend with him on your behalf, but if he comes forth while I am not amongst you, each person must contend on his own behalf, and Allah will take care of every Muslim on my behalf. Know that the Dajjal is a young man with twisted, contracted hair and one of his eyes is blind; he looks like Abdul-Uzza ibn Qatan (a known Jew at the time). Whoever survives to see him should recite over him the beginning of Surat Al-Kahf. He will first appear between the Levant and Iraq, and will spread mischief right and left (everywhere). O servants of Allah! Stay strong and be steadfast (on the Path of Truth)'. We said, 'O Messenger of Allah! How long will he stay on earth?' He (pbuh) said, 'For forty days; one day like a year and one day like a month and one day like a week, while the rest of the days are like your normal days'. We said, 'O Messenger of Allah! Then, will one day's prayers suffice for the prayers of the day equal to one year?' Thereupon he (pbuh) said, 'No, but you must make an estimate of the time (so to observe the five daily prayers)'. We said, 'O Messenger of Allah! How quickly will he move on earth?' He (pbuh) replied, 'Like a cloud driven by the wind. He would come to some people and invite them (to himself) and they would affirm their faith in him and follow him. He would then command the sky to rain, and they will get rain and their crops will grow for them. Their pasturing animals would return to them after grazing with their humps very high and their udders full of milk and their flanks stretched. He would come to another group of people and invite them (to himself), but they will reject him. As a result, he would leave them in drought and no wealth would be left with them. He will also walk through wasteland and command it 'Bring forth your treasures', and its treasures will come out and gather before him like swarms of bees. He will call a young man brimming with youth and will strike him with a sword and cut him into two and (make these pieces lie at a distance that is) between the archer and his target. He will then call the deceased man and he will come (alive) laughing with his face gleaming (with joy). Then, Allah will send down Christ, son of Mary, and he will descend at the white minaret in the eastern side of Damascus, wearing two garments lightly dyed with saffron colour, placing his hands on the wings of two Angels. When he lowers his head, beads of perspiration would fall from it, and when he raises his head, beads like pearls would scatter from it. Every non-believer who smells Christ's breath will die instantly. The breath of Christ will reach as far as his vision can reach. He will then search for the Dajjal until he will catch hold of him at the Gate of Ludd and will kill him there. Then, a people whom Allah had protected would come to Jesus son of Maryam, and he would wipe their faces and would inform them of their ranks in Paradise. Then, Allah will reveal to Jesus, 'I have brought forth from amongst My servants such people against whom none can stand; so take your people safely to Tur. Then, Allah will send forth Gog and Magog, swarming down from every slope. The first of them would pass by the lake of Tiberius and drink all of it. When the last of them would pass by, they would say 'There was once water here!' Jesus and his companions will then be besieged here (at Tur, and they would be so much hard pressed) that the head of an ox would be dearer to them than one hundred dinars. Jesus, the Messenger of Allah, and his companions will pray to Allah for relief; Allah will send unto Gog and Magog a kind of insects that would attack their necks, and by the morning, they will all perish like a single soul. Jesus and his companions will then come down and will not find on the land any space but filled with their putrefaction and stench. Jesus, the Messenger of Allah, and his companions will then again beseech Allah, and Allah will send huge birds with thick necks like those of Bactrian camels, and they will carry their dead bodies away where Allah Wills. Then, Allah will send rain which will fall on every house of brick or tent of goats' hair and it will wash the earth until it becomes as clean as a mirror. Then, the earth will be commanded to bring forth its good crops and restore its blessings. As a result, the pomegranates will grow so large that one of them would be enough to feed a group of people, and its skin would be enough to shelter them; one cow would be enough to feed a large number of people; one camel would be enough to feed a whole tribe; and one goat would be enough to feed a whole clan. Thereafter, Allah will send a pleasant breeze that will soothe the believers from under their armpits, taking away with it the souls of every Muslim. Then, only the wicked people will remain and live a vulgar life like frightened donkeys in the wilderness, and upon such people the Last Hour shall strike.

Beloved murid!

Be wise! Do not wait for the appearance of the individual Deceiver, the Dajjal; he has already appeared and you are still in his time suffering loss of faith and loss of great spirituality. It is part of his deceit that you do not realise when you are sucked into his ways and evil lifestyle. Awaken!

The Dajjal has already appeared and has changed the people's vision of life, and he continues to strive to corrupt the world. Now, he managed to reach you in your own Muslim lands and homes, each one in a different time, taking you away from the Path of the Truth - the Path of safety and salvation.

Those who are still deceived by the enormous developments in modern technology and the material lifestyle associated with it have actually fallen victims to Dajjal. Who or what can save you from such an evil fitnah if you believe it is good? Dajjal has done magic on you and you have become blind.

Another dark form of deception is that although Dajjal's fitnah came to you from the West, the Dajjal leader as a person will appear in the East, and both sides will come together to crush the faithful. Only the Light of Allah can make you see again. May Allah save us all!

Hadrat Usama (RA) reported that the Messenger of Allah (pbuh) climbed up one of the hills of Medina and then remarked, "Do you not see what I see now? I see the places where tribulations will fall within your homes, coming down like rainfall."

Hadrat Abu Huraira (RA) reported that the Messenger of Allah (pbuh) said, "There will soon come a period of tribulations. Therein, the one who is sitting will be better than the one who is standing, the one who is standing will be better than one who is walking and the one who is walking will be better than the one who is running. He who aspires to these tribulations will be consumed by them. Whoever finds a refuge or a shelter from them should remain in that refuge."

Hadrat Abu Huraira reported that the Messenger of Allah (pbuh) said, "The last Hour will not strike until harj (much bloodshed) will take place. They asked, 'What is harj?' He said, 'it is bloodshed, bloodshed.'"

Hadrat Ibn Omar (RA) reported that the Messenger of Allah (pbuh) stood outside the house of Hafsah (or Aisha) and, pointing towards the east, he said, "Tribulations will appear from this side, where the horns of Satan rise." He uttered these words twice or thrice.

Hadrat Abu Huraira (RA) reported that the Messenger of Allah (pbuh) said, "The Last Hour shall not strike until around thirty impostors, liars, would appear, all of them claiming to be a messenger of Allah."

(Narrated by Ibn Majah):

Hadrat Abu Hurairah (RA) narrated that the Messenger of Allah (pbuh) said, "When one of you completes reading the second Tashahhud (in prayer), let him seek refuge with Allah from four things: from the torment of Hell, from the torment of the grave, from the tribulations of life and death, and from the tribulation of Masih Dajjal (the False Messiah)."

(Narrated by Al-Tirmizi):

Hadrat Ali ibn Abi-Talib (RA) said, "The Holy Messenger (pbuh) said, 'when my nation bears fifteen traits, tribulations will befall them.' Someone asked, 'What are they, O Messenger of Allah?' He said, 'When wealth is shared out only among the rich, with no benefit to the poor; when trust becomes a means of making a profit; when paying Zakah becomes a burden; when a man obeys his wife and disobeys his mother, and treats his friend kindly whilst shunning his father away; when voices are raised high in the mosques; when the leader of a people is the worst of them; when people treat a man with respect only out of fear of his evil; when drinking alcohol is widespread; when men wear silk; when female singers and musical instruments become popular; when the last generations of this Nation will curse the first of them. When these happen, let them expect a red wind (to torture them), or the earth would swallow them up, or people may be transformed into animals.'

(Narrated by Abu Dawud):

Hadrat Abu-Bakrah (RA) narrated that Messenger of Allah (Salla Allahu 'alaihi wasallam) said, 'There will be a period of fitnah (tribulation) in which the one who lies down will be better than the one who sits, and the one who sits is better than the one who stands, and the one who stands is better than the one who walks, and the one who walks is better than the one who runs (in it)'. He asked, 'What do you command me to do, Messenger of Allah?' He (pbuh) replied, 'He who has camels should go stay with his camels; he who has sheep should remain with his sheep, and he who has land should go stay in his land.' He asked, 'If anyone has none of these, (what should he do)? He replied, 'He should break his sword on a stone, and then run away from all of this if he can.'

Another version adds, "He (pbuh) said, 'All the slain people in this fitnah will go to Hell'. Wabisah asked, 'When will this happen, Ibn Mas'ud?' He replied, 'This is the period of bloody turmoil (harj), when a person will not be safe even from his own associates.' I asked, 'What do you command me (to do) if I happen to live during that period?' He replied, 'Restrain your tongue and hands and stay at home. I then recollected this hadith when Othman (RA) was murdered...".

Beloved murid! Never underestimate any fitna and never overestimate your "withstanding" iman (faith). If you fall for anything that is contrary to the Sunnah of our Holy Guide, Sayyiduna Muhammad (pbuh), you may never pick up again. So, remain steadfast on your Tariqah, including its zhikr, supplications and Suhbah of the Shaykh and his companions. Remain close to his Zawiya and frequent it as much as possible, for in it lies the Light you need to see in the darkness of the tribulations around you.

Another means of safety from fitnah is to consult with your Shaykh about every major move you need to make in your life. At times, you feel satisfied with what your mind can see in a certain situation and you think you do not need to consult anyone as the matter seems very clear to you. Remember, this is what fitnah is, you think you see but in reality your vision is being tricked. A few months or a few years down the line, when negative results of your choices hit you, you will regret not asking your Shaykh.

O Allah! Show us the right path. Make us love Your Tariqah and the deeds that You Love. O Allah, give us steadfastness on the Path that leads to knowing You and pleasing You. You are Most Kind.

Our Most Glorious Lord! Accept my beloved murids in Your Glorious Presence of Mercy and Compassion. Most High Lord! Allow us to guide unto You all the people of the world You Wish to Guide, so that all can attain Salvation, Peace and Love.

SAFETY FROM GRIEF AND DISTRESS

My beloved seeker!

I am trying to warn you from dangers that are present on the way to the hereafter. I have crossed its highs and lows, and have seen its enemies on the side roads. Here, I want to warn you from emotional dangers that may put you down. Once you feel low and feel that faith has let you down, that is the moment when the devil will attack and finish off your Faith.

Extreme grief and distress harm your heart the way a narrow cage harms the feelings of a free lion. They form a heavy weight on your heart and thus prevent you from enjoying transparent spiritual experiences. This would lead a murid to struggle with his deeds and consequently with his inner vision and his journey to Allah.

Allah Almighty says addressing Prophet Musa (pbuh):

"... And you killed someone, but We saved you from distress and tried you with a severe trial..." (Surat Taha: 40)

Also, Allah Almighty says with reference to Prophet Yunus (pbuh):

"So We responded to his call and saved him from distress. And thus do We Save the believers." (Surat Al-Anbiya: 88)

In today's world, grief and distress related to worldly matters are very common due to the destruction the Dajjal has caused to human values and ways of life. Therefore, the culturally-oriented Sufi ways and the methods of the Sharia-based scholars are not working anymore. They are not giving the positive effects that they used to give in the past.

A murid may not escape this reality, but there is a way out for you when you have the sincere wish and intention. As you remain steadfast on your daily deeds that I have given you, you will gain more purity in your heart, your mind and your nafs. As you keep yourself to yourself, and observe regular presence in my company, you will have less and less worries and griefs that sadden and darken your heart and form a thick layer on your inner vision. Thus, your cure from distress and grief is in my Tariqah by zhikrullah with my blessed connection (Rabitah) with the Holy Messenger (pbuh).

Allah is the Lord of all. He is the One Who manages the events in the world, so do only as much as you can to help others but do not go far in as to destroy your heart with distress and grief. The more Divine Light comes into your faithful heart, the more you are a real help for others, as the calamities Allah Almighty sends down cannot be lifted by your effort, but by your righteous inner reality, enlightened by the Light of God.

To help you further, read these blessed hadiths frequently and contemplate on their meanings with great attentiveness.

(Narrated by Bukhari and Muslim):

Hadrat Ibn Omar (RA) narrated that the Messenger of Allah (pbuh) said, '... Whoever comes to the aid of his Muslim brother's need, Allah will be there for him at the time of his need; whoever gives relief to the distress of a Muslim, Allah will relieve him from a distress of the distresses of the Day of Reckoning; and whoever conceals (the faults of) a Muslim, Allah will conceal his faults on the Day of Reckoning'.

(Narrated by Abu Dawud):

Hadrat Anas (RA) said that he used to see the Messenger of Allah (pbuh) when he was concerned about a particular matter, wiping his head with his right hand, saying, 'bismillahi-llazhi la-ilaha ghayruhu, arrahmanu-rraheem, allahumma azhib 'anni-lhamma walhuzn':
(In the Name of Allah, there is no god other than He, The Merciful, The Compassionate. O Allah, relieve me from all worry and grief).

(Narrated by Ahmad):

Hadrat Abdullah ibn Ja'far (RA) said that the Messenger of Allah (pbuh) advised us to say this supplication at the time of grief (distress): "la ilaha illa-llahu al-Haleemu al-Kareem, Subhanallahi rabbil-'arshil-'azeem, walhamdu-lillahi rabbil-'alameen: (There is none worthy of worship but Allah, the Most Kind, Most Generous. Glory be to Allah, the Lord of the Great Throne, and all praise be to Allah, the Lord of the Worlds)."

(Narrated by Ibn Al-Sunni):

On the authority of Hadrat Abu-Qutada (RA), the Messenger of Allah (pbuh) said, "Whoever reads the Verse of the Throne (ayat al-kursi) and the last two verses of Surat Al-Baqara at the time of distress, Allah will relieve him."

(Narrated by Al-Tirmizi and Ahmad):

It is narrated that Hadrat Ubai ibn Ka'ab (RA) said, 'I said, 'O Messenger of Allah, I supplicate often to Allah, how much of my supplication should I devote to praying upon you?' the Holy Messenger (pbuh) replied, 'As you wish'. I said, 'shall I devote a quarter of it?' He said 'As you wish, but if you were to give more, it would be better for you.' I said, 'then, half of it?' He said, 'As you wish, but if you were to give more, it would be better for you.' I said, 'then, two-thirds?' He again said, 'As you wish, but if you were to do more, it would be better for you.' I finally said, 'Then, I should dedicate all of my supplication as prayers upon you?' He said, 'If you do so, then your worries will be relieved and your sins forgiven.'

Murids must pay great attention to Salawat (prayers upon the Messenger, pbuh) and practice them in great amounts and regularly. You should at least do 1000 Salawat a day, and keep increasing them over time, but with consulting your Shaykh.

Similar attention should be given to istighfar (seeking forgiveness from Allah Almighty). A murid should always begin his daily deeds with praying 1000 istighfar, and end his day with the same.

(Narrated by Abu Dawud, Ibn Majah, Ahmad, Al-Tabarani):

Hadrat Abdullah ibn Abbas (RA) reported that the Holy Messenger (pbuh) said, "Whoever practices seeking forgiveness profusely, Allah will give him a way out from every difficulty, and a relief from every worry and distress, and will grant him provision from ways unknown to him."

Remember, you have the advantage of being on a connected Tariqah, guided by your spiritual leader, your Shaykh. So be in his companionship (Suhbah) in every way he makes possible for you. Your Shaykh will help you stay away from situations of extreme grief and distress, and if you do fall into them once, your Shaykh will give you the strength you need to survive the situation.

Through your companionship (Suhbah) with me as your Guide, you will gain immense spiritual and intellectual knowledge which will be your provision during troubled times. Remember, states of the heart cannot be changed with your own effort. An enlightened Guide is as necessary for your spiritual and emotional rehabilitation as a doctor is for your complex physical conditions. If you are reading this book and you are not a murid of any credible Tariqah, you should immediately start searching for one. You are most welcome to contact the Zawiyah of my Tariqah for further guidance. Allah bless you wherever you may be.

Book of Safety

Book of Sacred Images

INTRODUCTION TO SACRED IMAGES

Since the descendance of our first parents on earth, Adam and Eve (peace be upon them), Allah Almighty has provided for us places and times around which we build up our spiritual experiences and develop our religious attachments so that we may have a physical focus to help us develop emotional and mental focus. An image can take you miles and miles closer to a reality and miles and miles higher in the sphere of real meanings.

In this Book, I have gathered for you some blessed images of some sacred realities in our world.

First come the images related to the Jewel of Faith and Master of God's creation, Sayyiduna Muhammad, the Messenger of Allah (pbuh). Everything that leads us to him (pbuh) or reminds us of him (pbuh) is extremely valuable as it increases our faith in him and our connection with him (pbuh). Along with his Muhammadi presence, comes the blessed presence of his shining daughter, Sayyidah Fatima (RA) and the presence of his two closest Companions and Vicegerents, Sayyiduna Abu-Bakr and Sayyiduna Omar, Allah be pleased with all of them. We are then further reminded with the Muhammadi presence by some of the holy belongings of the Holy Messenger (pbuh).

Then, we have images related to the Holy Ka'ba, the House of Allah, which forms the Centre of Focus for worshipping Allah on earth.

Lastly, we visualise great spiritual and holy meanings through the images of the Far Mosque and the Blessed Land in Palestine, which provided humankind with spiritual blessings throughout time.

May Allah bless us all as He Has Blessed the Masters and the holy places of the realities behind these images. Amen.

Book of Sacred Images

First, we begin with the Star of all Stars, the Master of all Masters,

the Beloved of Allah, the Fountain of Light, the Spring of Love,

Sayyiduna Muhammad, peace be upon him

And with him (pbuh) are Hadrat Sayyidah Fatima (RA),
Sayyiduna Abu-Bakr (RA) and Sayyiduna Omar (RA)

Book of Sacred Images

The Blessed Green Dome, sheltering the Holy Chamber of
Sayyiduna Muhammad (pbuh) in the Masjid Nabawi in Madinah

Book of Sacred Images

AS-Suffah Platform in the Holy Mosque in Madinah, where the
poor muhajirin (Companions from Makkah) used to stay during
the time of the Holy Messenger (pbuh)

The Blessed Rawdah (Garden) and the blessed Pulpit of the Holy
Messenger (pbuh) in Madinah. Also seen is the Mihrab (Niche)
marking the blessed place where the Holy Messenger stood when
leading the prayers in his Holy Mosque

Book of Sacred Images

The green gate marking the entrance of the blessed house of
Sayyidah Fatima (RA), in the Holy Mosque in Madinah.

Book of Sacred Images

The Blessed Chamber of Hadrat Fatima (RA), showing a green
cover over her blessed bed, and the private Mihrab (Niche) of the
Holy Messenger (pbuh), in the Holy Mosque, Madinah

مسجد النبوي - المحراب النبوي داخل الروضة

The Blessed Niche of the Holy Messenger (pbuh), marking the
location where he (pbuh) used to lead the prayers

The blessed Ghar Hiraa (Cave of Hiraa) in a mountain near
Makkah, where the Holy Messenger (pbuh) used to stay in
solitude just before he received Divine Revelation through
Sayyiduna Jibril, the Spirit Archangel (pbuh)

An old photo of The As-salam Gate of the Holy Mosque in
Madinah, when Madinah houses were adjacent to it.

Alas! A beautiful time gone forever!

Book of Sacred Images

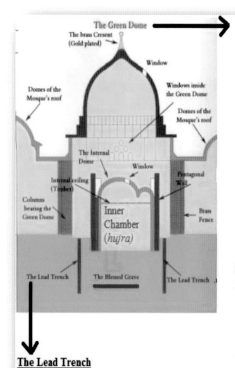

The Dome

The dome was first constructed in 1279 A.D; last renovated and painted green in 1837 A.D (initially grey)

Inner Chamber

The inner chamber is the room in which the Prophet(s) is resting. The walls of the room are built of black stones and the roof has a small black dome called Qubbat an-Nur. The chamber has no doors and it is completely sealed from the outside - except a small window in the dome which is closed by a grill.

In 1477 A.D, the mosque was destroyed in a fire. The walls of the inner chamber and the outer pentagonal wall developed cracks and had to be pulled down for reconstruction. This is the last time the sacred chamber become visible and open for entry. The chamber was resealed on Jan 23, 1477

The Lead Trench

Constructed around the chamber, by Sultan Nur-ud-din Zangi, in 1179 A.D because he feared that crusaders were trying to pull out the body of the Prophet (s).

The Pentagonal Wall

In 709 A.D, Al-Walid Bin Abd-al Malik constructed a 5 sided wall around the sacred *hujra*. This pentagonal wall has no door or windows and thus the chamber is completely sealed within this wall.

Diagram showing history and construction of the Blessed Green Dome and the Hujra Sharifa (Prophet's Holy Chamber)

Our Crown Masters: Muhammad the Messenger of Allah (pbuh), Abu-Bakr AS-Siddiq, Omar ibn Al-khattab, Othman ibn Affan (RA), {Ali ibn Abi-Talib, Fatima Az-zahra, Al-Hasan and Al-Husain (AS)}

Book of Sacred Images

The Blessed Masjid Nabawi (the Prophet's Mosque) from the
rooftop of the Ottoman structure

The blessed green turban, cloak and staff of the Holy Messenger,
Sayyiduna Muhammad (pbuh)

Book of Sacred Images

The Blessed Sandal that was blessed to touch the Holy feet of the Holy Messenger (pbuh), Kept in Topkapi Palace, Istanbul, Turkey

I wish I could just kiss it and put it on my eyes! A wonderful dream of mine! May Allah fulfil it for me.

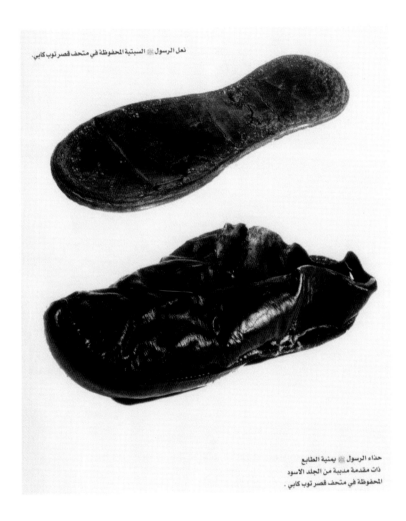

نعل الرسول ﷺ السبتية المحفوظة في متحف قصر توب كابي.

حذاء الرسول ﷺ يمنية الطابع
ذات مقدمة مدببة من الجلد الأسود
المحفوظة في متحف قصر توب كابي.

The Blessed Sabtiyyah Shoe of the Holy Messenger (pbuh), Kept in Topkapi Palace, Istanbul, Turkey

Book of Sacred Images

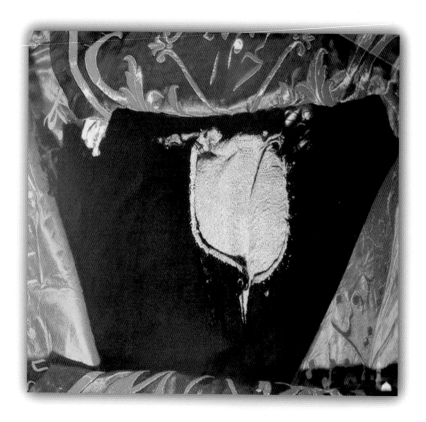

The blessed Shirt that was blessed to touch the Holy body of
Sayyiduna Muhammad (pbuh), Kept in Topkapi Palace, Istanbul,
Turkey Simplicity was his mizaj. In this simple shirt, the Holy
Messenger (pbuh) conquered hearts before lands. May Allah give
us his blessed mizaj. Amen.

Book of Sacred Images

The Holy Ka'ba

First House of God on Earth, in Holy Makkah. Upon it descend
great Divine Lights that guide the lost and the bewildered.

Our Crown Masters: Muhammad the Messenger of Allah (pbuh), Abu-Bakr AS-Siddiq, Omar ibn Al-khattab,
Othman ibn Affan (RA), {Ali ibn Abi-Talib, Fatima Az-zahra, Al-Hasan and Al-Husain (AS)}

Book of Sacred Images

Old photo of Holy Ka'ba and the Holy Mosque in Makkah during
the past days of simplicity and spiritual beauty

The Holy Black Stone in a silver casket, placed in the Holy Stone
Corner of the Holy Ka'ba. The Black Stone was shining white
when descended from Paradise but was blackened by the sins of
people on earth.

Book of Sacred Images

Al-Aqsa Blessed Mosque in Jerusalem, where the Holy Messenger
(pbuh) was taken by Jibril (AS) on the miraculous Isra Journey
from Holy Makkah

Book of Sacred Images

Mosque of the Dome of the Rock, in Al-Aqsa Area in Jerusalem

Book of Sacred Images

The blessed Rock from which Sayyiduna Muhammad (pbuh)
travelled to Heaven and beyond to Divine Presence on the Mi'raj
Journey escorted by Sayyiduna Jibril (AS). The Rock is under the
Dome of the Mosque of the Rock in Jerusalem

Our Crown Masters: Muhammad the Messenger of Allah (pbuh), Abu-Bakr AS-Siddiq, Omar ibn Al-khattab,
Othman ibn Affan (RA), {Ali ibn Abi-Talib, Fatima Az-zahra, Al-Hasan and Al-Husain (AS)}

THE AUTHOR

This poor slave of Allah, Al-Sharif ibn-Hashim Abdullah Al-Husaini, is an Arab scholar, descendant of Imam Al-Husain son of Imam Ali and Sayyidah Fatima (Allah be pleased with them), the daughter of the Holy Messenger (pbuh). I was born and raised in their Holy hometown, Madinah 'the Enlightened City', in the vicinity of the Holy Mosque of my Grandfather and our Master, Sayyiduna Muhammad (pbuh).

Allah has blessed me to become an authorised Master in spiritual and moral training, especially in the Naqshabandi Sufi Path which offers purification of one's heart and the inner self. I am the 37th Master (Shaykh) in the Blessed Siddiqiyya Chain, going back to Sayyiduna Abu-Bakr AS-Siddiq (RA), and the 44th Shaykh in the Blessed Golden Chain, that goes back to my grandfather, Sayyiduna Ali ibn Abi-Talib (RA).

In addition to learning at the Holy Mosque of Prophet Muhammad (pbuh) in Madinah, I have completed my religious education and secular undergraduate education in various schools of Holy Madinah, and then completed my postgraduate education in the United Kingdom. I have been also blessed to become a scholar in various Islamic and secular sciences, particularly in Quranic exegesis and holy recitation, the Prophet's Hadith, Hanafi Fiqh and in the Holy Messenger's Biography studies (Blessed Seerah). I am also a professor in Arabic and English philology and literature.

Most prominent of my teachers and guides are: Hadrat Shaykh In'amul-Hasan Kandahlawi (RA), Hadrat Shaykh Mahmudul-Hasan Saharanpuri (RA), Hadrat Shaykh Saeed Ahmad Khan Almadani (RA), Hadrat Shaykh Uwais ibn Abdullah Al-Husaini (RA), Hadrat Shaykh Muhammad Is-haq (RA), Hadrat Shaykh Ihsanul-Haq (RA), Hadrat Shaykh Saeed Hawwa (RA), Hadrat Shaykh Fazel-Azeem Madani (RA), Hadrat Shaykh Farooq Makki (RA), Hadrat Shaykh Sayyid Abdussalam Almadani (RA) and Shaykh Dr. Muhammad Hadrami Madani.

I have also met with and greatly benefitted from the following senior scholars: Hadrat Shaykhul-Hadith Moulana Muhammad Zakariyya Kandahlawi (RA), his son Hadrat Shaykh Muhammad Talhat Kandahlawi (RA), Hadrat Shaykh Moulana Az-zubair ibn In'amul-Hasan (RA), Hadrat Shaykh Omar Palampuri (RA), and many other great scholars in Holy Madina, India and elsewhere.

My unique message is my Divinely inspired mission of inviting people - men and women, Muslims and non-Muslims, to devote their lives for finding their inner peace with God Almighty as well as within themselves and with the rest of the world. I have been Divinely inspired to offer my Divine Gift of spiritual and moral guidance and mentorship to all those who realise they need to know who they are and Who Allah Almighty is, and who desire to establish a good relationship with Allah, The Glorious, The Compassionate. Peace, love and compassion for all are my main characteristics. We should not hate anyone nor look down upon anyone. Those who love me for my own sake for the Divine blessings in me will benefit greatly. Those who do not like me, I will forgive them whatever hurt they may cause me. We are all from Adam, and Adam is from dust. Let us turn our hearts to Love.

People who are blessed to join our highly spiritual Tariqah will be immediately blessed with peace at heart, with revival of the heart in remembering Allah and with unconditional love and compassion. I do not judge anyone, no matter what background or qualities they may have. I am here in this world to open heavenly channels for people to God Almighty, Praise and Glory be to Him.

I have been blessed to have seekers of The Divine Path in various regions in the world, especially in Hijaz, England, Morocco, Egypt, Australia and India. Al-Sharif is also keen on building strong bridges with people from other faiths through the power of love and compassion that I have inherited from my Grandfather, the Holy Messenger, Sayyiduna Muhammad (pbuh) and from my grand

Ahul-Bayt ancestors, Sayyidi Ali ibn Abi Talib and Sayyida Fatima Azzahra, peace be upon them.

May Allah bless all those who want Allah and all those who are still unsure about Him.

May Allah guide all those who do not want Him.

May Allah show Mercy to all.

May Allah grant our saints of this holy Tariqah the highest of heavenly stations, through the blessings and the Divine Secrets of Surat Al-Fatihah...

Zawiyat Alsharif (khanaqah) of the author,
is in the UK

Tariqah online:
puresunnah.blogspot.co.uk

For enquiry about the Blessed Naqshabandi Tariqah
and for guidance on spiritual purification,
Email of Shaykh Al-Sharif's personal assistant:
khadimofshaykh@gmail.com

Contacts' telephone numbers:
+44 7913 810160
+44 7718 126167